Praise for *Beeswing*

"*Beeswing* is thoughtful, well written and at times very funny . . . With his sophisticated songs and distinctive guitar work, Thompson has long been the thinking person's musician. Turns out he's also the thinking person's memoirist."

—*Minneapolis Star Tribune*

"*Beeswing* is wry, un-ponderous, anti-obligatory. Because the sound Thompson created with Fairport was rooted in centuries-old songs, he isn't captive to '60s clichés; and because British electric folk is off the classic-rock grid . . . the book's period accent makes it feel fresh and exploratory."

—*The New York Times Book Review*

"Mr. Thompson is a master showman. The balancing act of major and minor, strung together by his witty, self-deprecating banter, is the crux of Mr. Thompson's shows, and that same equipoise between dirge and ditty is the hallmark of *Beeswing*: it's everything you'd hope a Richard Thompson autobiography would be . . . It's both major and minor, dirge and ditty, light on its feet but packing a punch: like the very best Richard Thompson show."

—Wesley Stace, *The Wall Street Journal*

"A beloved musician's memoir is cause for celebration . . . The prose is smart and smartly moving . . . [*Beeswing*] documents a beloved band's prime existence."

—RJ Smith, *Los Angeles Times*

"An absorbing, witty, often deliciously biting read, as all rock memoirs should be."   —*Los Angeles Review of Books*

"[Reading] *Beeswing* is like sitting next to the author at dinner . . . Poignant."   —Minneapolis Public Radio's *The Current*

"Thompson writes exceptionally well, in a droll, very British way . . . If you love music in all its myriad forms, you'll love this book."   —*New York Journal of Books*

"Thompson has a reputation as a guitarist's guitarist and a top-notch singer-songwriter . . . With *Beeswing*, Thompson proves himself equally adept as a memoirist . . . Just as he has a knack for lyrics, Thompson has a way with words on the page, offering colorful portraits of his contemporaries and collaborators . . . Thompson's humor and insight also shine. He evocatively recreates a time and place, and, like his shows, his memoir leaves you wanting more."
     —*Booklist* (starred review)

"I admire Richard Thompson so much, and I found *Beeswing* as inspiring as his music. I devoured and savored it."
     —Steve Gunn, musician and songwriter

"Like his singing voice, guitarist Thompson's memoir of finding his way as a pioneering folk-rocker is homely in the best British way: inviting, down to earth and honest."
     —*Milwaukee Journal Sentinel*

"Lively, compact, and frequently funny."

—*The Philadelphia Inquirer*

"*Beeswing* is chockful of reflections on music and song . . . Wonderful."

—David Corn, *Mother Jones*

"A welcome revelation for both fanatics and casual fans. *Beeswing* is not music, but it sings, telling the story of one of our greatest contemporary guitarists in a voice as unique as his playing and composing. It is worth reading, even if you have never heard a note he has played (though you probably have at some point)."

—Bookreporter.com

"Gripping reflections on early tragedy, his conversion to Sufism, and a first marriage whose dramas were played out onstage . . . Enlightening . . . A quiet joy of a memoir."

—*The Guardian*

"[Thompson] offers plenty of insight into the early days of Fairport Convention and its ever-changing lineup along with charming anecdotes."

—*Kirkus Reviews*

"Readers who regard Thompson as a major figure in the arts will consider this a must-read."

—*Publishers Weekly*

"The book—like much of Thompson's best songwriting—is spare, sharply descriptive and filled with vivid characters."

—*New Jersey Monthly*

BEESWING

Losing My Way and Finding My Voice
1967–1975

RICHARD THOMPSON
with SCOTT TIMBERG

ALGONQUIN BOOKS
OF CHAPEL HILL
2022

Published by
Algonquin Books of Chapel Hill
Post Office Box 2225
Chapel Hill, North Carolina 27515-2225

a division of
Workman Publishing
225 Varick Street
New York, New York 10014

Library of Congress Cataloging-in-Publication Data
Names: Thompson, Richard, [date]– author.
Title: Beeswing / Richard Thompson.
Description: First edition. | Chapel Hill : Algonquin Books of
Chapel Hill, 2021. | Includes index. | Summary: "A revealing look at the
early years of Richard Thompson, one of the world's most influential
guitarists and songwriters, following the formation of his band Fairport
Convention, his revival of British folk traditions, and his journey
through Sufism—all before the age of 26"— Provided by publisher.
Identifiers: LCCN 2020051893 | ISBN 9781616208950 (hardcover) |
ISBN 9781643751702 (ebook)
Subjects: LCSH: Thompson, Richard, [date]– | Guitarists—Great Britain—
Biography. | Rock musicians—Great Britain—Biography. | Folk rock
music—Great Britain—History and criticism. | Fairport Convention
(Musical group)
Classification: LCC ML419.T47 A3 2021 | DDC 782.42166/092 [B]—dc23
LC record available at https://lccn.loc.gov/2020051893

ISBN 978-1-64375-253-2 (PB)

10 9 8 7 6 5 4 3 2 1
First Paperback Edition

CONTENTS

1

To Jump like Alice

I have nothing to say, I am saying it,
and that is poetry as I need it.
JOHN CAGE

THERE IS DUST, and then there is dust. It's thickest here, in my memory. This remotest room of my mind has been shut up for years, the windows shuttered, the furniture covered with dust sheets. Light hasn't penetrated into some of these corners for years; in some cases it never has. If something is uncomfortable, I shove it in here and forget about it. When was the last time I dared look? I don't want to remember, but now it is time to think back. The arrow is arcing through the air and speeding towards its appointed target.

Then there is the dust of London. When my story begins, in the 1960s, the fog is lifting a little. The choking smogs of my childhood, with visibility down to a yard, have been curtailed, for the sake of public health, by the Clean Air Act of 1956. The dust, dirt and grime of a million coal fires, hundreds of steam trains and massive power stations is receding as they are slowly replaced by cleaner fuel—but I miss it. I miss the sulphurous fog that linked you to the London of Sherlock Holmes and Dickens, that inspired visiting French Impressionists to paint the city's blurred sunrises and sunsets, and that made everything soft and mysterious. It was part of London, and part of being a Londoner. I suppose even poison is something you can grow fond of.

In the spring of 1967 I had just turned eighteen, and there was another kind of dust in my life entirely, so thick you could see it hang in the air, composed of 50 percent chalk, 30 percent boredom and 20 percent dull amusement. The dust of school gets into your lungs—molecules of it are still in there, I swear, clinging to the bronchioles like crabs to a sea wall, even fifty years later. No amount of violent coughing or deep breathing will shift it. It seems to have penetrated my DNA. Maybe that's why I still dream about school, guilty dreams, dreams of unfulfillment, dreams where I'm avoiding, running away, non-confronting. On a sunny day, and the sun still shone in black and white in 1967, you could see the dust hanging in the sunbeams like cigarette smoke caught in the projector beam at the local flea pit.

At least I was on the final lap. A few more months, a few more exams, and I would be paroled at last, free after thirteen years of incarceration. I had no stomach for further education, and I had no plan A, B or C. The thought of spending another three years in an institution did not appeal. Hospitals, prisons, schools, insane asylums—in Britain they all seemed to have been designed by the same Victorian sadist, and all shared the same decor: Urine Green and Despair Grey. I went to a "good" school, William Ellis Grammar, on the edge of Hampstead Heath. The Heath has been described as "the lungs of London," a rural enclave a fifteen-minute Tube ride from the center of the city. Sitting on London clay and Bagshot sand, it could never be built upon with reliability, which saved it from the developers. The school supplied a fair number of candidates to Oxford and Cambridge, and provided a fine education for those who could be bothered—but I drifted through it. I only cared about the guitar.

ONE OF MY earliest memories, from when I was about three, is of the attic at 23 Ladbroke Crescent. Notting Hill, just west of Central London, was a fairly run-down area in the early fifties, and our street was pockmarked with shrapnel damage from the war. In fact, one end of the street was a bomb site. It was fenced off, of course, but we kids found a way in and played joyfully among the smashed porcelain, knee-scraping rubble and broken artifacts of ruined lives. My family—my father, my mother, my sister Perri and I—lived in a flat in the upper half of the house, a few doors down from my mother's father at number 19. My grandad kept chickens in his back garden, and would often run out into the street with a shovel after a horse and cart had passed by to get the manure for his roses. I remember being taken up to the attic by my parents, presumably so they could keep an eye on me while they looked for something. I had never been in an attic before, so it was a new and thrilling experience. At one point, my father opened a case and pulled out a magical wooden box with strings on it. The box made noises, and you could change them by turning the pegs at the end. My father ran his hand across the strings. It sounded like heaven, and I wanted to hear more, but after a minute or so he put it back in the case, and I never saw it again. Did he sell it soon afterwards? Perhaps he thought it a luxury at a time when money was tight, but its sound stayed with me.

If Dad was not much of a guitarist, he did have plenty of records. In among the albums of show tunes that everyone's parents seemed to own, and the Perry Como and the Gilbert and Sullivan, there were jazz records—Fats Waller, Meade Lux Lewis, Duke Ellington—and among these were lots of guitar 78s. There was the Quintette du Hot Club de France, including the astonishing Django Reinhardt; there was Lonnie Johnson, playing with the Louis Armstrong Hot Seven; and then there was Les Paul, inventing multitrack recording. I remember lying on a sea-green shagpile rug in the living room, with my ear a foot from the radiogram speaker. I must have been all of five years old. Much of the furniture in the room was mid-century modern, G-Plan, but the dark walnut radiogram seemed ancient.

I liked some of my father's records and disliked others; I seemed to have some sort of critical instinct, even at such a young age. Dad would keep up a running commentary on the music, in his cockney-inflected Scottish accent. He'd talk mostly to himself, reverentially, like a tour guide at the Vatican. "Louis Armstrong Hot Five—recorded in 1926 . . . that's Earl Hines on piano . . . I saw him in Glasgow in the thirties." He'd always sound authoritative, but I could tell he was reading most of it off the back of the record sleeve. The next thing he put on grabbed me and held my attention. It started with percussion, before slowly sprouting wings and sounding like nothing I had ever heard. The only thing I could compare it to was the music played on radio or TV programs to evoke alien worlds and life forms. "Caravan," said my father. "That's a Duke Ellington tune, played by Les Paul on guitar. He did the whole thing himself." I didn't understand what I was hearing—I only knew that it sounded like it was from Mars, and that it was fabulous. I didn't know how to ask to hear it again, so I just waited for the next time.

My sister Perri was five years my senior, and when rock and roll hit Britain in 1956, first with Bill Haley and then with Elvis, she was strongly identifying with the baby boomer generation. Even back then, at the tender age of twelve, she pitched her look somewhere between Julie Christie and Brigitte Bardot. I don't remember a time when boys weren't hanging around—and some of them played the guitar and brought over records.

Here was music that was not controlled by the grown-ups. The great watershed had arrived—it was goodbye to the saccharine saxophones of the 1940s, to rationing and austerity, and your parents' world of wartime sacrifice and post-war peace and quiet. The boomers had arrived, and they wanted it loud, primitive and exciting. The rock and roll of Jerry Lee, Gene, Eddie and Buddy started to rumble through the wall from my sister's bedroom.

After our family moved to Highgate in the mid-fifties, to a better, newly-built flat, we went to the famous and ancient Hampstead Heath Fair twice a year, and there you could hear rock and roll properly—cranked up loud as a soundtrack to the dodgems, on huge speakers with tons of bass. The sound carried literally for miles. The noise thumped right into your chest and rearranged your intestines. It was a soundtrack for the beautiful ballet of rebellion of the spivs leaping from car to car to take the money, for the Teddy boys going to the insane edge of daring on the switchback to impress their girlfriends.

And because my father was born and grew up in Scotland, every summer we would drive up to the Scottish Lowlands for a two-week holiday. We would stay with my father's parents in Dumfries for a few days, before driving a few more miles to the Solway coast, where the family had a chalet. The seaside was special, but I especially loved tagging along with Perri as she explored Dumfries's three coffee bars. Each establishment had a jukebox, and they all played the records loud, with tons of low end. At night I would hang out of the bedroom window and listen to Buddy Holly being played in the cafe three streets away. This music seemed more important than anything else in my life, with the possible exception of model trains and the *Beano.*

Of course, guitars were central to this whole culture. They were starting to crop up on TV, on shows for teenagers like *Six-Five Special* and *Oh Boy!*, and on the variety show *Sunday Night at the London Palladium*, which my parents would watch, commenting on any rock and roll content ("Long-haired layabouts!" or "What a bloody racket!"). Joe Brown was probably the first home-grown British guitar hero. He'd appear backing the American acts on *Oh Boy!* and then do a spot on his own. Joe had a winning cockney manner and a great haircut, and he played with a certain streetwise authenticity. As I would find out in later years, he was also one of the nicest human beings you could hope to meet.

I started asking for a guitar for Christmas from about the

age of six. My parents warmly responded with a succession of plastic ukuleles, tin Roy Rogers mini-guitars that exploded upon impact and toy banjos covered in clowns' faces. Even at the age of six, I knew I was being fobbed off. I would really try to play them and would point out the deficiencies to my father. He didn't have an answer, except to put these pathetic toys into something approximating tuning and wander off, muttering to himself.

In 1960, when I was eleven, the situation became more urgent. Cliff Richard's backing group, the Shadows, scored a number one hit with "Apache." All over Britain, instrumental bands were trying to emulate Hank Marvin's fabulous tone on the Fender Stratocaster. Posing in front of a mirror with a tennis racquet would no longer suffice.

My father was in the Metropolitan Police, and at that time was serving with the Flying Squad. Charing Cross Road was part of his beat, and one of his old army buddies worked in a music shop called Lew Davis. They had a damaged guitar they were going to throw away—the side had split open in transit from Spain—and Dad, who had trained as a joiner, brought it home and repaired it. He had some idea that he was going to play it. My sister also had designs on it. And I had other ideas. It was as if this sacred object was being pulled towards me by a giant magnet. This was my destiny, and no one else stood a chance. Someone loaned me a guitar instruction manual, *Play in a Day* by Bert Weedon. If you saw or heard Bert on a radio or TV variety show, you would deem it impossible that he had replaced Django Reinhardt in the Quintette du Hot Club de France, as he always seemed slightly corny and "mumsy" as a player, but he was actually the most famous guitarist in Britain and had written a beginner's guitar manual that everyone seemed to start with. It must have sold a million copies, and it actually worked—you really could learn to play something in a day! Having mastered "Bobby Shaftoe," with its C, G7 and tricky D minor chords, the musical world opened up to me, and "Apache" proved not too difficult.

I was very shy, and from around the age of six I developed a stutter. The causes of this are not always clear—my mother thought it started for me after a bout of dysentery, but there was probably a psychological factor. I lived in fear of my father, who was sometimes drunk and always Calvinistic—a common Scottish combination—so I never knew when I was going to get whacked. My mother was loving, kind and always there for me, but her attentions could make me feel a bit claustrophobic. My sister would stay in her room, playing her records and smoking her Gauloise cigarettes. She did from time to time take on my father head to head, though—no one was going to tell her how to live her life. I'm grateful to her for that, because by the time I was fifteen and starting to stay out later, Perri had exhausted my parents, which meant that I got an easier ride. Music became my place of escape. I found speaking difficult, and schoolkids could be mercilessly cruel about it. Standing up in front of class to read out a passage of a story was torture and embarrassment, but I was able to communicate through music.

I remember sitting in the school cafeteria, totally in my own world, singing Elvis's "Don't Be Cruel" half out loud, my body jerking along with the rhythm of the words, my food untouched. A small crowd was gathering around me, but I didn't notice.

"All right, what's going on here?"

"It's Thompson, Miss. He's gone mental!"

"Go back to your seats. Thompson, snap out of it and eat your lunch!"

At the age of eleven, I went to secondary school and began formal music lessons, but I found it hard to relate what I was learning by ear to the notes on a page. Just a few years ago, I was sitting down to Christmas dinner at my sister's house, and there on my plate was my school report book, which Perri had found among some family papers. This odious document contained some ugly truths about me that I thought were but tiny specks in the rear-view mirror. Then, to the amusement of everyone, Perri read out a succession of reports from the music master, Herr Prinz, damning me as a musical no-hoper, not to mention a disruptive and lazy so-and-so. How they chuckled, but it's true that I used to have a hard time reading music. I'm still very slow, and can write it much faster than I can read it—I think I might be a bit dyslexic, because things sometimes get scrambled before my eyes. Anyway, after this embarrassing interlude, I pocketed the offending document and put it on the fire when no one was looking.

One of my best friends, Malcolm Fuller, who lived around the corner from me, also got the guitar bug and convinced his parents to buy him one. As a couple of twelve-year-olds, we could now jam along to the Shadows, to our hearts' content. I had about a week's head start on him, so I got to play lead and he played rhythm. Our parents soon found us a classical

guitar tutor, Pete, but I'm not sure how. He must have adver-
tized in the newsagent's window or in the local paper. Every
week, Malcolm and I would get the bus over to the Caledonian
Road for our lesson.

Pete lived in a house that was basically condemned. He
had managed to bypass the gas meter so there was heating,
but there was no electricity, so everything was candlelit,
which we thought rather exciting and bohemian. The stairs
were rickety, and the floorboards gave considerably as you put
your weight on them. Pete had the Brylcreem- and-sideburns
look of a Teddy boy, a style that was fast going out of fashion
in 1961, but he was a nice guy and a real guitar enthusiast—as
well as being a very good player. He shared his house with
another guitarist, and our time there was always focused. Pete
helped me to read music a bit better, and the introductory
pieces he gave us got my fingers moving independently, for
which I have always been grateful.

I soon got bored with Pete's guitar exercises and wanted
to go straight to the classics of the repertoire. I owned a few
classical guitar and flamenco records. I loved the French guitarist Ida Presti, whose duets with her husband Alexandre
Lagoya have never been equalled. She had small hands, and
you would occasionally hear some fret noise, but she had such
passion—in some ways, I try to emulate her musical soul even
now. That year, my parents took me to the Festival Hall to
see the man who developed the classical guitar as a concert
instrument, the great Andrés Segovia. He was nearly seventy
years old and seemed ancient. He had fat sausage-like fingers, but his playing seemed effortless and he sounded like

an angel. I was beginning to understand that while it is easy to play classical guitar simply, it is phenomenally difficult to play it well.

Our lessons lasted for a year or so, and then one week we turned up and Pete wasn't there. Neither was his house. It had been bulldozed to the ground, and we never heard from him again. Our parents speculated that he was in prison for defrauding the council and the gas board. That was the end of our classical lessons, and it was probably just as well, because we were both losing enthusiasm. I was also facing stiff competition. In my year at school, out of ninety boys, there were *two* classical guitar whiz kids. Carlos Bonell, Spanish by heritage, has had a long and successful career as a concert guitarist. The other was a kid called Paul Lomax, a pale, English working-class Mod. He was a student of Len Williams, father of John Williams, and even appeared on TV at the age of fourteen. I was seriously outgunned and sought refuge in the less crowded fields of rock and folk.

By 1963, at the age of fourteen, Malcolm and I had formed a band with some boys from his school—St. Aloysius' College, a Catholic school on Highgate Hill. On Sunday afternoons, we would rehearse over in Dalston at the house of Marrik, the bass player—his parents were the most tolerant of the racket we were making, and also had a tasty line in Polish pastries. Michael "Elvis" Burke was the lead guitarist and would go on to have a career in music, while John Wood was the drummer (not to be confused with the sound engineer of the same name). I still only owned an acoustic guitar, albeit a better, steel-string one, so I played rhythm alongside Malcolm. We would typically rehearse for an hour and then spend three hours arguing about a name for the group—we never managed to agree on one. After a year or so, a slot came up at the St. Aloysius school dance, and we decided that we were going to fill it. By this time, the Beatles had appeared on the scene, and the Shadows were old hat. We needed to sound more like a beat group, and beat groups had singers. We found three from the dubious well of talent that was St. Aloysius' College, making us a very unwieldy eight-piece.

This show was the lever that I needed to convince my father to buy me an electric guitar. Once again, we drew on the friendship of his army mate at Lew Davis, and I scored a very battered sunburst Hofner V3, with holes worn through the pickups, as well as a Selmer Selectortone amplifier, with a stunning fifteen watts of power.

As often happens with young bands, our first show was also our last. We were chronically under-amplified and probably sounded atrocious. The crowd jeered—perhaps there were also some school politics I was unaware of—and started to throw coins at us. Coins are a little lighter nowadays, but in 1963 the old, heavy pennies were still in circulation, and when you threw them, you spun them edgewise like a discus. If they connected with flesh, it hurt. At one point I looked over at Malcolm, who was still managing to smile heroically. He had recently acquired a blood-red Japanese electric guitar, with a white pickguard—except it was now the same color as the guitar's body because he was bleeding all over it from a gash where a penny had struck his hand. We finished the set and bandaged our wounds. There was a pow-wow soon after, and the core of the group sensibly reconfigured into a Johnny Kidd and the Pirates-style three-piece, with vocalist. The rest of us "resigned."

I gained a lot of inspiration from one of my sister's long-term boyfriends, a guy called Richard Roberts-Miller, who helped me with the guitar from the beginning. I'm still grateful to Perri for her lifelong habit of being an hour late for everything, including dates. Richard would come around to pick her up, and because she wasn't ready, I'd get a guitar lesson. "Big Muldoon," as I called him, could play all of Buddy Holly's songs—indeed, he had something of the look of Buddy Holly, complete with the horn-rimmed glasses. Muldoon could also play the Shadows' repertoire and a selection of other rock and roll. He lent my sister and me the first Bob Dylan record and a great EP by the New Orleans guitarist Snooks Eaglin, which helped me learn how to use the fingerstyle technique in a wider context. Muldoon was always friendly, funny and never condescending, even though I was six years his junior.

A subsequent boyfriend of Perri's was Bob Nadkarni, a fellow student of hers at Hornsey College of Art. As often happens with the sons of vicars, they either conform and go into the family business, or rebel, and Bob definitely did the latter—he was every inch the bohemian artist. He played good gut-string guitar; at the time, he was very influenced by the guitarist, lutenist and singer Desmond Dupré, and I stole a lot from Desmond via Bob. Bob would come round the house and perform with little inhibition, singing and playing at the top of his voice to an audience of one, and I would sit and make mental notes of his chords, harmonies and technique. My mind was like a sponge, and every single style and facet of music was relevant.

I found a musical ally at school in Hugh Cornwell, who would later have great success with the Stranglers. He was one of my closest friends—we were both lamppost-thin in those days, and bonded over a mutual love of cricket, a shared confusion over girls and a fascination with the music that you heard around London and on the radio—mostly rhythm and blues, and pop. Hugh, an upbeat and positive boy, was concentrating on sciences at school and was also a talented cartoonist. He bought a home-made bass guitar from another kid at school, before graduating to a Hofner Beatle. With Malcolm on rhythm and a lad called Dave on drums, we rehearsed regularly at a church hall in Highgate and played sporadically at clubs and parties around North London. At some point Malcolm dropped out—I don't remember why— and we became a three-piece. Then we recruited Nick Jones, another William Ellis boy, to replace Dave. Though he seemed a step up as a drummer, it is dangerous to have Keith Moon as your hero. Moonie would play impossible drum fills but land miraculously on the beat; Nick would try the same thing and land in a different song!

Nick's father was the great Max Jones, the jazz critic of the *Melody Maker*, and their house in Muswell Hill was groaning with jazz 78s. He liked me because I could answer his jazz trivia questions, having read his column since I was twelve years old: "Coleman Hawkins?" "Tenor." "Chet Baker?" "Trumpet." "Zutty Singleton?" "Drums." Max's close friendship with so many of the jazz greats, and his vivid descriptions of them, meant that as I listened to their music, it almost felt like I knew them.

Melody Maker had begun in 1926, in the early days of dance bands. A weekly music paper, it had two pages of jazz and two pages of folk, as well as covering every other scene, from Liverpool to Los Angeles and New York. It was where I first heard about psychedelia, John Coltrane, the Butterfield Blues Band and a young folk singer called Sandy Denny. And very importantly, it had a small ads section for recruiting band members. A typical ad of the time would read:

Wanted: Singer for Tull/Quo/Shack-type band that's going places. Must have own PA. Hair, passport, image essential. No time-wasters. No jazzers.

Over the years, the various bands I was in had occasional need of the *Melody Maker* ads page.

On Saturday mornings, I would take the Tube into town and tour the guitar shops, dreaming of owning some of the wondrous instruments on display. I would also visit the bookshops, and at some point I wandered into Watkins bookshop in Cecil Court—the occult theme of the window display was irresistible. I bought a book called *Zen Flesh, Zen Bones* by Paul Reps, and was hooked:

A dunce once searched for a fire with a lighted lantern. Had he known what fire was, he could have cooked his rice much sooner.

Though it was cryptic and puzzling, this made more sense to me than the Presbyterian Church services I had been dragged to from an early age. You could not solve it by thought alone—you had to become a different person. This started me on a quest for meaning in my life. I dreamed of Jesus, but he was mutated and weird.* I visited Watkins regularly over the next ten years.

Muswell Hill was a quiet and leafy suburb of North London, about as far from the center of town as my home in Highgate was. These commuter communities had been villages until they were swallowed up by urban sprawl between the wars. Around the age of sixteen, I started playing with Ashley Hutchings and Simon Nicol in a band that was to become Fairport Convention, and Muswell Hill became my musical focus. Inconveniently, my parents had moved from Highgate by that point, to the suburban wilds of Whetstone, perilously close to the end of the Tube's Northern Line. The journey to band practice now involved waiting for buses that would sometimes never arrive. If I went to see the Who on a Tuesday night at the Marquee Club, I could watch the first set and catch the last train home. If I wanted to see the second set, I knew I would have to walk home—and it was usually worth it—a distance of ten miles, on a school night. No wonder my grades were slipping. I would console myself on these strange nocturnal journeys with thoughts of Percy Bysshe Shelley, who, finding himself without the fare for the coach from London to Oxford one night, decided to walk, a

* See Appendix B, p. 274.

distance of fifty-five miles. They walked more in those days. There is also the story of Johann Sebastian Bach walking two hundred miles to another town to try out a new organ. Ten miles wasn't such a long way, and I broke it down into mile-long twenty-minute segments to keep myself sane. The world is different at night—inanimate things come alive, and once I was in the suburbs, I would often see not a soul. Many years later, I wrote a song called "Walking the Long Miles Home"*:

> *Oh the last bus has gone*
> *Or maybe I'm wrong*
> *It just doesn't exist*
> *And the words that flew*
> *Between me and you*
> *I must be crossed off your list*
>
> *So I'm walking the long miles home*
> *And I don't mind losing you*
> *In fact I feel better each step of the way*
> *In the dark I rehearse all the right things to say*
> *I'll be home, I'll be sober by break of day*
> *Walking the long miles home*

Whetstone might have been less convenient than Highgate, but it did have a folk club, held in the Black Bull pub at the end of our street. There you could see the likes of Bert Jansch, Davey Graham, the Watersons, Shirley Collins or Martin

* See Appendix A, p. 261.

Carthy. Everywhere else was a pain to get to, and I counted
down the days till I could move closer to the action.

In my final year of school, music and painting took up
all my headspace. I would spend as little time as possible on
English homework and zero time in French lessons—I was far
too busy playing gigs to attend classes at 9 A.M.—and would
take about sixteen hours on the weekend to complete a two-
hour art assignment. Okay, maybe I did have a plan D. In my
dreamy world, I might take a gap year and then apply for art
college, where I could waste a few more years, without making up my mind about anything. Looking back, "head in the
clouds" hardly begins to describe my mental state at the age
of eighteen. I had the greatest difficulty with the practical
world—I couldn't fill out a form, I'd daydream on the bus and
miss my stop, I could not confront responsibility and I had a
mortal dread of authority—and yet somehow I believed that if
I didn't deal with it, it would all go away and I could keep on
dreaming. I avoided my family as much as I could. The only
time I felt engaged was when I was with Ashley and Simon, my
musical companions. I knew I would feel free and fulfilled if I
could live that life all the time—but in 1967 that did not seem
an option. The only future that school, my parents and society
permitted involved a "proper" job—accountancy? Banking?

While I was in my final year, rescue arrived. The graphic
designer Hans Unger contacted the school's art department,
asking if any school-leavers would like to work for him on
a temporary basis before moving on to higher education.
Salvation! I applied and was hired. Hans, as I would quickly
learn, was a very accomplished poster designer; a Jewish

refugee from Nazi Germany, he had done some memorable poster series for the Post Office from the late 1940s onward, including "Post Early for Christmas." He also designed iconic "Keep Britain Tidy" posters and dozens of wonderful images for London Transport, many of which are now on display in museums. Hans and his partner Eberhard Schulze, a brilliant mosaicist, were at that point working on a large stained-glass-window project for St. Columba's Church in Chester and needed assistance. I was taught the basics of glass-cutting and how to work with epoxy resin—we did not use traditional lead, instead making the black outlines in the window from a mixture of black pigment and epoxy, which was sticky and tended to splash everywhere. In the afternoons, we would heat the workshop up to one hundred degrees to dry the glue faster—no wonder I was so skinny in those days!

The project consisted of a huge rectangular panel on each side of the church and an arched panel behind the altar. These were all divided into panes that measured four feet by two feet six inches. We would glue the stained glass onto plain glass panes and fill in the gaps with the black cement, keeping in mind that each pane was a small part of a large design. I worked mostly alongside Eberhard, who was charming, informative and forgiving while I learned what I was doing. Often I was left to work alone, as other projects were also running. I learned to distinguish between German glass, which was rolled flat with consistent color, and English glass, which was uneven with streaky color. The English stuff was a pig to cut and I picked up many lacerations on my hands, often in inconvenient places for a guitarist. I still have some scars on my fingers to this day. For my lunch break, I would grab a sandwich and head off into Highgate Woods, directly behind Hans's house. There I would sit on a bench and dream that the forest was absorbing me, sucking my life force down into the soil.

Hans and Eberhard loved to work to classical music, and there were two feeds in the workshop: one was Radio 3, the BBC's classical music station, and the other was the record player, which might be playing Wagner's "Ring Cycle" or something more to my taste, like Hans Werner Henze. The combination of the music and the intense colors of the glass on the light table could send me into sensory overload, and I'd often find myself tearful with emotion. Once a week there was a run to the library to pick up a new batch of records, and I might be asked if there was anything I would like to hear. I usually asked for Elgar or Vaughan Williams—music that I had heard on the radio at home and grown to love—but this would elicit a dismissive snort from Hans and a cry of "Not that English sentimental shit!" Still, he would borrow them and let me play them. Most of the playlist was German; Eberhard would discuss the virtues of good architecture in music and considered French composers like Debussy to be "frivolous." I once asked Hans how, as a refugee from Nazi atrocities, he could love the music of Wagner, a well-documented racist. He gave a shrug of the shoulders and said, "Nice tunes?" We both cracked up at that.

The epoxy destroyed clothing at an alarming rate. In those days I had little money to spend on clothes, so I would borrow old shirts from my father, each of which would last maybe a week. I relied on a couple of pairs of jeans for work, gigs and leisure. I had one good checked shirt that my sister had bought me from Carnaby Street, when the Walker Brothers were at the peak of their popularity and doing the lumberjack look. That was okay to wear on stage—thanks to the Rolling Stones, bands no longer had to wear a suit and tie to perform and I could stagger on in my street clothes.

My LIFE AT the age of eighteen consisted of equal parts frustration and joy. I was frustrated to still be stuck out in a suburban wasteland with my parents. School had been something to be endured but was happily over. I had a steady girlfriend by this point, which was an improvement on the occasional kiss and grope at a party. So much of my pleasure and self-esteem came from music and art, and I longed for a life where I could devote more time to them. I considered myself a reasonable electric guitarist—I wasn't very original but I had quite a wide range of influences, and I longed to play more music. I could be opinionated and socially awkward, but was less so on a stage. I lost my temper easily, which I was ashamed of and resolved to overcome. At my core, though, I was an optimist—like my mother, who had refused to go down into the bomb shelters during the Blitz, preferring to sleep in her own bed and believing that God would protect her. Though I believed in a more abstract version of a benign universe, I similarly thought that everything would turn out fine.

2

Instead of Bleeding

If a literary man puts together two words
about music, one of them will be wrong.
AARON COPLAND

I MET ASHLEY "Tyger" Hutchings through my schoolfriend Brian Wyvill, who lived a few doors away from him in Durnsford Road, Muswell Hill. Brian had been recommending us to each other for a while, so it was inevitable that we should cross paths eventually, and it finally happened one sunny afternoon across a suburban garden gate. You could bet your life that any band run by Tyger in 1966, of which there were several, would have an obscure repertoire. For Dr. K's Blues Band, he used to track down and play B-sides by artists who had been mere footnotes in blues anthologies, and for the Ethnic Shuffle Orchestra he revived the 1920s repertoires of Gus Cannon and the Memphis Jug Band. There certainly wasn't anyone else doing that in North London at that time! At twenty-one, Ashley was five years older than me. He was working as a journalist at *Advertisers Weekly*, and was good-looking in the pale and interesting way that Ashleys often are (think Ashley Wilkes, from *Gone with the Wind*). I filled in on occasion for some of his bands and must have passed muster, because he began to include me in his projects, which is how I ran into Simon Nicol.

Simon, who along with Ashley formed the backbone of the Ethnic Shuffle Orchestra, was affable and adept at the twelve-string acoustic guitar, which he was strumming when I first met him at his home in Muswell Hill. He was fifteen, but he seemed mature and worldly for his age. He had already left school by this point, and was working as a projectionist at the Odeon cinema in Highgate—it appeared to be quite a glamorous job, and I envied his freedom and earning power. Musically and culturally, the three of us were on the same page. I had been playing in bands for years, but this consortium of musical friends was far more thoughtful and musically inquisitive than any I had experienced before, and we were also more determined to be original. If the opportunity arose, we would happily turn ourselves into a blues band, an acoustic folk band or a folk rock band—whichever gave us a chance to play. Our drummer was Shaun Frater, who had gone to the same school as Simon, and we played at parties, bowling alleys, school dances and in the upstairs rooms of pubs.

Judy Dyble was another young Muswell Hill musician in Ashley's address book. Petite, pretty, shy and slightly eccentric, she sang in folk clubs with her own band, and would occasionally join Ashley, Simon and me to play an acoustic set at one of the many clubs in the area. Sometime in 1966, Judy and I started dating. Our common ground was English literature A level—we were both still at school—and our obsession with all sorts of music, from folk to Stockhausen.

Simon's family owned a large mock Tudor house called Fairport on Fortis Green. It had been the family home and also housed his father's medical practice. Ray and Dave Davies of the Kinks grew up literally down the road. Not long before I first met Simon, his father had tragically died of cancer, and he and his mother moved to a smaller flat nearby. Fairport was rented out, and Ashley was one of the renters. It was a large, sparsely furnished house, with a capacious living room that was ideal for rehearsing in—the only problem was that our PA system would sometimes pick up shortwave radio transmissions from the fire station next door. Ashley soon realized that his landlady's son Simon played the guitar, and recruited him to play in the Ethnic Shuffle Orchestra. Richard Lewis and Kingsley Abbott were two friends in the area who both had record collections that we could raid; Richard suggested the name Fairport Convention for the band, which seemed to sum us up nicely—plus, in keeping with bands like Jefferson Airplane, Quicksilver Messenger Service, Strawberry Alarm Clock and Hapshash and the Coloured Coat, it was suitably polysyllabic for the age.

We rehearsed whenever possible, polishing a repertoire of covers of the Byrds and the Lovin' Spoonful, along with a bit of blues and R&B and the odd country song. Our drummer, Shaun, was probably the weakest link in the band at that point. Our short-term ambition was to play competently together and have enough songs for a couple of sets. We were planning to play our first show as Fairport, but before that happened there was an important watershed moment in our own backyard.

The *14 Hour Technicolor Dream* was a concert at Alexandra Palace on 29 April 1967 that might be described as a "psychedelic happening." The idea of a happening had existed in the world of Pop Art for a decade or so—an artistic event that broke the norms of perception and behavior. This was my first experience of the LSD version of that, with loud music and light shows that were intended to disorient the participant and lead them to experience reality differently.

The sound hit me as soon as I walked through the door. It was like being inside a huge bell that was being hammered from the outside: the cacophony seemed to blend into one deafening drone. The hall was the size of a couple of middling cathedrals, and the music was bouncing off the ceiling. Standing in the middle of the hall, I could hear three bands at once! I got close to the stage and watched Pink Floyd, Soft Machine, Sam Gopal and the Crazy World of Arthur Brown. The music was loud, self-indulgent, theatrical and quite experimental. It was as if the shackles of pop music had been removed during the previous few months, and a kind of musical anarchy had taken over. The friends I had come with vanished and reappeared again through the course of the night. There were light shows and silent films from the 1920s. Some people were smoking dried banana peel and the smell of hashish was strong in the air, while a lot of the crowd were undoubtedly on acid. John Lennon was wandering around, looking every inch an impersonation of himself, with his moustache, NHS spectacles and Afghan jacket. Yoko Ono did a performance called "Cut Piece" that involved inviting members of the crowd to cut pieces from a girl's dress until she was naked. There must have been ten thousand people in there. One of the members of Soft Machine, Pink Floyd's rival for the most famous psychedelic band in

London, was wearing a top hat with the wings of a model glider attached to it, which seemed almost like the new sartorial normal. Was this what it was like at the famous Fillmore in San Francisco, on any given day of the week?

Here was proof of the arrival of a new culture. The Mods had ruled for a couple of years, with their Italian suits, parkas and Lambrettas, but now the hippies were taking over, with bell-bottoms, paisley shirts and long hair. There was a new spirit in the air.

Britain was already the global epicenter of youth culture, which had begun in around 1963 with the Beatles and the Stones, Jean Shrimpton, David Bailey, Mary Quant, the *Avengers* TV series and the pioneering Pop artists Richard Hamilton and Peter Blake. Carnaby Street was world-famous, and you could go to the King's Road for loon pants, military jackets and other Victorian cast-offs. Hair was growing longer—my own was barely an inch longer than school regulations but I was only a month away from leaving school for ever, so was working on it. I never wanted to be predictable enough to be part of a "scene," and looked on with detached amusement at the antics of my generation. At the same time, I was keen not to stand out as a "square"—that would have taken more courage than I was willing to muster. I also wanted a love life, so I realized that I needed to look a bit contemporary in this new hippie way. I endured my parents teasing me about my hair and clothes. My sister had by this time gone away to art college, leaving me directly in the firing line, but like teenagers before and since, I relied on the thickness of a bedroom door to insulate me.

And where did *we* fit in—Ashley, Simon and I, our little musical nucleus? Was our music viable for an audience that was getting off on Soft Machine and the Pretty Things, the Crazy World of Arthur Brown and the Social Deviants? Well, we didn't really care whether we fitted in or not. We had an extraordinary amount of self-belief, fueled by Ashley's visions and idealism, and loved the thought that we were ploughing new musical furrows.

We decided to launch Fairport Convention with a bit of a fanfare, so booked St. Michael's Church Hall in Golders Green, well within our North London catchment area, and put up posters in the fluorescent style of the times. Our set that evening consisted of covers of bands that we admired: "7 and 7 Is" by Love, "Killing Floor" by Howlin' Wolf and "Turn! Turn! Turn!" by the Byrds. There were about fifty people in the audience, and I'm sure we knew almost all of them. We repaired to a Chinese restaurant afterwards, and fed the band and immediate circle on the profits from the gig. £5 went a long way in those days.

Although the gig was meaningful as the first time we played under the name Fairport Convention, it came to be more significant as the completion of a puzzle. Martin Lamble, a young drummer in the audience who was a friend of Kingsley Abbott, suggested that he could play better than Shaun, and after giving him an audition soon afterwards, we agreed. Martin was a pleasant, studious and occasionally very funny young man of seventeen, with a fine head of blond, wavy hair. A grammar-school boy like the rest of us, he came from not-too-distant Harrow and very quickly became a part of the fabric of the group. With him in the band, we felt more like a real musical entity. Judy, who was still my girlfriend at that point, also joined permanently, and the gigs began to roll in. It was unusual at the time for a band to have a female member, and that distinguished us from other groups, although we felt that we were distinguished more by our interest in lyrics and our offbeat set list.

At this point, we were still singing the music of our heroes, like the Lovin' Spoonful or the Byrds, in addition to singer-songwriter material that we felt was worth covering. Our versions were a little different, sometimes as a result of our musical shortcomings and misunderstandings of what we heard on a record, and sometimes due to a conscious effort to be a bit different. Playing a Byrds song without a twelve-string guitar meant that I had to play riffs using octaves, while trying to "jangle" as much as possible under the vocal. Covering Leonard Cohen's "Suzanne," which we learned from the Judy Collins version, meant coming up with a whole new arrangement, and we managed to create a kind of bolero feel between the guitar and drum pattern that made it popular when we played it live.

At this point, regular gigs were beginning to trickle in, and that summer we were somehow offered a residency at a beach bar in Spain. We were all very excited about this, and everyone's parents were happy to let their kids go and enjoy this opportunity—all except my father, despite entreaties from my bandmates' parents. He had a misguided sense that he had to oversee my life, which did not help our already fractured relationship. Did he think I was too young to be playing in a bar?

Coming from someone who was so often drunk, I thought that was rather rich. I resolved to escape from the parental home at the first chance I got.

Musicians are notoriously flaky when it comes to financial matters, and bands often reach out to someone they know and trust to protect them from the sharks in suits. Their confidence can be misplaced when their friends sometimes turn out to be just as willing to sell them down the river as any cigar-chewing corporate sleazebag, but this wasn't the case with Fairport. We turned to our friends John Penhallow and Keith Roberts to be our manager and roadie respectively, and they did a good and honest job. We were soon signed to the Bryan Morrison Agency, who seemed to handle half the bands in London. Bryan's main interest was playing polo; he used to play with Prince Charles and also owned a racehorse with the great name of Gwaaanmyson! That alone is almost enough to forgive him everything—but not quite. Poor John Penhallow would sit in Morrison's office for days on end, trying to arrange for us to be paid for the gigs we'd played. We later learned that Bryan liked to keep the money that rolled in for at least three months to earn the interest from the bank, while we could really have used it ourselves. But being on the agency's roster meant that when a university phoned and asked for half a dozen bands to play an all-night rave, we would get booked, alongside Pink Floyd, the Social Deviants, the Incredible String Band and Tyrannosaurus Rex.

Due to the influence of our agency, we were playing gigs almost as soon as we'd formed, partly as a result of British government policy. Outside of London, there were very few clubs that catered to the underground music scene: the Van Dike in Plymouth, Mothers in Birmingham, Redcar Jazz Club were three, and there were a couple more dotted around. Most of the venues outside London were universities, polytechnics, teacher training colleges or art schools, all of which had an entertainment grant that was subsidized by Harold Wilson's Labour government. Anti-establishment and counter-cultural groups were thriving, and all thanks to the British taxpayer. A larger university like Manchester would put on huge all-nighters with as many as twenty bands, including psychedelic groups but also chart bands like the Hollies and the Small Faces. It never occurred to us that we should bend our style to fit in with the new musical scene and we were accepted by audiences, along with all the other acts.

We had been playing as Fairport only for a month or two when we were booked to play at the UFO Club in London. This was established in the Blarney, an Irish pub on Tottenham Court Road, and the house band was Pink Floyd—at least some of the time. The Floyd were Britain's leading psychedelic band then. Syd Barrett wasn't a great musician in the ortho-dox sense, but he had a good instinct for the possibilities of music. Audiences at that time were generous and tolerant of experimentation—songs could last for half an hour and they would lap it up. The fact that the crowds were just as stoned and zonked on acid as the bands probably helped enormously. I recently learned that Syd's father's great-grandmother was a cousin of Elizabeth Garrett Anderson, Britain's first female doctor, who was my mother's great-great-aunt. Syd and I were, in fact, distant cousins.

On 28 July 1967 Fairport opened for the Floyd. That was the night that Syd overdosed on LSD, and Dave Gilmour had to play Syd's guitar parts behind the stage. That was also the night we met Joe Boyd for the first time. Joe, who ran the UFO with John "Hoppy" Hopkins, was also a record producer and had by this time recorded the Incredible String Band, the Purple Gang and Pink Floyd. Joe was only in his mid-twenties but had quite a track record in roots music. He'd booked Lonnie Johnson while he was in college, stage-managed Newport Folk Festival when Dylan went electric in 1965, and had also run the UK office of Elektra Records. Joe was about six feet four, handsome and inescapably clean-cut. He looked like a cross between Ivy League and hippie, in seersucker jacket and velvet loon pants. Anyway, he seemed to take to our music—after our set, he met us backstage and said he'd enjoyed it. With a grin that suggested he was aware of the cliché, he said, "Let's make a record!"

So, just two months into our incarnation as Fairport, we were offered a record deal. We were incredibly excited—it felt like a vindication that our chosen style, far from the zeitgeist of psychedelia, was acceptable, at least to one American man whose taste was similar to ours. Looking back, I think I also felt a tiny bit of arrogant teenage superiority. I thought, "Well of course we're going to make a record!" But Joe was probably the only person in Britain who understood the musical roots of what we were doing and who would have "got" Fairport fully—we were lucky to have found him before we were forced into someone else's vision of us as a pop or psychedelic act. Joe knew the young Joni Mitchell, and gave us some of

her as-yet-unrecorded songs. And he had shared a room at
Harvard with Geoff Muldaur from the Jim Kweskin Jug Band,
one of our heroes. He was connected to many of the strains
of music that we loved, so we immediately felt a great affinity
for him, and as someone who was even older than Ashley, we
trusted him to serve our best interests.

Soon after our meeting with Joe, we went in to record for
the first time. For this dummy run we had learned how to play
Joni Mitchell's "Both Sides Now," a song that we felt was too
well known to be considered for a Fairport record but which
we could practice in the studio to get used to the recording
process.

Sound Techniques was on Old Church Street in Chelsea,
between the hippie bustle of the fashionable King's Road and
the grey procession of the River Thames. The studio itself was
a former dairy, and the building bears a sculpture of a cow's
head. It was hard to get past the Danish patisserie next door
without succumbing, and the Black Lion pub opposite offered
sandwiches and alcoholic refreshment, which fueled many
a session. The interior of the studio was workmanlike, with
functional decor that never seemed quite finished. Unusually
for a recording studio, it had a couple of windows, but the
sound was wonderful. On first impression the control room
looked like a spaceship, with impossible amounts of technical
gear wedged into a fairly tight space, a thousand lights blink-
ing. From then on, I was suspicious of studios that were shiny.

Geoff Frost and John Wood owned and ran Sound
Techniques, which was one of the first independent studios
in London. They had both previously worked at Levy's Studio,

Geoff building equipment and John in the mastering room. Before that, John had cut classical records at Decca. John and Joe Boyd had already established a good working relationship on previous projects. It wasn't exactly good cop, bad cop, but Joe would allow the musicians plenty of space to express themselves and would let things flow, while at the same time having a good idea of when a take was good and when to call a tea break—all while checking the baseball scores in the *New York Herald Tribune*. John would tell people exactly what he thought, and he did not suffer fools gladly. Between the two of them, there was a good balance. John taught us a lot about the studio. He told Martin how important it was to tune the drums properly, using Nick Mason from Pink Floyd as an example. He also told him he should get a deeper snare drum, and to hit the drums harder—Martin took tips like these to heart, and you can hear the difference after the first album.

After one session John took me down to the studio floor and showed me a guitar amp that belonged to the session guitarist Judd Proctor. My studio amp was the same as my stage amp at that time, a Marshall 4 × 12, because it was all I could afford. Judd's was a little single speaker, a ten-watt affair. Then John played me a bit of Judd's work, and it sounded full and even. After that I started to look for ways to get a more balanced guitar tone, which led me to the out-of-phase setting on the Fender Stratocaster, and for a smaller amp to use in the studio.

We got through our recording of "Both Sides Now" in about five takes. We could play it without making any mistakes, and that was enough for the first recording—we could think about feel, groove and emotion in the next session. Joe thought we should add more vocal power to the band, so we recruited Iain Matthews, who was then in a vocal group called the Pyramid. Iain seemed to have a good understanding of the singer-songwriter genre, and like us was into Tim Hardin and Tim Buckley. He also had a taste for country acts like Waylon Jennings.

Country music at that time was deeply unfashionable in London, and was considered the epitome of bad taste. In Liverpool, so many records came over with sailors and ended up in second-hand shops that it was more accepted as a part of every band's repertoire—so Ringo sang the Beatles song "Act Naturally," and every Scouse bass player played a modified country-style bass part on the pop hits. By contrast, Southerners who were into country music tended to dress in a cartoon American style, drive big American cars and go for the worst aspects of the genre—the sentimental tearjerkers that were all about Mama, prison and D-I-V-O-R-C-E. There was a famous club in Chelmsford that catered to hardcore country fans, where the audience dressed as cowboys and would carry replica Colt .45 guns, and there was always a wagon wheel and a bale of hay on the stage. Still, we appreciated the songwriting and musicianship of good country music that went along with the corny stuff. We were into Hank Williams, played some covers of Johnny Cash and appreciated the Byrds when they leaned in that direction.

Iain came down to the studio to meet us, but I don't think he ever had any kind of audition. It was more a matter of us saying to him, "Could you put a harmony on that?" or

"Can you do something over this section?" and that was that—he seamlessly became a member of the band. He was a bit more dapper than the rest of us. He had recently been working in Ravel's shoe shop in Carnaby Street as a day job, so I found myself wearing his cast-offs for the next few years.

Now that recording was part of our lives, we had to start writing our own material—the audience expected it. The days of divvying things up—singers singing, writers writing, producers producing, arrangers arranging and engineers engineering—had ended just a few years earlier, largely thanks to the Beatles, who wrote and performed their own material so successfully that everyone else had to play catch-up. Bands like the Stones and the Yardbirds had to write their own material in order to achieve credibility with the audience—it was the end of covers bands. The lines were blurring as bands produced themselves, engineers became producers and recording staff at EMI no longer wore lab coats, which had previously been obligatory.

Just about everyone in Fairport contributed to the songwriting. By this time, I had moved out of the family home and had taken a flat with a couple of old schoolfriends, Andy Horvitch and Paul Ghosh. Our flat, at 33 St. Mary's Road in deeply unfashionable Brent, had no central heating and was furnished with grey industrial carpet and brown furniture. However, it was wonderful to feel independent, and the future felt brighter than the decor. Brent boasted an Indian restaurant and a laundromat, but for anything else we would have to walk a mile to Golders Green, which was only slightly less unfashionable. We lived upstairs from a bunch of Australian girls. We thought there were nine of them; there were actually only three, but every day they would each wear a different wig—blonde, brunette or redhead—so it was about a year before we got the headcount right. They would endlessly play Stan Getz records—"The Girl from Ipanema" was a favorite—and I was always surprised by how many bum notes Stan hit on his recordings, until I realized that someone down there was learning the saxophone and playing along.

At least the lack of French bistros and stylish boutiques in Brent concentrated the mind. Having written a couple of tunes that I thought might work for the band, I recruited Andy and Paul as co-lyricists, having no confidence in my own abilities, and we worked together on the songs "Sun Shade" and "Decameron." At least now I had broken the creative ice and had compositions that I could take to the band. The songs were obscure in their meaning and were a hodgepodge of musical styles, but they had some originality. It felt like good practice for the next time.

As it turned out, the next time came quickly. Ashley and I wrote "It's All Right Ma, It's Only Witchcraft," the title being an obvious nod to Dylan. The song was a thinly veiled satire on Witchseason, Joe Boyd's production office, and its inhabitants, including Danny Halperin, who ran a design company in the adjacent office, and Joe's partner Tod Lloyd. Danny was an American who seemed to know everybody in the jazz and folk worlds, and he designed our first poster. He would occasionally harangue us through the door of his office, in a way that reinforced his view of himself as a man of vast experience and made us feel like a bunch of naive children. He had a few good stories, though—wasn't he at that party where Bob Dylan had hogged the record player, playing Robert Johnson for hours and making everyone hate him? And he'd gone out with the jazz singer Annie Ross—how cool was that?

One day, Tod took me down to the Ivor Mairants Musicentre, Britain's first specialist guitar shop, just off Oxford Street, to buy me my first "serious" guitar. They had a Gibson ES-175D, and I lovingly ran my hands over it. Jerry Miller, the lead guitarist in Moby Grape, played a big jazz Gibson L-7, and this was similar—by this time it wasn't really regarded as a rock and roll guitar of choice, having been overlooked in favor of solid-body instruments. Ivor Mairants had been a pretty good jazz player himself with the Ted Heath Band, and he looked down his nose at the sight of such a fine instrument in the hands of a rock and roll yob. Ivor was notoriously tight, but Tod drove a hard bargain and got him to change the guineas price to pounds, with the case thrown in, and we walked out of the shop with a serious upgrade. This was the guitar I used on that first album. Tod also sold me his John Bailey acoustic guitar and loaned me his sitar—after all, this was 1967! That year, I took lessons with Nazir Jairazbhoy, an eminent scholar in the folk and classical music of South Asia at the University of London, in a class with Andy Summers. Nazir would hold weekend concerts at his house, featuring touring Indian classical musicians. The standard of musicianship was staggering, and it was a privilege to see something that very few people knew about outside the Asian community.

Other tracks we recorded at that time included "The Lobster," an adaptation of a poem by George Painter, which

I had discovered in *The Penguin Book of Sick Verse*. "Jack o' Diamonds" was a song that had survived from the days of my band at school. The actor Ben Carruthers had set the poem by Bob Dylan to music, and Nick Jones had unearthed it from among a pile of demos at *Melody Maker*. We also did a couple of Joni Mitchell covers, "I Don't Know Where I Stand" and "Chelsea Morning," from her early demos that Joe had obtained.

We also covered "Time Will Show the Wiser" by the Merry-Go-Round, which I think we'd found in Kingsley Abbott's record collection. And I co-wrote another song with Iain, "If (Stomp)," which I was never totally satisfied with. We were trying to be like a jug band and witty, and I don't think we quite managed either. "One Sure Thing" came from the American folk duo Jim and Jean, and Judy also contributed a track, "Portfolio." One of our best live performances was the cover of Leonard Cohen's "Suzanne," but for some reason it didn't make it onto the album—perhaps it was becoming too well known by that point.

We were playing a lot more live shows by now, and we'd slot in recording on our days off, or sometimes late at night after a show. We had also recorded a single, a version of the 1930s jazz arrangement by Maxine Sullivan of the folk song "If I Had a Ribbon Bow." It was not particularly representative of Fairport's style, but what was? Singles were a slightly delicate subject at the time. All the underground bands saw themselves as album artists because albums gave them the space to stretch songs and improvise, but everyone would also put out singles to gain some radio attention. I remember being in the bath when "If I Had a Ribbon Bow" got played on Radio 2's

Night Ride—this was around 12:30 A.M. I remember the DJ, Dwight Wylie, absolutely hated it and kept saying, "Oh dear, oh dear," as it was playing. I knocked the radio into the bath and still have no idea how I failed to electrocute myself.

In the studio, the length of a song was limited by the amount of tape available and the amount of space on the disc or cassette where the recording was going to end up. Though a band might think it was okay to have a single song take up one entire side of an LP, they would probably choose to have more tracks. When playing live, it was a different matter. Long instrumental passages were part and parcel of a band's performance in 1967, and Fairport was no exception. I think it must have started with bands like the Grateful Dead, who would play when they were basically out of their skulls, and lose touch with time and space. It did not seem indulgent at that time for me to play a guitar solo for ten minutes—in fact, it was expected. Half an hour would not have been exceptional, as audiences were increasingly stoned and hearing things from an altered perspective—we, on the other hand, were relatively sober. It also helped when we needed to come up with three sets of material. I got into the habit of musical excursions into semi-charted or uncharted waters, and would drag the audience along for the ride.

There wasn't much time for leisure outside of the band. Judy and I might grab a meal occasionally or go to an exhibition, and there was also a small social scene at number 33—friends would come and go, usually with an LP or two under their arm. When Andy and Paul moved on, Simon and Iain moved in, making pick-ups and drop-offs for gigs a little more straightforward. Above all, our idea of a good time was to soak up some of the wide range of great music and art that was coming through London in those days—Albert Ayler at Ronnie Scott's, Humphrey Lyttelton at the Gate House in Highgate and Alberto Giacometti at the Tate Gallery.

We were working three or four days a week, but most of our shows were still in and around London. We drove a borrowed butcher's van that was lined with metal in the back so that it could be hosed down at the end of the working day and then rented to us. However, it would still smell strongly of meat, and there were no seats—the gear and most of the band would slide around every time we went round a corner. We then graduated to an old Securicor Commer van, which, though it had seating for all and room for equipment, also had a large hole in the floor where the rust had eaten through. We used this van through the winter of 1967, huddling together for warmth, as we began to play gigs in a few more out-of-town venues. We also had a new roadie called Phil Dudderidge, who had worked for Joe Boyd's poster company and the Incredible String Band. An affable fellow, Phil got us through traffic jams, snow drifts and freezing fog. He worked for Led Zeppelin a few years later; eventually he started companies called Soundcraft and Focusrite, which were very successful at making mixing consoles and outboard studio gear.

Our bread-and-butter gigs, and the core of our audience, were still in London, at places like the Country Club in Belsize Park, the Speakeasy Club on Margaret Street and the Electric Garden in Covent Garden. The Country Club was the bar of a tennis club, and it felt like our "local" venue. The place probably held 150 people, and it was always completely packed. On a summer's evening, the audience would spill out during the intervals into the pub next door and down the hill towards Belsize Park Tube station. If we ever truly felt among our fanbase, I would say it was there—middle-class teens in North London who liked their rock with a bit of folk mixed in, or vice versa.

We must have played the Speakeasy once a week in the early days. It was a late-night club in London's West End that didn't really get rolling until about 9 P.M., and it would often fill up with bands who had driven back from Birmingham or Manchester after their gigs. We would play two or three sets a night at the club, but could never afford to eat there. Clearly the idea of a sadist, the only free food that was ever on offer was lettuce sandwiches. A leaf of lettuce between two slices of dry Wonder Bread, it would make you incredibly thirsty—which was the whole point. There were always a lot of musicians in the audience. One night, the songwriter Graham Nash was sat at a front table, and Ashley was making some between-songs patter, saying that Fairport didn't seem to have much luck with money—that we were "sort of like King Midas in reverse." A little later, this showed up as the title of a Hollies hit. Another night, I looked up after playing a solo to see Cilla Black a few yards in front of me, frugging wildly.

Jimi Hendrix was a regular at the "Speak." His arrival in London had made a huge impact. He combined Pete Townshend's stage act with lessons that he'd learned on the Chitlin' Circuit in the States, and married that to some ground-breaking musicianship. A superb blues player, Hendrix was one of the first people to really exploit the possibilities of feedback. He was a good singer, a fine composer and a wonderful arranger. His appearance on the scene made many British players, most of whom had learned their skills by copying records by Chicago bluesmen, start to question themselves. Here, suddenly, was the real thing—he wasn't just on tour, he was living in London. There was a new kid on the block, who could play, perform and sing better than anyone else. The stars of the British blues scene suddenly seemed outgunned—where did Jimi's arrival leave Eric, Jeff, Peter and Pete? Seeing him perform made me feel as inadequate as anybody, but I thought that if I could not compete, perhaps I could jump sideways—above everything else, I was striving for originality.

Jimi would finish his dinner and have a few drinks, and then he would feel like playing. On several occasions he got on stage with us. He would borrow one of our guitars and play it just fine—even though he was playing it upside down, it was still strung the wrong way round for him, but genius will find a way. I particularly remember him playing bass on "East–West" by Paul Butterfield and guitar on "Like a Rolling Stone." He seemed personable, likeable, a little shy, and he had a beautiful honey-colored complexion and a delightful smile. It seemed to me that he epitomized the look of the time better than anyone else—a military jacket from the Portobello Road boutique I Was Lord Kitchener's Valet, velvet flares, perhaps a feather boa from Biba, a paisley headband and a Spanish dancer's hat. My sister, who had by now graduated from Hornsey College of Art and had her own boutique, counted Jimi as a client.

Some of our earliest shows in Central London were at the Electric Garden, or Middle Earth as it was later known. It was essentially a large basement in Covent Garden, which at that point was the main fruit and vegetable market in London. The atmosphere, but not the murder rate, is accurately depicted in Hitchcock's 1972 film *Frenzy*, which was set in the area. If you were one of the smaller bands on the line-up, it was quite possible that you would find yourselves playing one set at 9 P.M. and another at 5 A.M. In the meantime, you could either go home and grab six hours' sleep or stay to watch the other bands, who might include Elmer Gantry's Velvet Opera, Mighty Baby, Graham Bond or Tyrannosaurus Rex. The gaps between performances at the club inspired a long-running joke: "What's the biggest break of your career?" "Eight hours between sets at Middle Earth!" It held a couple of hundred people, and three stages were squeezed into the space. Sometime in 1968, the club closed down. It had been hit by a couple of police raids, and the place suffered severe damage when a band called the Tribe of the Sacred Mushroom performed a play there, and a rumour, completely untrue, went around the market workers that a child was being burned at the stake. Outraged, they stormed into the club with axes and box hooks, destroying everything they could.

Outside the club there was always a strange meeting of cultures. There would be hippies dressed as deranged peacocks, and among them there would also be the market workers, in their flat caps and leather aprons. The Royal Opera House was just around the corner, and in those days audiences would dress to the nines, with the men in black tie and women in evening gowns. There was a famous sausage sandwich stall in one corner of the market square, and there, at around 11 P.M., the three cultures would collide. It was always friendly, with the normal barriers of age and class for some reason not applying. For me, another bizarre layer to all this was the fact that my father was then stationed at Covent Garden police station, not a hundred yards off the market square. Being a plain-clothes officer, he would dress like a market worker to "blend in." Fortunately, he and I always timed our shifts slightly differently and never ran into each other. Given the police raids on the club that I often played in, it would have been strange. The police always stuck out like a sore thumb. I remember going to a festival at around that time, and wandering into the crowd to listen to the music. It was densely packed, but right in the middle there was a big space about twenty-five feet across. Standing in the middle of it were two plain-clothes drug squad coppers with short hair, dressed in kaftans and beads and fooling absolutely no one.

I did ask Dad about another incident, though. The market had its own licensing hours for the benefit of the market workers, so the pubs there stayed open all night. I was in one of them having a quiet pint one night when there was an altercation, with much shouting and a threat to throw somebody out. A voice then rose above the noise and said, "How dare you! Don't you know who I am? I'm Josef Locke!" I had no idea who that was, but the people in the pub certainly did. "Give us a song, Josey!" "Give us 'A Shawl of Galway Grey'!" Josef Locke was a famous Irish tenor, from a later generation than Count John McCormack, but with a similar repertoire of the more sentimental Irish folk songs, plus a few light classics. He was in exile from the UK because the Inland Revenue was after him for unpaid taxes. In his absence, imitators were touring Britain, performing under his name, so it was unclear whether this was the real man or a phony. Anyway, this man did sing and he sounded pretty good, with just an occasional crack from a fine voice that had been semi-neglected and an occasional slur from an over-lubricated tongue. He then left in a fairly bad humor, swaying slightly and cursing about the insults he had suffered. The next day, when I told my father about it, he said it was probably the real Josef Locke and dug out one of his 78s. I still don't know for sure, but many years later I wrote a song about it,* which began like this:

> *My name is Josef Locke*
> *God bless all here and state your pleasure*
> *If you'll refill my glass*
> *I'll sing "Ave Maria"*
> *I'll sing "The Old Bog Road"*
> *Or "A Shawl of Galway Grey"*

Locke was incredibly famous to one generation, and then almost unknown to the next. His sentimentality and showmanship were anathema to the baby boomers in Ireland and the UK, who sought a comparatively no-frills, traditional approach. In Fairport, we looked at fame warily and would never admit to wanting it for ourselves. We were pleased to see

---

* See Appendix A, p. 262.

our names in print, our concerts and records reviewed by the music press and our worth assessed by others, but our intention was always music first. We always thought our way was best, whether anyone else understood it or not.

In February 1968, our single "If I Had a Ribbon Bow" had come out on Track Records, the label run by Kit Lambert and Chris Stamp, managers of the Who. It sold about three copies, and I resolved never again to get excited about success or failure—I would keep an even keel and see success on my own terms. Joe, hopeful that our chances might improve if we were on a larger label, moved us to Polydor for our first album, the eponymous *Fairport Convention*. The artwork for the cover became an urgent matter. Cover concepts are often an area where everyone from the band themselves up to the senior echelons of management feels qualified to contribute ideas. Some junior executive somewhere, no doubt wearing a suit at a meeting in an office, had the bright idea of us all sitting in a rowing eight in the middle of the Thames, at dawn, to "capture the light." So we were dragged from our beds at about 4 A.M. and taken down to the river in taxis; there we sat for two hours, miserable and freezing, in a remarkably flimsy vessel. We did not drown, although for quite a lot of the time it felt like the better option. Predictably, the pictures came back and were unusable, though the aforementioned executive escaped with his scalp intact. We had more luck with the photographer Donald Silverstein, who was flavour of the month, having recently shot iconic images of Hendrix. He sat us around a Tiffany lamp in a London studio with a few favorite objects, marbles and Marx Brothers, faces floating in a sea of shadow.

With the album in the can, our live shows now took us all over Britain. If I have one abiding impression of the time we spent touring during the winter of 1967, it is of never being warm. The van was freezing and dressing rooms were often unheated. Pubs north of Watford figured that real men who drank eight pints were heated from the inside, so why waste fuel?

We stayed in terrible guest houses. We shared rooms, and occasionally beds. All bedding appeared to be damp nylon, which had the remarkable quality of being neither warm nor cool when needed. When we checked into our rooms, they were like icebergs, but we could turn on the single-element electric fire, which would cozy things up after about three hours. We'd slip into bed with all our clothes on. It was better to sleep slightly drunk, to take the edge off these minor discomforts. Some guest houses consisted of a whole row of terraced houses knocked together—echoes of the Beatles' *Help!*, when they all go in different doors, but it's the same house—so you might get your key at one end of the street, then walk up and down twenty-five flights of stairs going from house to house, to reach your room at the other end. Some guest houses became regulars; one was the "Lay-By" (pronounced "Lie-Be") at Five Ways in Birmingham. The couple who ran it seemed to consider how young we were, Simon being a mere sixteen, and looked out for us as best they could. They prided themselves on their full English breakfast, and we prided ourselves on mimicking their very strong Brummie accents—"Meekst grrreel" (mixed grill) and "Twurn royt oyer" (turn right here). Mostly we avoided staying overnight anywhere, preferring to save money by driving back to London.

After just a few months on the road, we were asked to do some sessions for BBC radio. All the bands did them, and we welcomed the extra cash. Because of a deal between the BBC and the Musicians' Union, the Beeb could play only a limited number of hours of recorded music per week, known as "needle time," and had to supplement this with "live" sessions on the popular music channels. This was supposed to keep the union's members from being put out of work; I suppose it did to some extent, unless you were a trombone player who was never going to be employed anyway. We would go into one of the BBC's many recording facilities in London and usually cut four or five tracks, which would be broadcast the week after. When our first session was broadcast that December, we were so amazed to hear ourselves that we swerved our van off the road! *Top Gear*, John Peel's show, was probably the one we played for the most. Those sessions were always great fun, and Bernie Andrews, John's producer, would let us hide in the corner of the studio during other people's sessions, such as when our American heroes Leonard Cohen and Tim Hardin were in town. Ashley chatted with Cohen between takes, hitting him up for any unrecorded material. To us, he seemed grown up and sensible—he was wearing a suit—and more the picture of a poet than the kinds of musician we were used to. Hardin seemed strung out, a little dangerous and unpredictable, but he was totally present when he performed. They were both backed by some very fine British jazz musicians, though we felt we would have been a more sympathetic choice of backing band.

Many bands in the 1960s would have been impoverished without Peel, and he subsequently continued to support generation after generation of up-and-coming musicians. He did so while working at the BBC, fighting against a bastion of conservatism and championing styles of music that would have baffled the controllers, had they ever bothered to listen to it. There was no equivalent of American FM or college radio, and so many bands owed their first radio plays to Peel.

The BBC had fabulous recording gear, if your idea of sonic perfection was 1938. Microphones were mostly pre-war, old ribbon RCAs and Coles that are coveted today for recording brass or used as room mics for drums, but there wasn't much else. Men in white coats would plug your amp in—the union would not allow you to do it yourself. Everything was recorded in mono, so if you wanted to do an overdub, you had to replay the track and add the new part onto another mono machine, causing you to lose a generation in quality. That is why many of those old Fairport tracks done at the BBC have so much wow and flutter—the more generations you recorded, the wobblier it got. The studio at Maida Vale was the most impressive. Submerged under the unsuspecting leafy suburbs like a giant ichthyosaur, it is a truly massive converted roller-skating rink that contains seven recording spaces. Maida Vale One was huge—it was bigger than Abbey Road Studio One—and it was a wonderful orchestral room. We used to fantasize that the BBC had tunnels running all over London, connecting all these buildings; to some extent, this turned out to be true.

Our entertainment on long journeys to out-of-town gigs was limited to BBC radio and whatever games you could come up with. However, I hardly remember the radio being on—we tended to amuse ourselves with jokes, anecdotes and games of Twenty Questions. Fairport had a great sense of humor from the beginning, and sharing a generational viewpoint, we loved to spoof the likes of John Betjeman, a popular poet and broadcaster. He not only had a uniquely high-pitched and slightly quavery delivery, but his poetry was unmistakable in its form and content, and was ripe for parody. He had grown up in Highgate, so I also considered him one of my "local" poets. Martin in particular seemed to catch the nuances to perfection. Another very funny book that went round the band was *Owning Up* by George Melly, which described his life on the road around Britain in the 1950s with the Mick Mulligan Magnolia Jazz Band. We liberally borrowed phrases and ideas from this fine volume, and it helped us develop a vocabulary to deal with what was still a relatively new lifestyle. People who lived south of the Thames were considered to be a bit lower on the social scale, and were described as "transpontine," while people on a pedestrian crossing were awarded scores according to the desirability of running them over. Melly's descriptions of guest house horrors reflected our own experiences, as did Roger McGough's poems in *Gig*, which came out a few years later. We also found humor in *Let's Talk Strine* by Afferbeck Lauder, a brilliant presentation of the Australian lexicon, written phonetically so as to appear like another language, and its sister volume *Fraffly Well Spoken*, which did the same thing for upper-class British vowels. And we shared a love for the "Molesworth" books by Ronald Searle—the badly spelled, ink-spotted diaries of a disruptive British schoolboy.

By this time, and at our request, Joe Boyd's office had reluctantly taken over our management. We needed more support than John Penhallow could provide, and when we looked at the shark-infested waters of the British music industry, it was daunting. At least we trusted Joe. He asked us what the minimum amount was, per week, that we needed to survive. We came up with £12—given that I had been paid "apprentice" wages of £6 with Hans Unger, it felt like a raise! So now we had proper management in the actual office of Witchseason Productions at 83 Charlotte Street, where we could take meetings and feel important. The office was where we might run into Joe's other acts—John Martyn, Nick Drake, the Incredible String Band, Chris McGregor or Dudu Pukwana. Joe's roster would come by just to hang out, or to pick up some float or wages on their way to a gig.

Towards the end of 1967 and in early 1968, our touring began to take us further afield, and we made our first trips over to the Continent. It was all very new and exciting. In January 1968 we played the Cannes Music Festival as part of a Polydor Records promotion, with the likes of Captain Beefheart. In April we did the *Bouton Rouge* TV show in Paris, looking very stiff and self-conscious. And then in May we joined a large contingent of British bands at the Rome Pop Festival.

We had played a show at Middle Earth the night before, so we arrived in Rome having had barely an hour's sleep. In the lobby of the hotel, I realized I had two guitars and a suitcase to carry. With bleary eyes and a bit of a hangover,

I looked for assistance and spied a man in uniform. "Excuse me," I said, speaking slowly so that he could understand me, "could you help me with my luggage?" I made lifting motions and pointed to the stairs. The man eyed me with what looked like disbelief. He was still a little out of focus. I made another gesture. "Bags?" I said. "*Baggagio*?" He didn't respond as I'd hoped he would.

"Just who do you think you're talking to?" he said.

"Thank God," I said. "You speak English. I could really use a hand to get my stuff upstairs."

He eyed me up and down. "Who do you think I am? I'm a colonel in the United States Army!" I could now see, as my sight improved, that he was speaking the truth. He continued to look incredulous, and I suddenly saw myself through his eyes, hairy and buckskinned. I backed away slowly.

It was my first time in southern Europe, and Rome was warm, humid and beautiful. The Trevi Fountain! The Circus Maximus! Trajan's Column! Years of school Latin lessons suddenly came to life. Unfortunately, it seemed that we were the first men with long hair to hit Rome since the Visigoths in AD 410, and about as welcome. Everywhere we went, we were followed by gangs of curious males. Were they hoping we were girls? We had been told that good Catholic girls got locked away at 9.30 P.M. Were these *ragazzi* just intent on a bit of fun? More likely. Staying in the hotel quickly became preferable to venturing down the street. The festival itself was held in the Palazzo dello Sport, an arena in the north of the city, which could probably seat ten thousand comfortably—sadly, it only attracted about two thousand. We had plenty of time to take in the other acts. Italy's home-grown contribution was a band called I Roboti, who dressed like a Quaker version of the Four Seasons and sang smarmy doo-wop, which was much to the taste of the Italian crowd. The audience had a remarkably childlike reaction to all of the music; if they liked a line, a harmony or a solo, they would all stand up and applaud, before promptly sitting down again. And if they really *loved* something, they would stand on their chairs for three seconds, and then promptly sit back down. It was the strangest audience reaction I've ever seen.

I was in the crowd when the shit hit the fan. The Nice had pushed the envelope a bit in their set, throwing knives and treating the Hammond organ like a bronco that needed breaking in. But the Italians were unprepared for the Move, who were well known for their anarchic stage antics. The authorities must have been tipped off that the long-hairs were out to destroy the palazzo, for when the Move began chopping up a TV set with an axe, the riot police moved in. Sitting dead center in the auditorium, I could just see two lines of riot cops with face masks, shields and truncheons, making their way down either side of the front stalls. When they reached the stage, they started hitting anything that moved: bands, crew, audience—it was merciless and random. They arrested a lot of people. I was far enough back to be able to head for the exit. To say that they panicked and overreacted would be an understatement. There may also have been an agenda to close down the festival by fabricating an incident. The hippies were not welcome. Everyone got out of jail fairly quickly—a small cash bribe was all it took.

The festival relocated to the Piper Club in the center of the city the next day, and that night we saw the Byrds play there. They had been our heroes from the earliest days of Fairport, and we loved their new blend of rock and country. At this point, their line-up included Gram Parsons and Doug Dillard, and Gram in particular was friendly and sociable between sets, as we chatted outside in the warm evening air about their new musical direction. A week later, the Byrds would play at Middle Earth, and we had the privilege of lending them our PA system.

JUDY, WHO TO my mind shone in a quieter setting like a folk club, did not have the vocal strength to sing over a band that was becoming more muscular. She ended up sounding strained, and it was doing her a disservice. She had been with us from the beginning, sharing vocals with Iain both on stage and on our first LP, and had been a friend even before she joined the band. She was also my girlfriend, although our relationship had slowly faded away over time under the constant demands of Fairport. She and the band parted ways. We all lived for the band, and very little was able to exist outside that. At eighteen years old, I was fairly hopeless as a boyfriend. I had seen a lot of French cinema, where the men were moody and monosyllabic, but while that somehow worked like magic for Jean-Paul Belmondo, it just made me incredibly hard to get along with. It took me a while to get past that.

AT THAT MOMENT, Fairport seemed to be swept along by the fates, with possibilities opening up wherever we turned.

We put the work in, of course—writing songs, arranging, recording and touring—but the energy we expended seemed to open doors without us having to knock. We were lucky that we were carried along by the tide of the "psychedelic" music scene, similar enough to appeal but also different enough to stand out. All I wanted to do was to play music, and nothing mattered beyond the plans we made for the next month or so. It never crossed my mind to consider even a year or two ahead.

We felt in good company. Joe, to our minds, had fine taste in the bands he chose to record. There was some kinship there, as well as a sense of similar intention and aesthetic. Witchseason seemed a sane sanctuary compared to the rest of the music business. It even seemed sane compared to the sometimes radical and progressive music around the London psychedelic venues. The Kinks, the Beatles and the Stones all appeared to inhabit a different world—they were also from a different generation, being five or so years older than us. We would listen to the new Beatles albums with amazement, but were more interested in the new records by Dylan, David Ackles or Joni Mitchell. We were caught up in our obsession with lyrics and with our own version of instrumental music, with our own unique blend of influences. Like a group of mountaineers roped together, we were isolated and interdependent, focusing on the summit. We did not realize then how frequently the rope that bound us together would unravel.

3

A Dialogue Set to a Tune

I can tell a fair old story
Which I'm sure ain't no surprise,
Of the places I have been, oh,
And they ain't no lies.
SANDY DENNY

WE HAD A reputation for being a band that had a female singer, and we saw no reason to change that. We wanted someone to replace Judy, so in May 1968 we began asking around the folk and rock scenes. I think we had all heard of Sandy Denny through the grapevine—she was up-and-coming as a folk singer, sang well and wrote some of her own songs. Joe Boyd knew her, and knew that she wanted to get beyond the folk clubs—but he never brought her up as an option for Fairport because he thought she might stomp all over us. Sandy had figured out that to survive in the folk scene at that time, which was male-dominated and sexist, you had to act tough, drink and swear as much as any man, and hide any vulnerability. Joe saw us, perhaps misguidedly, as polite, well-mannered lads from suburban North London, with moderate habits. Compared to Sandy, we seemed like chalk and cheese. Joe was away in the States at that point, so Sandy came to us independent of his opinions.

On 13 May, we held auditions in the Eight Feathers Boys' Club in Fulham. After a couple of unimpressive contenders, it was Sandy's turn. She came in wearing a brown leather waistcoat over a green dress. She was about five feet two, with dirty blonde hair. From the initial greetings and pleasantries she seemed prickly, almost confrontational, like someone who had spent years having to stand their ground. Then she sang the Jackson C. Frank song "You Never Wanted Me," which gave her voice the scope to effortlessly go from a whisper to full power. She had learned Jackson's guitar arrangement well, with its quirky bent fifth interval, and the immediate impression was of a complete artist in command of her musical skill, with a unique vocal quality. There was nothing not to like about her performance. Then Sandy set her guitar back in its case. "Okay," she said. "Now I want to hear what you do." Although it was unexpected, it was a fair question—she wanted to audition us. Sandy knew enough about her own worth to demand a certain standard from would-be bandmates. Iain sang the Tim Buckley song "Morning Glory," which was a regular part of our stage repertoire. She seemed to like us, and we definitely loved her. There was no withdrawing to another room to discuss, and no "We'll get back to you." We just looked at each other and nodded, and that was it.

We were working constantly, so we had to add Sandy into the fabric of the band slowly. It was easy to drape ourselves around a song like "You Never Wanted Me," keeping Sandy's voice and guitar intact, and adding a fairly sensitive arrangement of bass, drums and guitar around it. We did the same with "She Moved Through the Fair"—it was probably the first traditional song that Fairport tackled, and would start us on a whole new direction a year later. We did a BBC session just weeks after Sandy joined, and our progress when you listen to those tracks is obvious. We sound a lot more accomplished and musically complete. The voice at the front of a band is a vital focus, carrying all of a song's emotion, and if that voice is as strong and intriguing as Sandy's, with such an ability to tell a story, it just lifts everything else. Ashley said at the time that if we never did anything else, we had really achieved something here. As great a singer as Iain was, the longing in Sandy's voice brought an elusive quality to our music.

Sandy was an extraordinary bundle of contradictions. She thought herself not thin or tall enough, and yet when men went nuts for her, she always wanted the ones who resisted her. She was both very sure of herself musically and then not so sure, and you were never quite certain which Sandy you were dealing with. If you offered her reassurance, she could suddenly get irritated and dismiss you. She could be side-splittingly funny and then turn on you, screaming, or collapse in tears or hysterics. She possessed a tremendous empathy for others. She lacked a layer of skin. When I remember Sandy, which is often, I choose the funny moments—the ridiculous stoned games of Scrabble, when she would put down some word that didn't exist with a completely straight face, before exploding with laughter. Most of our Scrabble games were never finished. She was also famous for her stream-of-consciousness introductions on stage, which would start coherently enough and end up in an increasingly complicated cul-de-sac and fits of laughter. Sandy could routinely crack herself up. One of her favorite expressions, in the face of the unexpected, the adverse or the overwhelming, was "I suppose it's all part of life's rich tapestry," at which she would dissolve into hysterics, as would everyone else, even if it was the hundredth time we had heard it.

Another bonus to Sandy joining the band was an increase in wages. She had been singing in folk clubs, which was generally more lucrative for solo performers than being a band member on the rock scene, so although she was reaching a wider audience now, she was losing out financially. With her on board, we were able to negotiate more from Joe Boyd. Our wages crept up to £20 a week, which was wonderful for us, but barely enough for Sandy to subsist on: she took cabs and drank champagne. She did the odd commercial and solo gig to keep afloat, but she tried to keep the commercials secret—we were such a bunch of idealists that we would have sneered at the thought of playing music in return for filthy lucre. Sandy swore blind that it wasn't her singing the TV jingle "We're all much better for butter," and we were happy to believe her explanation that it was someone trying to sound like her rather than the ugly alternative.

Every week or so I would go over to Sandy's small flat just off the Gloucester Road in West London, on the top floor of a white-rendered Victorian terrace. She would play me songs she was writing that she thought might be suitable for the band. "Fotheringay," a song about Mary Queen of Scots, was one of her recent compositions. It seemed logical, as with the traditional songs she sang, that we would fit around her guitar arrangement. I seem to remember that I suggested the baroque instrumental passage. We recorded it fairly soon afterwards, with Simon's electric autoharp made to sound like a string quartet and Iain's vocal sounding like a choir, thanks to the wonderful echo plate at Sound Techniques.

A side of Sandy that we were less aware of was the pianist and the piano-based songwriter. She never played keyboard on stage with Fairport in that era. Half the venues we played didn't have them anyway, and the state of those that were on offer was something to behold—they would have missing or damaged keys, cigarette burns everywhere, and they would invariably be out of tune. We heard her only occasionally, in the rare venues that had functioning pianos backstage, working out song ideas, but she did start to add some piano in the studio, as we slowly began to record tracks for our next album.

Sound Techniques was becoming busy. We were competing for studio time with the Incredible String Band, John and Beverley Martyn, Al Stewart and most of the folk rock scene. When we couldn't get time there, we would record in Morgan Studios in Willesden or at Olympic Studios in Barnes, which was a bit more glamorous. Olympic, a converted cinema, was spacious and airy, and the Rolling Stones and the Who used it sometimes. Once, at the end of a session in the smaller studio, I noticed that the door to Studio One was ajar, and peered in. It was very dark in there, but I could just make out Keith Richards, in the middle of the studio floor, doing an overdub on what turned out to be "Sympathy for the Devil." Mick Jagger was in the control room directing operations, dimly lit and in his *Performance* persona, with dyed black hair and lipstick. They must have done about a hundred takes—it was a painstaking process. I had seen the Stones in the early days, and hadn't thought much of them as a live band. I think they had a genius for making great-sounding records, finding a deep groove between Keith and Charlie Watts, but it seemed clear that they didn't just go in and kill it in a couple of takes.

For reasons not clear to me—but it could have involved someone slipping something in my tea—that night I dreamed vividly about Keith.*

One morning, after another all-night recording session at Olympic, I emerged from the big studio at about 10 A.M. and stuck my head around the door of the small studio. An ad for Ski yogurt was being recorded, and the wonderful jazz guitarist Ike Isaacs was playing some menial riff that was far beneath his lofty skills. I reminded myself not to become a jazz musician, which seemed to involve playing at Pizza Express to twenty people and subsidizing my art with commercials. Rather than becoming a jazz musician, just steal from them.

I was keen not to sell my soul musically, but I was doing an increasing amount of session work for friends. From our earliest time in the studio, Joe and Tod had encouraged me to record with other artists, and it was a steep learning curve. With the first couple of things I tried, I did not make the cut. I overdubbed some electric guitar onto a Tom Paxton song, "Cindy's Cryin," but my style was not sympathetic enough—it was all vibrato and no space. I then did a track for a Dudu Pukwana record, with Bob Stuckey playing organ, but I was

* See Appendix B, p. 273.

lost, both rhythmically and harmonically. I had never really heard South African music, and couldn't get the hang of the swing and the timing. I studied more for the next opportunity with Dudu, which came a year or so later. The whole Fairport rhythm section played on Al Stewart's *Love Chronicles* album, and we welcomed the opportunity to further hone our skills in the studio.

Later that year, Sandy and I received invitations in the post to Paul McCartney's birthday party. It shows how much of a musical snob I was at the time that I decided not to go—to me, the Beatles were a "pop" band and not to be taken seriously. Sandy went, of course, and she had a great time. If I could speak to that nineteen-year-old snob now, I'd give him a good shake, tell him not to be so damn judgemental and to get down there and enjoy himself.

We worked constantly, but that was okay by us. We were young, and it was still new and exciting, although the stretch of the M1 between London and Birmingham was becoming all too familiar. We would stop on the way to a gig for breakfast or lunch, and on the way home for a late supper. The service station that received most of our custom was the Blue Boar at Watford Gap. You could almost guarantee running into another band, whatever time of the day or night you were there. The food was greasy transport-caff fare and only slightly preferable to the Wonder Bread sandwiches that may have been on offer at the venue. But eating was not a reliable practice in those days. I rarely ate three meals a day, and eating after a show was always tricky, at least until more Indian restaurants began to pop up around the country.

We were always on bills with the same bands. We played alongside Family, the Incredible String Band and Blossom Toes most, and regularly with Arthur Brown, Traffic and the Social Deviants. Despite our different styles, there was a great camaraderie around that whole scene. If your van broke down, you might be towed back to London by another band's vehicle, attached by speaker cables—everyone helped each other out. It was a true underground movement, which encompassed a big range of styles and personalities, from the deeply eccentric Ivor Cutler and Duster Bennett, whose mum was his roadie, to the psychedelic folk of the Incredible String Band and the lyric-conscious Fairport—but, elitists that we were, we always felt we were unique and on our own path.

The bands' road crews were also interconnected. If you needed a spare part, someone would have it. If you blew a speaker, you could borrow one from another band and return it later. If you needed something for a guitar, the roadies for Jimi Hendrix or the Who would each have a suitcase full of broken bits, wiring and pickups, and you could just help yourself. However, at one point, every music shop in London's West End had a sign that said "No credit for the Who"—their destructive live performances had led to the death of too many Rickenbackers.

Going up the M1 was getting to be routine, but there was something meditative in the repetition. Every trip yielded more detail of the countryside as it sped past: a stand of ancient oak trees blasted by wind, rain and lightning for hundreds of years, gnarled, part-amputated and defiant, surviving even the lead of a million vehicles; a distinctive Chinese-looking gate that might have come straight from a willow-pattern plate, opening onto an empty field; and what might have been a lodge to some larger estate, now truncated and isolated by the motorway, but with beautiful, intricate carving on its white bargeboards. Going to somewhere like Hull took us off the beaten track and onto back roads, through the strange, misty fenland of North Lincolnshire, across canals called drains and sluices. It was a world that seemed unaltered from a hundred years ago. There were still very few clubs to play outside London. The journey to the north-east of England and Redcar Jazz Club took us past the ICI chemical works outside Middlesbrough, which at night was lit up like some dystopian city straight out of Philip K. Dick. His novel *Do Androids Dream of Electric Sheep?* came out in 1968. Science fiction was about a third of my reading material then, alongside books about Zen meditation and astrology and more mainstream literature and classics—I was trying to catch up on a formal education cut short. Some books would be passed around the group, especially those with a musical connection, like the early novels of Leonard Cohen and Richard Fariña.

We also regularly played at the Van Dike Club in Plymouth, where we were always made to feel welcome by the wonderful Peter Van Dike and his son Greg. All the major bands played there in their early incarnations, including Led Zeppelin, Pink Floyd and Jethro Tull. It was entertainment for the area, though of course the police tried to shut it down. Drugs probably did change hands there frequently, but when 170 police officers raided the club during Fairport's gig there in 1971, they were only able to charge two people with possession of cannabis. They thought Dave Swarbrick's violin rosin was hashish.

Frank Freeman's Dance Club in Kidderminster was unusual. It was a ballroom dancing studio during the day, and usually when we arrived before a gig, Frank himself would be escorting some ample middle-aged lady around the dance-floor. He would give us a wave, say, "I'll be with you in a minute, lads," and point to a large tray of sandwiches and a pot of tea, which we thought was the ultimate in hospitality. The club was popular and our shows there were well attended, but the audience was mostly female and rather young, aged thirteen to eighteen. Fairport was never a band that relied on its looks to win favor with the public, but our resident heart-throbs, usually considered to be Iain and Martin, seemed to set young Black Country hearts racing. I doubt Frank would have approved of the occasional knee-trembler that happened behind the bike shed.

In September 1968, we played the Festival of Contemporary Song at the Festival Hall in London, our first gig at such a prestigious venue. Al Stewart was also on the bill, as was Sandy's old boyfriend Jackson C. Frank, whom she did not seem thrilled to see, and a young Joni Mitchell, who was making her UK debut and performed with poise and polish. While Joni was finishing her set, I went backstage to tune up and did something reprehensible—I took a peek in her notebook. For a songwriter, this is like looking into someone's private world—I would hate it if it was done to me—but it can be very informative. I was struck by the similarities with Sandy's notebooks, which were easier to sneak a look at because they were usually lying around open. Every page was dense with ideas, and every space and margin was decorated with abstract and figurative doodles, cartoons and sketches of people and objects. Joni was as much a visual artist as a musician. Perhaps out of guilt, I had a dream about Joni that night.*

We would devise games in the van to pass the time during the longer trips—London to Plymouth in those days could be an eight-hour drive, for instance. I Spy, usually a challenging game for four-year-olds, took on a whole new life when Sandy was playing, as she had an unfailing eye for the preposterous and unsolvable, such as "R" for the rabbit we had passed in a field an hour before. There were also various games with car number plates, one of which was trying to make a phrase out of the first three letters. For example, "VVS" would be "Varicose Vein Sandwiches" or "SNI" would be "Spottiswood's Nuclear Icecream." Heavens, we must have been bored! Before Eddie Stobart became the haulage king of the UK, there were other famous trucking firms on the roads of Britain, and points could be scored by spotting the logo of your assigned one. The largest firm at the time was Christian Salvesen, a Scottish whaling company that had moved into the haulage business when whaling became controversial. After about a year on the road with us, Sandy said, with a straight face and wanting a serious answer, "What do they actually put in all those Christian Salvation lorries?"

On days off, we might play a game of poker or liar's dice with Joe and Tod at Bob Squires's house. Bob was a small-time

---

* See Appendix B, p. 275.

villain who loved jazz, and he also loved winning my wages. Other Witchseason acts like Nick Drake or John Martyn might be there too.

I also enjoyed visiting art galleries when I had time off. My favourite was the Tate and I saw many outstanding exhibitions over the years, by artists including Victor Pasmore, L. S. Lowry and René Magritte. I used to love the walk along the Thames from Westminster Tube station to the gallery at Millbank, the river suitably grey and in those days very quiet, with just a few barges slowly bringing their cargo of coal or cement to and from the London Docks. While watching the river, I could imagine a medieval or a Roman London—even the Embankment, where I was standing, was Victorian, and carried within it Joseph Bazalgette's sewers. At low tide, clay pipes and Roman pottery and coins would still be uncovered, and the Thames often haunted my dreams.* I felt connected to history, a feeling that was reinforced by the music we listened to and were now playing. I could feel the old songs reverberate through history with the echoes of the voices that had sung them down the centuries.

We had always listened to folk songs, and now, with Sandy in the band, we were slowly adding them to our repertoire, taking them out of the folk clubs and into rock venues and a wider audience. Those old songs can really haunt you, with their picked-over sparseness and their occasional lack of logic. Boys can sing girl songs and girls can sing boy songs—it doesn't matter. The singer is less important than the song.

* See Appendix B, p. 276.

We were starting to connect to a lineage that was ancient, pagan and alive with the dreams of the dead.

When I was a teenager, traditional British songs and dance tunes were always played in the folk clubs—they were part of the learning experience. There were also great singers and guitarists to learn from. One of the early pioneers was Davey Graham. Half Guyanese and half Scottish, he was the first of the great British acoustic guitarists of the 1950s and 1960s. He pulled influences from jazz, traditional Irish, Caribbean and North African music into a unique style. Playing his instrumental "Angi" became a rite of passage for many younger musicians, including Paul Simon, and he is credited with pioneering the guitar tuning DADGAD. I saw him play a folk club only once, but it was revealing to watch not only his fingers but his eyes, which were as restless as his musical curiosity.

I was also watching Martin Carthy a lot in those days. He came from a strong socialist North London background and began singing in folk clubs in 1961 as part of the Thames-Side Four, before forming a famous duo with Dave Swarbrick. He was another unique stylist, whose focus was always on the song. How do you accompany something that was probably originally sung unaccompanied, without reducing it to the Western chordal tradition? How do you keep the ambiguity of key, and how do you preserve the lack of resolution in the melody? Martin had become one of the great originals of the guitar, and his playing introduced me to a world of possibilities.

Bert Jansch was a Scottish transplant to London, influenced by Davey Graham and Big Bill Broonzy. In turn he would influence a wide range of guitarists, including Jimmy Page and Neil Young, with his blend of Scottish, blues and baroque styles.

I saw Bert, Davey and Martin all play around this time. There is nothing like seeing someone live and not quite grasping what they are doing. If you understood it, you might just try to copy it; not understanding might lead you to experiment and maybe arrive at something different and original. I'm glad I didn't just slavishly copy any of them, or I might never have crawled out from under their influence.

On the rock side, of all the UK blues and pop guitarists I saw, Peter Green probably impressed me most. He really had wonderful touch and sensitivity. I saw Mike Bloomfield playing with the Paul Butterfield Blues Band in the Refectory in Golders Green, and I also saw Hendrix in the same venue. Bloomfield was a revelation. He came from Chicago and had studied with the masters, and yet he sounded like himself. He was a true original, far more so than the armies of British blues guitarists, who all seemed to come from places like Macclesfield and Penge, and could "do" Buddy Guy to a T. I loved his passion, and tried to copy his vibrato.

I was always trying to learn from the best, and soloing was something I thought about a lot. The actual construction of a solo was a much-discussed matter, as the possibilities seemed endless. Should a solo have a beginning, a middle and an end, like a story? Many do, and that's one way of thinking about it. I saw George Van Eps, the great jazz guitarist, play two shows a night on two consecutive nights—four sets with a pickup band, so the set list was the same every time. He played Duke

Ellington's "Satin Doll" in his full chordal style, also playing bass lines on the lower strings of his seven-string guitar. Each of the four versions was totally original—they would all start, develop and conclude differently. Very few musicians can reach that level of proficiency, with a large enough technical vocabulary and well of creativity to pull it off. I spent a long time digesting that experience, and wished I could match it. In contrast, I saw the wonderful blues singer and guitarist Albert Collins on several occasions, and I swear he had only three licks, but he could still keep you on the edge of your seat. He was all about tone, intensity and emotion.

I thought it was okay to be a rock musician or a folk musician and borrow from the jazz greats, or to steal ideas from Debussy or Stravinsky if you could shoehorn them in, while also trying to play with the intensity of Albert Collins. Every time I thought there were rules to follow for a solo, I found exceptions to break them all.

On other nights off from Fairport, I loved to be swept away by a musically enriching experience, and I saw plenty of strange and interesting tours that came through London. There was the extraordinary jazz guitarist Barney Kessel, and the Gary Burton Quartet, featuring Larry Coryell. There were the country musicians Conway Twitty, Loretta Lynn and Bill Anderson, and the obscure but legendary blues magician Magic Sam. I also saw Ornette Coleman and Albert Ayler, both of whom broke down the barriers of jazz and pointed to the future. How abstract could music become?

I kept returning to the tone of the guitar, and how it had to sing with one's own voice. It was time for me to switch to a solid-body instrument, to get more sustain from the notes and less feedback. An American gentleman intent on making a small profit had flown to London with a couple of Les Paul Gold Top guitars to sell at a reasonable price, at a time when HM Customs and Excise didn't know about such things. They had both been manufactured in 1955, and I chose the one with the better tailpiece. That was the instrument I used in the studio and live at the end of 1968. I passed the jazz Gibson that Tod had bought for me on to Simon.

In 1968, the Beatles' *Revolver* was two years old, *Sgt. Pepper* was a year old, and Fairport was experimenting in the studio with flanging, phasing, recording at half and double speed, and running tape backwards. When we went into the studio to cut Joni Mitchell's "Eastern Rain," I went back to an earlier influence, Les Paul. I wasn't aware of too many people using double speed since Les had done it twenty years earlier, and it seemed to fit the exotic mood of "Eastern Rain" well. We did the backwards guitar thing that the Beatles had used on "Tomorrow Never Knows" on "Book Song," under the guitar solo. After feeling our way on our first album, we were much happier with our little musical experiments while working on our second. On a song like "Tale in Hard Time," we could have three guitars on the intro, thanks to there now being a staggering eight tracks on the tape machine. We could also multitrack the harmonies, which gave Iain and Sandy scope for four parts. They nailed some unusual intervals.

We always thought long and hard about our musical style, but we were stopped in our tracks by a new record from Bob Dylan's backing group. *Music from Big Pink* by the Band had an immediate influence on Fairport when it appeared in July 1968, as well as on the rest of the London underground scene. After a couple of years of acid-fueled, occasionally pretentious and increasingly predictable output from San Francisco, New York and London, here was something completely refreshing. The Band had short haircuts and dressed like funeral directors. They played a synthesis of American roots styles very unpretentiously. There was rock and roll, country, gospel, Appalachian, soul, jazz and blues in there, and they mastered all of it—not bad for Canadians. Many British bands started writing in the slow 4/4 time of the Band's signature tune "The Weight," but never quite captured the elusive swing and looseness.

For Fairport, it was a strange watershed. The Band's style was in one sense what we had always aimed towards— roots-based popular music, with few concessions to popularity. Yet when we were presented with such a perfect synthesis, it was clear that their roots weren't the same as ours. The authenticity that I felt was lacking in British blues musicians was also lacking in us. We too derived a lot of our style from American records. We were more sneaky about it in the sense that we imitated the obscure rather than the obvious, but still, we didn't come from Nashville, New Orleans or Chicago— not even close. Enthusiasm and a talent for mimicry will carry you so far, but rarely to the pinnacle. If you come from Tufnell Park, you'll never be Howlin' Wolf, Otis Redding or Buck Owens. There were very few musicians like Steve Winwood, who managed to sound authentic despite hailing from Birmingham. We slowly began to realize that the small steps we had taken in the direction of home-grown music—playing Sandy's arrangements of traditional songs from England, Ireland and Scotland and composing our own music—might be leading to our salvation.

The material we were now coming up with was like the Fairport approach of the first album, but with an increasing awareness of our roots. "Tale in Hard Time" reflected something of my Scottish upbringing, with echoes of the bagpipe's drone. Sandy's song "Fotheringay" channelled the British folk tradition but existed in its own stylistic world, with references to baroque forms and modern folk composers like Ewan MacColl and Cyril Tawney. But mostly it was Sandy's musical landscape, in which she was growing in confidence, and which she would plough, hoe and winnow for the rest of her short life.

Collaborations can work wonderfully, and some of the greatest songs are written that way, but I thought writing a song with my own words and music might be rewarding and emotionally authentic. I also realized that my self-esteem would improve by leaps and bounds if I saw my name next to a song on an album, like George Harrison or Robbie Robertson.

I don't remember much about the process for writing "Meet on the Ledge." I was sitting on the bed in my tiny room at 33 St. Mary's Road in Brent, and the words and music both came to me fairly quickly—perhaps the Muse looked kindly on me.* I wrote down lyrics that sounded harmonious and easy

---

* Speaking of the Muse, I treat her with great respect. I swear she came to a band rehearsal in Highgate in 1964, dressed as a Camden schoolgirl but deathly pale, with black hair and bright red lips. She disappeared afterwards, and no one knew who she was.

to sing, without thinking too much about their meaning. In that sense, it was a bit stream-of-consciousness—I had to look at them afterwards and ask myself what the hell they meant. I can translate the song's meaning in various ways: it's a spiritual song; it's a song about wasted ambition; a song about the full circle of life; a song about old friends being the best friends; a song about the contemplation of ending it all—all very ambitious, given my narrow worldview at the age of nineteen.*

"Meet on the Ledge" made it onto the second album, along with a song Ashley wrote called "Mr. Lacey." Professor Bruce Lacey had been Ashley's neighbor in Durnsford Road, back in Muswell Hill. The phrase "performance art" had yet to be invented, but it fits at least part of what Bruce did. I first went to his house with his next-door neighbor, my schoolfriend Brian Wyvill, in 1965, when I was sixteen. It was Guy Fawkes Night, and I could not imagine a better place to be for a fireworks display. Right by the front door there was a female robot, erotically explicit in places and bare-bones Meccano in others. The house was filled with junk and more robots. I felt immediately at home. Why wasn't my house like this? Why weren't my parents raving eccentrics? Everything was about creativity and freedom, and I loved it.

In 1968, we saw Bruce perform at the Marquee Club with the Alberts, including Barry Fantoni, in an evening of Dadaist eccentricity and humor. We also experienced one of his installations at the Arts Lab, which was basically a huge human digestive tract made of plastic that one walked, crawled and

* See Appendix A, pp. 263.

slid through—in at the mouth and out through the rectum. We knew him from an earlier project, *The Running, Jumping and Standing Still Film*, which he had made with the Goons. The Tate had two of his robotic sculptures in their collection—and this was the man who went to see Stanley Kubrick's *2001: A Space Odyssey* in a space suit.

For the recording of the track we arranged for Bruce to come down to the studio with a few of his robots, and they took a "solo," their motors whirring, switching in and out, running up to speed and back down. It was perhaps baffling unless you knew about Mr. Lacey, but I'm glad we were able to pay tribute to him.

The last track on the record was "I'll Keep It with Mine," a Bob Dylan song we had found on a Judy Collins B-side—even then, we were still hunting for the obscure. We slowed it down and made it more reflective, which seemed to let it breathe. It proved a great vehicle for Sandy's voice and became a mainstay of our live set. Perhaps something of the Band had filtered through, helping us relax into the music.

For the record cover, we remembered a chalk drawing that Sandy and Martin had done on a dressing-room blackboard at the University of East Anglia a few days earlier and managed to photograph before it was rubbed off. It's a lovely piece of Fairport self-parody, including chalk-rendered effigies of the band on stage, with cartoon exclamations and expressions. The cartoon, and thence the album, was titled *What We Did on Our Holidays*.

We felt more confident about the second album than we had been with the first. In truth we were better musicians by

now, with a better sense of how to perform with each other—
and the songs were better too. We also had a pair of great
singers in Iain and Sandy. The critical response was fair, but
the album did not trouble the chart compilers—our audience
was still building. "Meet on the Ledge" came out as a single,
and even had a couple of cover versions, but nothing stuck.
Sometimes we hardly noticed album releases—there would be
ads in the music press, but launch parties and fanfares happened only occasionally, and to other people. In any case, we
were busy wearing deep ruts in the major roads of Britain in
our workhorse of a van, singing to a dozen drunk students at
a May Ball, or to a packed club of the more musically discriminating. The road owned us, clothed us and fed us, paid us in
Monopoly money and demanded respect. And from time to
time, it exacted a tribute.

4

Eggshells

I see them walking in an air of glory,
Whose light doth trample on my days:
My days, which are at best but dull and hoary,
Mere glimmering and decays.

HENRY VAUGHAN

FAIRPORT NOW SEEMED to be on a path. Even if we could not truly articulate our destiny, the ingredients were there—playing some traditional British songs and writing our own material in a more British style. All we lacked was a mission statement. If anyone was tugging in a different direction, it was Iain. At that time, he was sharing the flat in Brent with me and Simon, and he would enthusiastically play me songs from albums he had bought by the latest crop of American singer-songwriters such as Dr. John and Waylon Jennings. It was great to listen to, and some of it was inspiring, but when Iain suggested we should cover some of these songs, I felt it was a backward step—it was something we had embraced a year ago, but we had moved on since then. Sandy and I really wanted to keep writing, and our new songs sounded increasingly free of American influence. It was becoming hard to see where Iain would fit on the traditional songs we were starting to play—a crack was appearing in the band. Finally, Joe Boyd and Iain had a meeting, and Iain and the band parted ways. This all happened just before we left the Witchseason office to drive to a concert. As we piled into the van, Iain jumped in with us from force of habit, and we had to remind him that he was now on a separate musical path. There was some ill feeling at first, but the split was unavoidable, given the musical divergence. Iain continued to live with me and Simon, and we remained friends. It was gratifying to see him quickly move his career in a new, country rock direction.

At the start of 1969, Fairport was back to being a five-piece: Ashley, Simon, Martin, Sandy and me. Sandy was the sole vocalist and interpreter of material, front and center of our live shows, but she never pushed herself to be more than "one of the lads." The rest of us took over Iain's harmonies, a sizeable chunk of repertoire was retired and replaced, and we continued working on the new album we had just started. Before Iain left, he had contributed to a cover of a fairly obscure Dylan song—a song we felt was "rootsy" enough to take a more British interpretation. Dylan seemed to survive our purge of all things American, perhaps because his influences were so close to England, Ireland and Scotland.

In the D. A. Pennebaker film *Don't Look Back*, about Dylan's 1965 tour of the UK, Joan Baez sings a single verse of "Percy's Song." We saw the film at the Arts Lab on Drury Lane, and managed to track the song down to an early songbook, probably the first collection of Dylan's songs available in England. The song uses a traditional chorus, "Turn, turn to the rain and the wind," which Iain, Sandy and I harmonized on. The song's sixteen verses presented a challenge to rock audiences, who, unlike folk crowds, were not used to something so strophic, so we planned two crescendo points—one halfway through the song and one at the end. We recorded the basic track with vocal, bass, drums, acoustic guitar and dulcimer, and electric guitar and organ were overdubbed. We had Joe Boyd down on the studio floor with us, holding up verse numbers and reminding us of the desired intensity at various moments. The drums sounded big because the sound engineer, John Wood, had the idea to put the dulcimer about ten feet from the drum kit, which meant that the dulcimer mic was acting like a room mic. It's one of my favorite Fairport tracks and one of our best interpretations of a Dylan song, and by this point we had done many. At around the same time, and intended for the same record, we did "Million Dollar Bash" from his *Basement Tapes*, and "If You Gotta Go, Go Now," but we recorded the latter song with a difference. A few weeks earlier, we had been playing at a cinema in Notting Hill, which was being used as a temporary venue for the UFO Club. We were sitting back-stage and running through the song, and for some reason someone said, "Hey, let's do it in French!" We didn't trust our own fading memories of school so put out an announcement over the PA, asking for any francophones at the gig to head to the dressing room. Two men and a woman appeared, and for the next hour argued heatedly over rhyme, syntax and collo-quialisms. The finished result, even I could tell, was a typical committee job, no *panache*, no *esprit* and not enough *aisance*. Sandy managed to wrap her tonsils around it, and we recorded it with the addition of a melodeon in a faux-Cajun style, with Martin imitating a rub board on a stack of chair backs.

We had still not quite shrugged off our American roots. I had also written a song for the album called "Cajun Woman." I had discovered a mother lode of Arhoolie Records vinyl imported by James Asman's Record Centre in Covent Garden, and I thought we could adapt some of the infectious dance rhythms to our own culture and style. When I met real Cajun and Zydeco musicians years later, I was embarrassed to learn that they were familiar with Fairport and had heard their culture coming back at them in this strangled form. However, I was relieved that they seemed flattered and surprised to have been noticed by a band on the other side of the Atlantic.

I was consciously trying to write songs that fitted into the musical neverland between rock and traditional music. "Genesis Hall" was one such attempt. It was the name of a squat on Drury Lane in London, which had previously been a hotel. It was occupied by "hippies"—or at least that's how they were described in the newspapers following their violent eviction by the police. I thought this was a subject worthy of a "protest" song, though the fact that my father was still stationed at Covent Garden added some conflict to the narrative.

I'm not entirely sure how Sandy's song "Autopsy" arrived at band rehearsal. The part of the song that was in 5/4 was there already—Sandy had been playing a version of Alex Campbell's "Been on the Road So Long" around the folk clubs and it had become a comfortable time signature for her. Maybe the 2/4 section was there already too, and we added the 3/4 section during rehearsal. It all sounds more complicated than it is, which is a beautiful, free-flowing song that shows Sandy at her best as a composer and singer.

Sandy would often sing songs from her folk club repertoire when we were noodling backstage, and she talked a lot about her friends on the folk circuit, some of whom I knew and some I didn't. Being a female solo artist in that world and taking the milk train home after gigs, trundling for hours through the night, sounded like it could be a very lonely existence. We were backstage before a gig at Southampton University in January 1969 when Sandy started singing the eighteenth-century song "A Sailor's Life," in which a young girl takes to sea in a small boat in search of her beloved William, only to discover that he's feared drowned; beside herself with grief, she gives up the will to live and runs her boat onto the rocks. We jammed along with Sandy, droning under the first few verses, and then kicked into more of a four-square rock tempo about halfway through. This was pretty much just for fun, but we decided to play it that night to see what happened. It's only Southampton, it's only our careers on the line—what could possibly go wrong? We were quite pleased with the performance and thought it might be something special, so we asked Joe to come down and hear it at an upcoming show in Bristol. He liked it, and we decided to record it, with a view to including it on the next album.

Two weeks later, we went into Olympic Studios to cut "A Sailor's Life." We thought it would be interesting to invite someone who was familiar with the British tradition to add some instrumental weight to it, and Dave Swarbrick came to mind. Swarb turned up at the studio, I think somewhat trepidatiously, and with good humor agreed to have a pickup attached to his violin. This was the first time he had ever

played through an amp. It was probably also the first time
he had improvised in the free-form sense that Fairport used,
although as most traditional music involves spontaneous variations, the addition of harmonies and general thinking on
one's feet, in many ways he was prepared for how we played.
We knew we were going to roughly follow the template we
had tinkered with live. Beyond that, it was wherever the
music carried us. Before we started, I asked Swarb whether
he considered the song to be in a major or minor key. "Well,
I suppose both," he said, and that was the extent of our discussion before the red light went on.

Out on the studio floor, the balance was different from in
the control room, and not perfect. At Motown, they used to
say, "If you can't hear everybody else, then you're too loud."
My uncle Alan, who was a fiddle player, always used to say,
"If you can hear the drums, they're too loud!" These days, by
wearing headphones that have independent mixes, you can
get a balance that works for you, but at Olympic in 1969, we
were sharing one or two mixes. I took off one can so I could
hear the room, but kept one on so I could hear Sandy, who was
singing in the booth next to the control room. At that point
Olympic recorded in eight-track, which usually meant seven—
maintenance issues there were a running joke. Martin and his
drum kit were part-screened in the middle of the room, with
the rest of us forming a loose semi-circle around him. I said
to Joe before we committed to tape that we'd have to get it in
one—it was a long song, and playing it took a lot out of us.

We did a first take, and it sounded good out in the studio,
but we were interested to hear what kind of result we were

getting, so we went into the mixing room to listen. I was quite amazed by the way the track sounded on the big monitors— I don't think I've ever felt such a contrast between playing a song and listening back to it. Sandy's vocal sucked you into the story immediately, and Simon's guitar rippled and bubbled like water, directing the intensity of everything. At a certain point he brought in a riff that he had never played before, which gave the song a real solidity and fresh harmonic interest.

At this point, Swarb and I were feeling each other out. I would play a phrase and then he would play one back, as though we were having a conversation that increased in familiarity and intensity over five or six minutes. It switched between major and minor—it was as if we were building a bridge towards each other, and at some point the buttresses met, the keystone was set and our languages became mutually comprehensible.

Martin's drumming was extraordinary in its restraint. He played most of the song with beaters, increasing in intensity all the way through. When he finally kicked into a more orthodox rock rhythm with bass drum and snare, the whole thing soared to another level. Ashley was a bit critical of him for not breaking the tempo sooner at the end, but that was a minor quibble. We all agreed that there was no need for a second take—this first take had blown the doors off and revealed another world on the other side.

In the spring of 1969 we had acquired a real van—a Ford Transit, a familiar workhorse on British roads at the time. We could now ply our trade up and down the trunk roads and motorways of the country more efficiently. We also by now had a proper roadie, Harvey Bramham, who had worked with Iain previously, and also for Procol Harum. A rail-thin Yorkshireman who did not tolerate fools, he also had mildly larcenous leanings, which usually seemed to benefit the band—our stock of equipment seemed to multiply all by itself.

Harvey took a suitcase on tour, but there never seemed to be any clothes in it. Instead he carried his bedspread, a table lamp and a rug from his house, so that wherever he was staying he could feel at home. He also had a German shepherd called Bradford, who became an important part of the crew. He was supposed to be a guard dog but was far too friendly, and he would often take a nap on stage during our set.

On 24 April we were playing at the students' union of the City of London College. We had finished our set, and because the gig was in an auditorium with no backstage, we unglamorously jumped down and waded through the audience. A female voice said, "Can I carry your guitar?" This barely registered, so I kept walking, but the voice grew more insistent. "Hey you! Can I carry your guitar?" I looked around and noticed a skinny girl, about five feet nothing, with blonde hair in ringlets and wearing a red satin trouser suit. She was half running to keep up with me. Our road manager was busy sorting out the amps and PA—instruments in those days were the responsibility of the musicians. She persisted, and somewhat embarrassed, I handed over my weighty Les Paul to this small and attractive girl. She did not visibly flinch under the weight.

When we reached the classroom that was serving as a dressing room, she introduced herself as Jeannie, producing a card that said "Genie the Tailor." "Do I call you Jeannie or Genie?" I said. "Either will do," she replied. She was from Los Angeles and had a shop on Santa Monica Boulevard in Hollywood, where she catered to the sartorial needs of bands including Paul Revere and the Raiders, the Buckinghams and hipper clients like Cream. She spoke unabashedly about a previous liaison with Jack Bruce, from which I concluded that she went for pale Celtic men with dodgy teeth, but she had also lived with the American comedian Lenny Bruce for a couple of years. She mentioned, early on in our conversation, that she had been featured in a *Rolling Stone* issue on groupies—she was in there along with Cynthia Plaster Caster and Pamela Des Barres.

In 1969, I was still having a hard time saying no, and I allowed myself to be swept along by all this. I lacked confidence and self-esteem, and usually relied on Dutch courage to get up the nerve to talk to attractive girls. Sex, or the promise of it, was probably what pulled me along more than anything. I was not in a steady relationship at this point, and a bit of "how's your father" on the road was always appealing—even though it was very hit-and-miss in terms of satisfaction.

I took Jeannie back with me to Brent, the romance capital of Western Europe. Over the next couple of weeks, she tagged along to gigs with us—being what might be called pushy, she did not endear herself to the band—or we would visit her friends in London. At one point, that included going to the Beatles' headquarters on Savile Row to meet their publicist

Derek Taylor, who was every inch the British gentleman. We took a weekend trip to Paris, strolled through Saint-Germain and dined with another friend at Le Drugstore on the Champs-Elysées. On Saturday mornings in London, we shopped for jewelry in the antiques markets on Portobello Road. Life seemed good, and things were going well with Fairport. Our new album was due out soon, and the word was that we would tour America for the first time later that year.

On 11 May, Jeannie came with the band to one of our regular haunts, Mothers in Birmingham, a club we played every couple of months. We shared the bill that night with Eclection, another folk rock band with a female singer, Kerrilee Male. Kerry had been responsible for turning me vegetarian, encouraging me to make my own bread and eat more healthily, which was never easy on the road. Sandy's boyfriend Trevor Lucas was also in Eclection. Like Kerry, he had come to the UK from Australia. He stood out in a crowd, being tall with a mass of red hair, and he was a fine singer of traditional British and Australian songs. The show went well, with both bands getting a good reception. Sandy rode back to London with Trevor, while the rest of us piled into the Transit van and headed south down the A6 to the M1.

As we neared the end of the motorway, it was starting to get light. Nearly dawn . . . nearly home. The post-gig euphoria had worn off, and we were tired now. I was sitting in the front middle seat, with Jeannie next to me and Ashley and Martin behind us. Simon was suffering from a migraine and was stretched out on top of the equipment in the back of the van, trying to sleep it off. Harvey was at the wheel next to me.

He had been ill with a stomach ulcer for weeks, which had been badly affecting his sleep.

Approaching the last service station at the end of the M1, it was quiet in the van. Everyone was asleep, but being in the most uncomfortable seat, with nowhere to lean, I was struggling to nod off. We were doing a steady seventy miles per hour when I noticed that the van was moving slowly to the right, towards the central reservation. This was before motorways had crash barriers, so there was nothing to stop us drifting right into oncoming traffic. Nothing except a large pole, that is, which we were careering towards and would hit in about two seconds. I looked over at Harvey, and saw that his eyes were closed. I grabbed the wheel and pulled it hard to avoid the pole, but it was a drastic change of direction and the van's wheels came off the road. Harvey woke up and tried to correct the steering, but it was too late. We began to roll to the left, and as we spiralled into a long tunnel, all I could silently scream to myself was "NO, NO, NO—THIS IS NOT HAPPENING." After a few seconds I was battered into unconsciousness.

I felt as though I was floating somewhere high above the scene, and then with a whooshing sound I hurtled suddenly back into my body. I was lying propped up on my elbows, staring at the grass and mud on the embankment next to the motorway. I was finding it hard to breathe, and was almost blinded by the pain in my head. I looked around and saw Jeannie lying a few yards away, upside down, where the embankment sloped down from the road towards a golf course. I slowly crawled over to her. She was unconscious, but frowning, as if she was struggling to remember someone's name but it was on the tip of her tongue. There were small trickles of blood coming from her nose and in the corner of her mouth. Otherwise, she looked like she was sleeping peacefully. I felt for a pulse. It was hammering incredibly fast. This did not seem like a good sign. I took a wider look at the scene. Simon had walked up to the road and was flagging down a passing car. Harvey had been flung what seemed a huge distance onto the golf course, and was crying out in pain. Ashley and Martin were out of my line of vision. The van looked as though a thoughtless giant had stepped on it. It must have rolled many times and landed the right way up, squashed like a bug. There were instruments and amps scattered far and wide.

I drifted out of consciousness for a few minutes. An ambulance arrived and paramedics began to help the wounded. I went over to Jeannie again. She looked unchanged, but this time I couldn't find her pulse. I checked every place I knew a pulse should be. I went over to the ambulance.

"There's one over here," I said. "I think her heart has stopped beating."

"We're on it," they said. "How are you?"

"I can't breathe," I said.

They felt around my torso. "You've broken your ribs, son," they said. "Get in the ambulance."

There was blood dripping from my arm onto the ambulance floor. They put a dressing over it. I have no memory of the ambulance ride. I remember a hospital room, a nurse stitching up my arm in a couple of places. A doctor came in.

"That's your girlfriend?" he asked. I nodded.

"I'm afraid she didn't make it. Internal damage." I started saying the word "NO" quietly to myself, over and over.

"And the other lad—I think he was the drummer? He didn't make it either." The word "NO" was getting louder, and I was shaking my head. "If he'd survived, he would have been crippled for life. He had severe internal injuries."

The word "NO" was now a scream, and I couldn't help it. They gave me an injection, and the hospital receded and echoed, turned grey and then black, and the pain stopped. When I woke up, I was in a ward of four beds, with Harvey in the bed diagonally opposite me. If I tried to sit up, the room spun around. My ribs didn't feel as bad, but I must have been on painkillers. I was unconscious most of the time. Harvey's leg was in plaster and raised up. I didn't know what other injuries he had sustained, but he looked bad.

On the second day, Ashley wandered in from another ward. His face was cut, swollen and bruised. He asked me if I had any news of Martin. I couldn't believe that they hadn't told him. I couldn't bear to tell him, so I just said that we had to prepare for the worst. That seemed to be as good as telling him, anyway, and he let out a cry of anguish and walked back to his ward.

There were visitors, but I was not all there. Did my parents come? My sister? I have no idea. I remember the Social Deviants, a band we had shared many a stage with, being upbeat and cheerful—bless them for that. Sandy came in and fainted—not very good for an ex-nurse—and had to be treated herself. The Beatles and the Stones both sent flowers, which impressed the nurses. I was being kept in mainly because of concussion. My ribs weren't strapped up—they would heal by themselves.

After about five days in hospital, my parents came to pick me up. I had hardly seen them since leaving home, and it felt strange to be driving with them in these circumstances. They wanted to take me home for a few days, but I got them to drop me at the flat in Brent—I couldn't deal with questions. Simon was back at the flat, and he was probably the best person to be around—steady, sensible and had survived the same horror, so we each understood what the other was going through. We were all in deep shock. I found it hard to concentrate on anything for more than a few minutes, and when I tried to write something to articulate my feelings, I didn't recognize my handwriting—it seemed to belong to someone else. As a result, I stopped writing longhand and went back to printing, slowly and deliberately. We talked a little about the future of the band, which had been the focus of our lives for the last two years. When Ashley got out of hospital, the three of us went over to Sandy's flat and had what I suppose was a band meeting. What would we do now?

The cost of being musicians on the road was too high. As a band we were not really into drugs or hell-bent on self-destruction—maybe that would get us later, as the lifestyle became tedious or if we started to believe our own press. Just being on the road was dangerous, and if you threw in planes and helicopters, there were so many ways we could be cut down in our prime. But it wasn't as if we were accomplished in other fields and could walk into safer jobs. We were basically not very good at anything apart from being a band.

We had to go on—for the memory of Martin and Jeannie, if nothing else.

However, we knew things would have to change. We didn't want to play the songs that we'd played with Martin—it would be too painful. We decided that maybe this was the time for a new project. We had been moving towards the British tradition—perhaps now we should embrace it fully and make an album of traditional songs played with bass, drums and electric instruments.

When Martin died, he was aged just nineteen. How do you measure a life that short? Perhaps by the effect he had on others, how much he endeared himself to all who knew him and how people still enjoy his recorded legacy. I never saw a negative side to Martin; he had a sweet nature, fitted instantly into Fairport and had developed quickly as a drummer. His hero and role model was probably Jim Capaldi—Jim had a fine sense of swing in everything he did, and Martin aimed for the same. Those tips John Wood had given him were paying off, and his drum sound on *What We Did on Our Holidays* and *Unhalfbricking* was stellar.

It is hard to list all the "what-ifs," but Martin was a special human being, a special musician and someone I have remembered fondly my whole life. His funeral, at Golders Green Crematorium, was tough to get through. I sat with his girlfriend Helen, and when they played "I'll Keep It with Mine" from our previous album, we cried our hearts out, as did most of the congregation.

My relationship with Jeannie had probably been heading nowhere. I had known her for barely two weeks when she

died, and I'm not sure I could have let her run our lives much
longer. She was a talented designer and an extraordinary person, and her death froze our romance in midstream, so for a
while it seemed more important than it really was. It was easy
to idealize it, because it had no end. Joe was given the task of
sending Jeannie's luggage back to her family in the States, and
he asked me if I wanted the photographs of her that she'd had
with her, head shots and fashion shots. I kept them for a while,
but couldn't look at them.

So the band would carry on. Dave Swarbrick would join
us, we hoped, and we would hold auditions for Martin's
replacement. By throwing ourselves into a new project, we
would distract ourselves from grief and numb the pain of our
loss. In 1969, no one thought of counseling or therapy. With
British fortitude you soldiered on. We were too fragile; to
think beyond fumbling forward while leaning on each other
for support would have destroyed us.

Harvey recovered following the accident and was still our
road manager, at least in theory. He drove us just once more
after that. He seemed to think that confrontation therapy
would help us all get over the accident, but our nerves were
shot and our confidence in him was broken. We had to let him
go, and he had to face trial for causing death by dangerous
driving. We all gave evidence at the committal proceedings.
The last thing I wanted was to see Harvey in prison, but I was
having a hard time distinguishing reality from fantasy at that
point, and was useless as a witness. Harvey received a six-
month prison sentence, and I saw him only briefly after that.

5

Onward

Tho' you're tired and weary still journey on,
Till you come to your happy abode,
Where all the love you've been dreaming of
Will be there at the end of the road.

HARRY LAUDER

MY BROKEN RIBS knitted back together and my stitches were removed, but the mental scars took longer to heal. I felt like I was teetering on the edge, as if at any moment I might lose control and plunge into insanity. There would be a couple of weeks before we could reassemble as a band, and I was not looking forward to them. Joe Boyd came to the rescue. He and his partner Tod decided to take me, along with Simon, Simon's wife Roberta and Sandy, to the States for a couple of weeks, both to distract us from thoughts about the accident and to acclimatize us to a new country, before we toured there for the first time.

I sat next to Sandy on the flight from London to Los Angeles, and just after take-off she tipped a large vodka and tonic into my lap—she was well known for spilling drinks. Sandy was not a good flyer, so getting her tipsy helped the journey along. My trousers were nearly dry by the time we landed eleven hours later. LAX airport smelled of the ocean, subtropical vegetation and aviation fuel. While we waited for our luggage, Simon and I wandered over to a refreshment stand that sold grape juice, which seemed very exotic. In Britain, the choice was generally between orange or grapefruit out of a tin, so we were excited to try something different. However, when we tried it, only our British sense of manners prevented us from spitting it out onto the terminal floor. Would America continue to be a series of enticing lures and crushed hopes?

Our first real taste of the States was a party, the next day, at Phil Ochs's house. Phil was one of the great lyricists of the folk scene, and one of our heroes. We had bought his albums the moment they were released, and we had also covered his songs, so meeting him was truly special. His house, a large California contemporary up a winding road in the Hollywood Hills, was packed with musical luminaries: the pop band the Association was there, as were Judy Henske and Jerry Yester—we had records by all these people! Phil himself was hardly the tortured introvert I might have expected—he was quite full of himself, entrepreneurial and very political. In spite of being jet-lagged and more than a trifle inebriated, I went home with a beautiful woman called Liz, some ten years my senior, whom I had met at the Rome Pop Festival the previous year. I began to feel that the disappointing grape juice was not an omen after all—America was a wonderful country and a land where dreams were realized, and any evening might end up at Phil's house.

Nothing else in the following days was quite so spectacular, but the trip helped to distract us from the trauma of the crash. Sandy, Simon and I played a few songs at the LA Troubadour on the club's famous Monday-night open mic. On other nights, we saw the Esso Trinidad Steel Band, conducted by Van Dyke Parks, opening for Little Feat, who clearly had a huge local following but weren't quite the household name that they would later become. We also saw the obscure bluesman Earl Hooker open for his cousin, John Lee. We piled into a Ford station wagon and drove up the picturesque Pacific Coast Highway. Landmarks from the novels of Jack Kerouac whizzed past as the Pacific Ocean glinted far below us. Our driver, Walter Gundy, a former crew member with the Lovin' Spoonful, fancied himself as a bit of a rally driver and took every hairpin bend with the tires screeching and the back of the car hanging over the cliff. If this was also supposed to be some form of confrontational therapy to heal us after the accident, it didn't work. We stopped at Joan Baez's house, perched precariously over the ocean, but she wasn't home, so we drove up to San Francisco and dropped in on her sister, Mimi Fariña. She and her husband Richard were also our heroes, but he'd died tragically in a motorcycle accident a few years earlier. We started up a small jam session there, and she dragged Richard's dulcimer out of the cupboard. For us, this was a holy object.

We somehow ended up at the house of Bill Keith—banjo player extraordinaire, inventor of the "Keith Peg" for tuning and latterly a whiz on the pedal steel guitar. Bill was a member of the Jim Kweskin Jug Band, whom we had long adored for their rootsiness and sense of humour, and also at the house were Fritz Richmond and Geoff Muldaur, veterans of the same band. We spent some happy hours playing with Bill's collection of Victorian electrical hair restorers—terrifying devices that sent electrical stimulation to the scalp, which in Bill's case were clearly not working—and listening to bouzouki music on Bill's jukebox. I was impressed by a beaded curtain that he had made from ring pulls from beer cans, and resolved to make my own.

The short trip had served its purpose. It had been an absorbing week, full of new friends and new places, but now it was time to get back to Fairport and its future. Back in the UK, we held auditions for a drummer. I hated auditioning at the best of times, and in these circumstances was gripped by a fresh wave of sadness. We set up Martin's kit and tested the applicants with Sandy's song "Autopsy," with its three different time signatures. Most of them fell at the first hurdle, unable to handle the 5/4 section.

The third applicant was Dave Mattacks, who had spent the last couple of years playing for ballroom dancing in Belfast and Glasgow with the Ray McVay Band. This did not sound promising, and Dave looked suspiciously like a "jazzer," with shortish hair and the kind of roll-neck sweater Buddy Rich might have favored. But he handled the time changes flawlessly, said he didn't understand what the hell we were doing—and got the job. Dave admitted later—about thirty-five years later—that he had bought the album before the audition and had done his homework.

With Swarb and Dave Mattacks, or DM as we called him, now on board, we needed somewhere to live and rehearse without distraction. It was the fashion at that time to repair to the country, though I'm not sure who started this trend. The Beatles and the Stones had purchased huge houses in the stockbroker belt around London, where they could indulge themselves, their music and various substances without distraction. Our Island stablemates Traffic had rented a similar place in the Home Counties, and it seemed a good way to live and work cheek by jowl. There was also a neo-ruralist movement, mostly consisting of townies naively trying to reconnect with nature. Collectives sprang up in Europe and America, often made up of city kids attempting to figure out the rural economy with no previous experience. In some cases this also meant going "off-grid." The idealism of it all failed to reckon with human nature; in any kind of communal living, people can be greedy, selfish, domineering, controlling, promiscuous and devious, and most of these projects foundered after a year or two. But we needed something temporary to get us through the summer, so Joe started looking around. Those of us who had been through the crash needed to heal, with work as a distraction. And Swarb and DM, the new boys, needed to be integrated into the group, both musically and socially.

Without a map we would never have found the place that Joe arranged for us. We drove down single-track roads in the Hampshire countryside that looked like tiny scratches on the map, with sunlight filtering through high hedges on either side. At the end of a private drive was Farley House, a former rectory dating from the early eighteenth century. It had a facade of whitewashed brick, with windows and doors trimmed in pale blue. There was a flat lawn to the rear, and beyond that some elegant trees, including a commanding Lebanon cedar. The charming place seemed to fit the bill very well—it was secluded but only twenty minutes' drive from

Winchester, it had enough bedrooms to go round and the living room was large enough for rehearsal space. A Hampshire rectory—it was all very Jane Austen.

I arrived at the house first with our new roadie, Robin Gee, on a fine June afternoon. Robin had come to us from the band Family. He was handsome, eccentric and loyal, and he and I struck up a good friendship from the beginning—in fact, his first job was to pick up the gear and me, and drive to Farley. The rest of the band trickled in over the next day or two, Swarb with his wife Birgitta and young daughter, and Sandy with Trevor in tow; girlfriends, fiancées and wives would descend at the weekend. The living room was our workspace and the kitchen became the social hub of the house, but in truth we worked long hours on our British folk rock project, considering potential songs, collating versions from written sources and then rehearsing our ideas, taking strides into what was an unknown musical landscape.

Ashley, Swarb and Sandy were the main collectors of the material that became the album *Liege & Lief*. Swarb was probably the main source of the traditional songs, some of which he had learned during his association with Martin Carthy; had we known this, we might have vetoed them as being a bit plagiaristic—we would not have wanted to step on Martin's toes. We did go for some big ballads, reckoning that the drama would suit the amplified genre—powerful lyrics, loud music. With hindsight, it would have been interesting to have tried some industrial songs or more love songs—things like "The Blackleg Miner" and "The Blacksmith," which Ashley worked so well into his next project, Steeleye Span. Striking

a balance between modern and traditional was a challenge—
some things worked when updated, and some did not. We
rehearsed a version of "The Seeds of Love," a beautiful traditional English folk song, but I felt it sounded too bucolic in a
rock setting. Its sentiments struggled to convert from the pas-
toral setting in which Cecil Sharp had heard it in Edwardian
times to the world of rock and roll, so that one fell by the
wayside.

From time to time Ashley ran up to the English Folk
Dance and Song Society headquarters in London, where he
consulted their archive of ballads and recordings. They had
transcriptions of field recordings from the early days of the
Victorian folk revival that were originally on cylinder, including such wonderful singers as Joseph Taylor, recorded by
Percy Grainger in 1906. They also had a substantial library
of traditional music, which in those days was very valuable;
many books and collections were out of print, the recorded
coverage of music was patchy and finding versions of songs by
other musicians was hit-and-miss. In putting together songs,
we checked all the possible sources and compiled the clearest,
most poetic and narratively straightforward version; we might
use one from a fellow musician, a version or two from Cecil
Sharp House and a recorded version by someone like Ewan
MacColl, and sometimes we'd call a folklorist like Bert Lloyd.
We also had in our possession the ballad collection of Francis
James Child, an invaluable authority, comprising multiple
versions and fragments of four hundred-odd ballads from all
over the British Isles. Songs like "Sir Patrick Spens" and "Tam
Lin" were pieced together from various sources in that way,

rather than learned at our mother's knee—we were revivalists, after all. Perhaps coming from the rock world made us
less precious about the process—we didn't mind altering a few
things here and there to make a better song. Just the act of
playing these ballads with amplified fiddles and guitars was
divisive, at a time when some folk clubs did not permit songs
to be accompanied by instruments at all.

The power of the material was undeniable. Take a song like
"Matty Groves,"* with its immediate, descriptive language:

> At that Lord Arnold he jumped up
> And loudly he did bawl
> He struck his wife right through the heart
> And pinned her against the wall

Coupled with the volume of our rock rhythm section, this
made for powerful stuff, though the song also had a very dry
sense of humor:

> A grave, a grave, Lord Arnold cried
> To put these lovers in
> But bury my lady at the top
> For she was of noble kin

* This is an old song. One early variant, "*The Lamentable Ditty of the
Little Mousgrove and the Lady Barnet*" from the seventeenth-century
collection of Anthony Wood, has a handwritten note by Wood on the
reverse stating that the protagonists were alive in 1543. The tune we used
was the American "Shady Grove," which may or may not be connected.

"Tam Lin" is another ancient ballad—it is mentioned in the "Complaynt of Scotland" from 1549, but must be even older. The scene of the action is Carterhaugh, near Selkirk. Tam Lin is a prisoner of the Fairy Queen, and if Janet, the heroine of the song, can hold firm in the face of his magical transformation into all manner of beasts, she will free him and return him to the mortal world—as indeed she does. And although we regarded it as fantasy, or superstitious tale-telling, people in south-eastern Scotland will show you exactly where a song's action took place, and in some cases where humans were carried off by fairies. For rural people at least, the fairies were real—creatures existing in a parallel dimension. Dave and Toni Arthur, who acknowledged themselves to be white witches, were excellent interpreters of folk song and used to sing "Tam Lin" in the clubs. When they reached the line "Then up spoke the fairy queen / And an angry queen was she," there would occasionally sound a peal of thunder. Swarb was very into all that stuff. The strange carving of a doll-like effigy on the back cover of the *Liege & Lief* album, which always gave me the creeps, belonged to him, and was probably used for magical purposes at some point.

Swarb and Birgitta would organize the occasional Ouija board session at Farley House, which most of us would attend. I always got the feeling that we were tapping into a world that was beyond our understanding, and definitely beyond our control. It could also be unnerving—at one point we summoned the Fairy Queen from the song, and she did not seem to be a happy camper. The energy in the room was utterly strange, and superhumanly violent.

"Reynardine" is another supernatural song. I have read speculation that the subject of the song is a werewolf or a vampire, but it seems more likely that he is a fox in human form, leading innocent young girls over the mountain. In rural mythology, it was common to view the fox as something sinister. This version appears to be from the eighteenth century. When we began to rehearse it, it seemed to serve the song better to keep it out of tempo, just maintaining a violin drone and letting the vocal unfold at its own pace. We marked certain words in Sandy's vocal with emphatic chords from the guitars and bass, and cymbal splashes, which seemed to be all the arrangement the song needed. The weird, creepy narrative and Sandy's voice pull it along.

"The Deserter" is easy to date, as it mentions Queen Victoria's husband Prince Albert, but it is a broad update of a number of songs that go back to at least 1700. These songs often mention the Ratcliffe Highway, a notorious street near the London Docks in Stepney, where sailors would find lodgings, dodgy women would ply their trade and innocents would find themselves on a ship or in the army, sometimes after a sharp crack on the head. Swarb brought in a 3/4 version, based on a version he heard by Luke Kelly of the Dubliners. It became clear in rehearsal that performing the whole song in 3/4 was throwing away a lot of the drama in the story. We settled on a version that goes back and forth between 3/4 and 4/4, giving us more scope to build climaxes between the verses. Our take on the song has a happy ending, with Albert proving the hero.

Mummers' plays are a type of British folk play, usually performed at Christmas or Easter. Together, Sandy and Ashley wrote an opening track for the album—a kind of "calling on" song, akin to what you might hear before such a play. It mentions the various members of the band, just as the actors in a play would be introduced to the audience.

I wrote two songs that were "trad" enough to be considered for the project. For "Crazy Man Michael" I originally used the tune of "The Bonnie Hoose of Airlie," but Swarb reset it in three-quarter time to his own tune, and his version, with a few lyrical adjustments, became the one we all preferred. I also wrote the words of "Farewell, Farewell" to the tune of Child Ballad 101, "Willie o' Douglas Dale." I can hear in these songs the terrible sense of loss and confusion we were all still feeling at the time; they both sound like requiems for the departed.

Swarb brought us four dance tunes, which we arranged into a medley and attacked with rock-and-roll relish. I believe we were the first rock band to play traditional British dance music. DM had to invent a new drumming style to accompany these tunes, something more contemporary, not to mention more brutal, than the polite snare drum of a Scottish dance band.

The traditional music of England, Scotland, Ireland and Wales was familiar to those of us who had grown up in North London. It was educational policy, for as long as I was at school, to teach folk songs in music class, and these would be sung from primary school onward—often the cleaned-up Victorian versions. A song like "Sir Patrick Spens" would feature in poetry anthologies, sometimes in its original Scots dialect. We also visited the folk clubs as we were growing up, so a certain amount would have been absorbed there—we just didn't think it was particularly relevant to what we were involved in as a band. We probably thought it was too twee to have a musical place—after all, it was hardly very rock and roll. I was fairly unenthused by a band like Pentangle, who did some traditional songs with jazzy arrangements and light amplification—I preferred the music they made as individuals to what they did as a band. It wasn't until Sandy joined Fairport that it all came into focus.

My own childhood experience included listening to my grandmother singing around the house. She was from the Isle of Skye, and sang in both Gaelic and English. I can't remember too much about her Gaelic repertoire, but she would sing the English version of "Mingulay Boat Song" and a few other traditional songs. My father, a typical exile, was more Scottish than the average Scot. He had been recruited to the Metropolitan Police from the Borders prior to the Second World War. Besides his jazz records, he had many albums of Scottish dance music by Jimmy Shand. He never missed a Burns Night—his party piece was "Tam o' Shanter"—and the bookshelves at home were lined with Scots subject matter, as well as a number of books on criminology, a combination that might explain some of my musical obsessions!

All through the 1950s and 1960s, there were times when I was seriously forced to provide my own entertainment. There is an expression, "the long, dark teatime of the soul," referring to the lull in broadcasting between about 2 P.M. and 7.30 P.M. on a wet, miserable winter Sunday in England during those years. What was there to do between the end of *Round the*

Horne, a brilliantly witty, risqué gem of a BBC radio show, and the start of *Hancock's Half Hour*, an astute TV satire on 1950s attitudes? (Sometimes I thought my father *was* Tony Hancock—the resemblance was that close.) Being occasionally bored to distraction, when my friends were not available I would read from the family bookshelves. I got into Walter Scott, starting with *Ivanhoe* around the age of ten, and then moving on to *Rob Roy* and *Waverley*. I also liked Robert Burns, whose songs we had sung at school. There was a weighty tome of Border ballads, which included such nuggets as "The Dowie Dens of Yarrow." I always seemed to be getting in trouble with my father, but reciting a couple of stanzas of Burns would usually get me a pat on the head and a "don't do it again." So when we started to think about writing songs much more in the style of the British tradition, I thought, "Oh—I know how to do this!" I'd been paying no attention to any of this for the last ten years, but somehow I was already trained for it. The strands of my musical life were weaving together.

For recreation during the summer at Farley House, we'd play football on the lawn, go to a local pub or head into Winchester. While exploring the attic one day, Robin and I came across a box kite, a huge canvas thing about seven feet tall. We resolved to give it a test run, and after buying about six hundred feet of rope, just to be on the safe side, we headed off towards the local high point, Farley Mount. It was a pleasant summer's day, but there was a good stiff breeze blowing at the top of the mount. Having launched the beast, we tied the rope to the back door handle of the Transit van, as two of us couldn't hold it. The kite performed splendidly, but the further up it went, the stronger it pulled. We managed to use all the rope, watching in admiration as our white canvas angel soared over the forests of Hampshire. However, after about twenty minutes, the rope slackened and our kite slowly tumbled to earth. We followed the rope to its end and searched for a long while all around, but still the kite eluded us. It was probably caught in a tree, we concluded, and we retreated sadly back to the house.

During our time at Farley House, we had regular deliveries from a milkman; by the end of our stay there we had run up a considerable bill of £14, which was more than half a week's wages for us. We could have all chipped in and raised the money, but we decided that it would be more fun to busk for it. We went to the Cathedral Close in Winchester and set up under an arch, where we fancied there would be enough passing trade. We played a mixture of early Fairport and some older songs, including a couple of Ethnic Shuffle Orchestra numbers like "Blues in the Bottle" and "Boodle Am Shake," right up to medleys of jigs and reels. The money came rolling in—by the time we were moved on by the police, we had about double the amount needed for our milk bill, and quite a crowd had gathered. We donated the surplus cash to the cathedral's restoration fund.

One morning I was woken by a huge crash. A thunderstorm was sitting right over the house. I went to the window to smell the summer rain, and was just in time to see lightning strike the crown of the Lebanon cedar. There was a tearing sound, and a huge branch of the tree came away and fell to earth.

In early November, we went into the studio at Sound Techniques to record the fruits of our summer endeavours. Right on the first day, we told John Wood that we wanted DM's snare drum to sound more like Levon Helm from the Band, to which John replied, "If you want it to sound like Levon, get Levon to play it!" Levon used an old military snare drum and calfskin heads because he liked the dead sound, and it made the Band's records sound unique and timeless. John compromised by rolling higher frequencies off the snare drum mic, and we left it there. Today, to my ears, it just sounds wrong— John, of course, had been right. We were well rehearsed, so our recording sessions went fairly quickly, and in a couple of weeks we had completed our third album of 1969! That seems an impossible work rate, looking back, but *What We Did on Our Holidays* was recorded in 1968 and released in January 1969, so that flatters the picture a little. *Unhalfbricking* came out in July, and *Liege & Lief* was released in December.

It was time to get back on the road and take the music to a live audience. Although there was great joy in playing to a live crowd, I dreaded those fatigued late-night drives back to London, unable to doze off and trying to keep the van on the road with sheer nervous energy. Fortunately, Robin was a conscientious and steady driver, and he made me feel reassured.

You can rehearse forever and think you have written the best material, arranged to perfection, but until you actually stand in front of an audience, you will never know if other people "get" it. The new songs went down very well, which was fortunate because we had jettisoned everything older, on which we had built our fanbase. Our first show was back at the Van Dike in Plymouth, a familiar and welcoming venue to ease us into our new beginning. The reaction of the crowd was everything we could have hoped for; they responded well to Sandy's reading of the new songs, and especially to Swarb leading the dance tunes. This was loud, urgent music. People have been dancing to jigs and reels for centuries; the Van Dike audience knew none of the formal and sometimes complicated social dances that go with them, but felt an instinctive urge to move their bodies in primitive ways—by stomping their feet, clapping and jumping up and down. They wanted encores, and we did our best to supply them until we ran out of material.

Our time at Farley House was coming to an end. The spell of the summer was broken, and we abruptly re-entered the real world. We went on *Top of the Pops*, because our current single was doing quite well—in fact, it was at number nineteen in the singles chart. It was the Dylan song in French, "Si Tu Dois Partir," not exactly representative of Fairport, but TV was TV, and it had to be done. It was my first and last time on the program. Tony Blackburn was the DJ that week, a nice man but incredibly vanilla. It felt strange to interact with the world of pop, having been sheltered from it for our whole career up to that point. It must have been even stranger for Swarb and DM, with their backgrounds. The Bee Gees were also on the show and were acting like prima donnas, so I thought we should do the same. When the producer complained that we had too many members on stage—we had recruited a couple of extras from the Witchseason office, partly for visual effect but also to confuse and annoy people—I explained with a straight face that we were a tribe that lived communally, and the others would be devastated not to be included. The poor man, who must have dealt with acres of bullshit every week, just rolled his eyes and adjusted the cameras. We hammed up the French thing—wearing Breton shirts and berets, and bowing the bass with a baguette. Number nineteen remained our highest chart position, and we were happy to leave it at that.

The month after that we played the Festival Hall in London. This was the first major exposure of the *Liege & Lief* material, the big statement of intent before an audience of friends, critics and fans, who we hoped were prepared to be open-minded.

Opening the show were John and Beverley Martyn and Nick Drake, all stablemates from Joe's Witchseason roster. I had got to know John quite well, and had played guitar on one of Beverley's records. John and Beverley's stage persona was upbeat, with John talking nineteen to the dozen between songs while he tuned up. Although this could easily last as long as the songs themselves, it was usually really funny and they were all we could have asked for in an opening act.

Ashley had recently seen Nick play live, and he had recommended him to Joe as a potential recording artist. I had played on Nick's first record, on the song "Time Has Told Me." In an era when a lot of people didn't say much, myself included, Nick stood out at that end of the spectrum. We would nod at each other in the Witchseason office—just as I would nod at Syd Barrett in the dressing room, or at Jim King from Family on the bus—but that was about it. I suppose it was felt that words were unnecessary—after all, we all shared a generational vision of the world and the state of humanity, so why speak? So my acquaintanceship with Nick was mostly restricted to averted eyes and half-smiles. We both lived in Hampstead at one point—we would occasionally pass each other in the street, and there would be some shy, embarrassed acknowledgement.

I did have one meaningful conversation with Nick. I was on the Tube platform at Hampstead, heading into Central London, and he walked by and nodded. He was uncomfortable meeting anybody, but he must have thought it would be more embarrassing to walk past without acknowledging me before waiting further down the platform, so he came and sat down next to me. This was now awkward for both of us, so I had to strike up a conversation, or what would have to pass for one, between two socially inept introverts. I knew he liked Frederick Delius, so I asked him what his favorite works were. It was the right question. After some shaking of the head as he gave thought to the question, he came up with "Song of Summer" and "Brigg Fair." I asked if he thought Delius was too much under the shadow of Debussy, to which Nick said that though he was clearly influenced by him, Delius was an original. He said he liked Delius's English-sounding work more than the works he wrote in other countries. Then the train came. We both got on and sat opposite one another; it was noisy enough to stem conversation, to our mutual relief. Fifteen minutes later, he got off at Goodge Street, before I disembarked at Leicester Square.

Nick was also a little different on stage. He had a certain charisma, but did not attempt to ingratiate himself with the listener in any way. His need to tinker between songs was even more acute than John Martyn's, because every song he played seemed to require a different tuning. He never spoke to the audience; he played and sang exquisitely, but the crowd got restless and were less inclined to pay attention. As a result, he was less well received. At the time he was unknown, having played just a handful of gigs in his life. Ashley had seen him at a multi-band all-nighter at the Roundhouse in Camden, but his gig opening for us was the most important concert of his career to date, and the audience didn't get it. They may well have kicked themselves, such is the importance given to Nick's music—his reputation has continued to grow in the decades following his tragic death in 1974. Sometimes the public has to be told by a critic or fellow musician, "You really need to listen to this guy—he's incredible." Putting him on the bill was our way of trying to make that happen, but it unfortunately wasn't to be during Nick's brief life.

I saw nothing of Nick in the later years of his life, and when John Wood played me some tracks from his 1972 album *Pink Moon*, I was disturbed. Part of what had made Nick's earlier music so appealing was a balance between dark and light. The sadness inherent in the music had been veiled behind beautiful arrangements and an intriguing voice that drew you in. However, his third album seemed a stark cry for help, the voice of a man teetering on the edge of sanity. I worried for Nick as I also worried for Sandy, but as I knew him less well it wasn't always uppermost in my mind. When I heard of his death, it shook me badly, and I questioned a universe that could take away one so young and talented. I hope the soul of Nick is still around somewhere, and I hope he can see that his music, so neglected during his lifetime, has become accepted and revered. I meet artists all the time who claim Nick as a major influence on their music, and I hope he also finds peace and comfort in that.

At the Festival Hall we played a number of *Liege & Lief*'s songs more or less in sequence, with a few additions. We opened with "Come All Ye," which was more powerful live with the visual element, featuring the succession of band members. "Reynardine" followed, with its proto-metal guitar chords and Sandy's bare and expressive declamation of the lyric. She then sang "Sir Patrick Spens," a song that had arrived too late for *Liege & Lief* but ended up on the next record. The instrumental medley of "The Lark in the Morning" came next, in what felt like the most powerful opening quartet of songs in Fairport's history to date. Sandy also sang "The Quiet Joys of Brotherhood," a poem by Richard Fariña set to the traditional Irish tune "My Lagan Love." The audience responded well, seeming to get what we were driving at, and we finished with "The Ballad of Easy Rider" and Swarb singing the tongue-in-cheek "Don't You Think It's Time We Had a Talk with Jesus?" Again, the reaction was loud and physical.

Backstage in the bar after the concert, people were complimentary. Bert Lloyd, who had helped us assemble some of the versions of the traditional songs we had played, said it was the most exciting thing he had seen for some time. Lou Killen, stalwart of the folk revival and a terrific singer, was magnanimous. It was hard to gauge how many people left the venue disappointed that we had jettisoned the old repertoire, but we weren't thinking about that. We felt vindicated that our choice of direction had been met with approval, and the omens were good for the release of the album—still a couple of months away.

During that autumn we played a dozen dates across the UK, including another London show at the Fairfield Halls in Croydon, a couple of dates in Scotland, an attendance record-breaking appearance at Manchester University and a not-too-traumatic return to Mothers in Birmingham. We were treated with sympathy wherever we went, and though we didn't care too much about that, we were pleased that the music was going down well. All seemed to be set fair. Fairport was on the up and America again beckoned, if we could get Sandy onto a plane.

Sandy and Trevor were by now a firm item. Trevor would drive Sandy to and from many of our gigs, and we frequently shared a bill with his band Eclection. One evening, as we sat in our dressing room, we heard Sandy and Trevor singing a beautiful a cappella two-part harmony to "A Sailor's Life" in Eclection's dressing room next door, with Trevor improvising a harmony underneath Sandy's tune. It sounded like a million dollars, and we looked at each other with a growing realisation that Sandy's first loyalty wasn't to us. She was a brilliant frontwoman for Fairport, one of the great singers of her generation, and she was helping us carve out a whole new genre of music—we did not want to lose her.

Sandy was high maintenance—she could be drunk, lived emotionally on a knife edge and would sometimes be late or not turn up at all—but the quality of her musicianship outweighed the negatives. An obvious way to keep her happy and in the band, while also keeping Trevor away from the temptations of life on the road, would be to bring him into Fairport. Simon suggested this as we sat there backstage, but also acknowledged that he himself would be redundant—who would need a second rhythm guitarist who didn't sing as well as Trev? But we were not going to dump founder members. Simon was much more than a rhythm guitarist, anyway. And bringing Trevor in as a bass player and dumping Ashley was never even suggested. The growing unease about Sandy remained in the background most of the time, but we carried on cheerfully enough. We'd had enough to endure in 1969 and were still trying to heal. We were young and living in the moment, without thinking ahead too much.

Swarb had connections with Denmark—his wife Birgitta was Danish, and he and Martin had played shows over there. He was friends with a promoter called Walther Klaebel, who booked us for a tour that November. We assembled at Heathrow for the flight to Copenhagen, but there was no sign of Sandy. After some frantic phone calls, Anthea Joseph, Joe Boyd's assistant at Witchseason, found her at home. She hadn't turned up for the flight because she was terrified of flying, and also because her faith in Trevor's fidelity was zero. Separation from him was becoming an issue. Anthea arranged for her to get a later flight, but something had snapped within us, like the neck of a beloved guitar that had been mistreated by baggage handlers. It followed a series of minor sins that would have been tolerated forever, but this truly seemed like an act of betrayal. At the baggage carousel at Copenhagen airport, there were mutinous mutterings.

The tour of Denmark ended up being two shows instead of ten, after Mr. Klaebel turned out to be somewhat flaky. We were slowly learning that Swarb's connections, brainwaves and sources of potential income needed to be taken with liberal doses of salt—his somewhat romantic view of the world didn't always align with reality. Before we flew home, we decided to fire Sandy. I don't remember who asked her to leave—it was probably Ashley, who usually did the dirty work. She was reportedly shocked that we would take that step. She may have been fragile beneath the confident facade, but she still knew her worth.

Why would you fire the best singer in the land, who in hindsight is one of the greatest singers Britain ever produced? I suppose we felt that in her mind she had already left; our vision of Sandy and Trevor forming their own band became a reality just a few months later. Our own loyalty to Fairport seemed unshakeable—it had been a huge effort to recover from the accident, and we did not want to throw that away. Our new material and direction had been hard-won, and our determination to persevere may have been our way of concealing our mental frailty. We were a little crazy, in the sense that the crash had unbalanced us, leaving us restless, unpredictable and irrational. We were probably suffering from post-traumatic stress disorder, though there wasn't a name for it back then.

My mind ran through the "what-ifs," which is always a futile exercise. What if we had shoehorned Trevor into the band somehow to keep Sandy happy and modified our tour schedules, allowing her time to travel by boat or train?

That band might have swept all before it, though I think with Trevor there would have been conflict. I had always liked him and he was unfailingly generous to me, but he was ambitious for Sandy, and for himself as a producer too. He liked a comfortable lifestyle and had no problem spending money, whether Sandy's or a record company's. In Fairport, he very likely would have taken over the band, locking horns with Ashley, Swarb and myself—there would have been too many egos. Sandy and Trevor's relationship was also pretty volatile, loving but not particularly loyal. To watch that on a daily basis would have not always given one a feeling of peace and stability.

Hard on the heels of losing Sandy, we found ourselves facing another crisis. Ashley was suffering more than the rest of us following the crash. His way of keeping on an even keel was to throw himself into project after project, and his next vision for Fairport was not meeting with universal approval. *Liege & Lief* had been a great artistic success, pioneering a new form of music. Musicians in Spain, the Netherlands, Scandinavia and even the US had heard it and were responding by applying the same contemporary approach to their own traditional cultures. The face of folk music in the UK had been transformed forever, and this was a sea change for which Ashley deserves immense credit. Some of us saw *Liege & Lief* as a project that would reshape the direction of Fairport, after which we would get back to writing new songs that would represent at least half the band's material. However, Ashley was keen to pursue traditional music—there was much left to explore, as his subsequent career attests. At one point, he wanted to bring in

Terry and Gay Woods, Martin Carthy and Bert Lloyd, making us a nine-piece. This idea had redundancy written all over it—three singers and three guitarists was a fine formula for a jam session at a festival, but Simon and I were used to something more intimate. I had felt redundant in an eight-piece at school, and I knew how long that had lasted. At some point economics comes into it too—it was hard enough feeding a band of five or six.

Ashley duly quit the band. It must have been agony for him—Fairport really was his baby, and the rest of us had been smart enough to cling to his coat-tails. From our days in Muswell Hill, it was clear to everyone that he had the vision. However, he was first and foremost an idealist, and I cannot deny that in many ways, the move he made enabled him to do wonderful things for English music that would not have happened had he stayed.

Swarb seemed to take all this change in his stride. DM must have been surprised at the turbulence he had seen in his six-month tenure, but we all figured that the band would continue—at these junctures, we would look searchingly at ourselves and realize that a job in social services would be much less fun, plus we'd be lousy at it. We had to soldier on and find a new bass player to take Ashley's place. Swarb recommended a guy called Dave Pegg. We all knew more about electric bass players than Swarb, whose reliability in these matters had already come into question—he was a folkie who had crossed bows with the occasional upright bassist, and his knowledge of the lower octaves was mostly learned from playing with Beryl Marriott's band, watching her left hand on

the piano. Besides Swarb's approval, this Dave Pegg seemed to
have a few other strikes against him: he was from Birmingham
and he had played acoustic bass with the Ian Campbell Folk
Group.

We had played in Birmingham frequently, but whenever
we approached it there appeared to be a green smog hanging over the city—whether as a result of its light industry or
of an ancient and long-lasting curse by a Druidic god. It also
had the ugliest modern city center in Britain, now thankfully
demolished, as well as the most baffling ring road known to
man. We had nicknamed it "The Celestial City."

The Ian Campbell Folk Group was a mainstay of the
Birmingham folk scene. Ian and his sister Lorna had moved
there from Buchan in Aberdeenshire, and were fine singers.
They ran the Jug o' Punch folk club at Digbeth Civic Hall
every week, which was also broadcast to hospitals in the
area. Their repertoire included some international songs, in
keeping with the socialist spirit of the 1950s; they would do
"Guantanamera" and "Kumbaya," as well as the more common
English and Scottish favorites. It was a set list that overlapped
with that of bands like the Weavers and the Spinners, but it
was becoming corny by the late 1960s. This did not seem a hip
résumé for a potential bass player.

Swarb could judge a good fiddle tune or a bargain in an
antique shop, but bass-playing? We thought not. However, we
summoned a degree of generosity and agreed to give Dave Pegg
a try. We were auditioning at the Roebuck pub in Chiswick,
south-west London, not an easy commute from Birmingham,
but we were still surprised when he turned up an hour late. He

later revealed that his own car wouldn't start that morning, so he'd had to borrow his dad's. There was something wrong with the steering, though, and it couldn't make right turns, so Dave had had to figure out a route from Birmingham to Chiswick only turning left! But he played fabulously, and we had forgiven him about two minutes into the session. Ashley was a fine player with a very distinctive approach, and early Fairport rhythm sections have a unique feel to them. Dave was a monster, though, much funkier and more technically adept. There was a bit of James Jamerson, the great Motown bass player, in there, and some similarities to the bass players of Birmingham bands like the Spencer Davis Group and the Moody Blues. We soon realized that he hadn't learned these skills with Ian Campbell—he had played in bands with Robert Plant and John Bonham, had been in chart band the Uglys, and was a lead guitarist who had converted to playing bass.

We liked Dave instantly and hired him on the spot. The fact that two-fifths of the band were now from Birmingham hardly registered—the immediate crisis facing us was having three Daves. So no one got called Dave—we had "DM' (Mattacks), "Peggy' (Pegg) and "Swarb' (Swarbrick). Peggy played one more show with Ian Campbell, fulfilling his final obligation. At the end of the set, he threw the double bass down off the stage and jumped through it—an unorthodox way to hand in your notice, and all broadcast on hospital radio.

Our next issue was where to live. We had loved our time in Farley House, finding it vastly preferable to renting rehearsal rooms in London, and we currently found ourselves geographically scattered. Swarb was in Haverfordwest, about as far away as you can get in Wales without falling into the Irish Sea, Peggy was in Birmingham, DM was in Sussex, and Simon and I were still in North London. We searched for another country dwelling that would not break the bank, and then Robin and Simon went to look at a disused pub near Bishop's Stortford, forty-five minutes north of London. They rejected it as being freezing, damp and inhospitable, not to mention right on a main lorry route.

A day later, Swarb phoned from Wales. "What's the address?" he asked. "I've got everything in the van—all my furniture, Birgitta and the kid. We're on our way." The freezing, disused Angel suddenly became the only option, and our fate was sealed.

6

The Angel

Come, bring hither quick a flagon of wine,
that I may soak my brain and get an ingenious idea.

ARISTOPHANES

THE ANGEL WOULD have been far more appealing if it had been a hundred yards further away from the main road. The front was Georgian and well proportioned, and there were parts that dated back to the sixteenth century. Its elegance, however, was partly obscured by the large black-and-white chevron warning traffic of a sharp left turn. It was built as a house, but had more recently been a pub. Stripped of taps and optics, the bars were still in place, as well as a long function room that had once been a skittle alley. Swarb and his family grabbed a couple of connecting rooms upstairs, as did Peggy and his family. The rest of us found space as best we could, with Robin in the remains of the saloon bar. I was the only unmarried member of the group, so the privations were less of an issue for me. Peggy had a young daughter, Stephanie, who I think was only two at the time. All these people and only one bathroom—and one toilet. Hot water came from a wall-mounted Ascot gas heater. It would dribble a couple of inches of water into the bath, and then give up for about thirty minutes; it was advisable to attempt a bath at four in the morning, to avoid queues. We also had crew with us: in addition to Robin, we had recruited David Harry, who had previously worked for Family, as a general dogsbody. He was something of an acid casualty; formerly a sharp operator, he remained a sweet human being but was not firing on all cylinders. He helped load and unload the gear, as did Jack (whose last name I never knew), who came from—I'm not sure where. Jack had a notorious appetite. Anything not nailed down in the refrigerator would disappear by morning, hence his nickname, "Jack the Gannet." We did pay him a pittance, so perhaps it was no wonder. Jack famously fainted full length onto the floor of the local pub one evening. It was his turn to buy a round, so a novel way of avoiding the expense!

There was no heating in the place, so we bought storage heaters and spread them around. These ingenious devices used electricity at night, when it was cheapest, and then retained that heat for the rest of the day—or at least that was the theory. They seemed next to useless, though maybe the spaces they were required to heat were too large. The kitchen was generally warmer, there being a bit of residual heat from cooking, and it became the place where we hung out. I don't remember doing any cooking myself—in fact, I don't remember eating much other than cereal during the year we were there, apart from the occasional meal out in Bishop's Stortford.

My room was upstairs at the right-hand end of the building. There was a mattress and rush matting on the floorboards, a couple of shelves for books and records, a turntable, nice Quad amplifiers, and KEF speakers that Robin and I had built from kits. In the corner was a large Victorian harmonium, which I had inherited from Swarb, and which I painted white with silver trim. It was fun to do impersonations of Captain Nemo, and I did write one song at least on it—"Bad News Is All the Wind Can Carry." The traffic from the road was very loud. The A120 was a main route to the docks at Harwich, and hundreds of trucks would thunder past every day. There was a long, straight, downward slope and then that sharp left turn just before the pub, so the lorries would slam on their air brakes and change gear. The noise started at around eight in the morning, but eventually I learned to tune it out and would doze fitfully, dreaming of blitzkrieg and apocalypse, until noon, a respectable hour for a musician to rise.

We would light a fire in the fireplace in the function room, burning whatever we could scavenge, and then get down to rehearsal. This was an ideal space, and the neighbrs weren't too bothersome—the landlord lived next door, but didn't complain. Some evenings, Swarb and I would bank up the fire and write. Swarb would usually start the process with a tune he had come up with. I would figure out a harmonic structure and then try to come up with a lyric. Swarb's sense of melody was fairly unique; when I asked him about his influences, he'd mention some obscure music-hall duo from the 1920s. I never knew if he was pulling my leg, but his tunes didn't sound like anyone else's. I think the first song we wrote together was "Sloth."*

> *Just a roll, just a roll*
> *Just a roll on your drum*
> *Just a roll, just a roll*
> *And the war has begun*

* See Appendix A, p. 266.

The title may be misleading; we were rehearsing two new songs, one slow and one up-tempo. The slow one had the working title "Slowth" and the fast one "Fasth"; the latter became "Walk Awhile," while "Sloth" never shrugged off its temporary name. I still get people asking me if it was the first of a series about the seven deadly sins. Or maybe it was about indifference in a time of war? As with most songs, it is what you want it to be.

These writing sessions usually took place after our regular trips to the Nag's Head, the pub in the next village. The moustachioed landlord Cyril knew good customers when he saw them, and treated us well. The evening usually concluded behind locked doors and into the small hours; our drive home sometimes ended up in a ditch.

Not everyone in the area received us as well as Cyril. The local paper put us on the front page, with a headline that read something like "Little Hadham Invaded by Hippie Musicians!" The article voiced concerns about drugs, hedonism, the safety of their daughters, and so on. Their concerns were reasonable considering what we got up to, but we were never a big drug band. Swarb and the crew smoked a bit of weed, but the rest of us were really just drinkers. We had been partly trained by Sandy, but Peggy ramped it up a few more notches.

My own drug experience was haphazard and brief. I never wanted to take acid, because I didn't want to be like everyone else, all love and peace, without any edge, without any balls . . . but avoiding it was impossible. I know of three occasions when someone spiked my drink, with varying results. I felt that amazing oneness with everything, not knowing where I ended and the table began, roots growing out of my arm and into the furniture; the painful sensory overload of being in a crowd, all filters stripped from me; the horror of watching a steam train turn into a living, fire-breathing animal that chased me down the platform; and seeing *Sgt. Pepper* turn into curlicues of colors and patterns, the reverb on the vocals echoing back thousands of years, into the tombs of ancient Egypt. I had never smoked cigarettes, having a real phobia from looking at my parents' ashtrays, so I never smoked dope either. I did eat the odd brownie, with predictable results, but ultimately it put me to sleep. I preferred stimulants like speed or cocaine, but never to the point of becoming addicted. Cocaine made me deeply paranoid, so I skipped that after a while, and I saw what speed did to your teeth within a year or two. Drinking, on the other hand, was a social necessity in Fairport (and is to this day), and while I was in the band I enjoyed the effect it had on me, loosening my inhibitions, unknotting my tongue and knocking me out at night.

We were frequently away from the Angel, playing shows all over Britain and the US. We were diminished vocally without Sandy, but instrumentally we were tighter and more powerful than ever. In March 1970 we played at the National Stadium in Dublin. It was a boxing venue, so we played in the ring, surrounded by the audience! The only way we could think to perform was to face outwards on all four sides. The Chieftains opened for us—I think it was early in their career, before they became the very definition of Irish traditional music— and it proved to be a fantastic night. After the show, there was a party with the Chieftains and the Dubliners, and some mighty jamming and drinking took place. The next day I had the privilege of walking through the streets of Dublin with the Dubliners, which felt a bit like going for a stroll through Memphis with Elvis.

Swarb, coming from the folk world, was not always up to speed on the subtleties and protocols of a rock band. He was used to a more leisurely pace, with no sound checks or hotel check-ins to negotiate. He had a frequent need to stop the van, usually every thirty minutes:

"Can we stop? I need a gypsy's." (A gypsy's kiss: rhyming slang indicating "I wish to void my bladder.")

"Can we stop for a cup of tea?" (We just did that.)

"Awww, did you see that? Fantastic antique shop! Pull over, quick!"

This became such a regular set of requests that stopping the van for any reason whatsoever became known as "piss/tea/antiques." It goes without saying that such requests were rarely acknowledged.

When you travel together, and spend so much time on top of each other, you develop your own private language. Another phrase common to Fairport members is the expression "curly fish." We were playing on the Continent somewhere, when the promoter uttered the magic words, "I am taking you out to dinner before the show." This usually meant a good restaurant, and in most of Europe, pretty good food—the promoter not wishing to appear a cheapskate. On this one occasion, there appeared on the table a pile of over-fried fish, of indeterminate species, and a few vegetables. The fish were so dehydrated that they had curled up, and you might have considered them edible if you had been in a lifeboat for a month and cannibalism really wasn't your thing. From that point forward, and to this day, a "curly fish" means a free meal paid for by the promoter.

After we had been at the Angel a good few months, the local vicar asked us if we would play a concert to raise money for the church organ fund. This seemed an opportunity to show the good people of Hertfordshire that if we were decadent and debauched hippies, at least our hearts were in the right place. We performed in a field in the neighboring village of Much Hadham, and the well-attended event was deemed a success. Money was raised, along with our status in the community.

There was a knock on the kitchen door a week later, and without invitation, a uniformed figure came in, trailed by other uniformed figures. His epaulets dazzled and sparkled. I had grown up with these people and knew a superintendent of police when I saw one. There was a sudden rush to hide the drugs under the table, but he put out a reassuring hand. "Stand easy, lads," he said, "I'm here on unofficial business." He explained that the local constabulary had been impressed with the concert for the church organ fund. Would we like to do something similar for the police orphan fund?

This did not seem like an offer you turned down, just as you would probably not turn down the offer to play at Al Capone's wedding. These were people you did not want to piss off, so we readily agreed. If we could do organs, we could do orphans. A date was set, the venue was the same field and the band Trees agreed to play too.

It turned out to be a beautiful summer's evening. The show was unexpectedly mentioned on BBC Radio 1 that afternoon, and thousands of people headed out on the short drive from London. The police were unprepared for the massive success of what was, after all, their idea. The single-lane country roads were jammed, pubs ran out of beer and parking was a nightmare, with coppers drafted in from neighboring towns to direct traffic. The show, however, went terrifically well.

The next morning, there was another knock on the kitchen door. It was the same superintendent: "Well done, lads. I want to thank you personally on behalf of the force. The orphan fund received a wonderful boost. Is there anything we can do for you? Anything you need?"

A moment's thought. "Well—we could use a dishwasher."

Later that afternoon, a brand-new dishwasher showed up. No longer would the dishes pile up in the sink for weeks on end. In addition to this, we began to receive some preferential treatment. We had been getting a couple of parking tickets a week before that, but we never saw another one in the rest of our time at the Angel.

It was around then that Swarb convinced us that we could demand a higher weekly salary—our fees had increased, after all. Like Sandy, he was used to a more comfortable lifestyle. We agreed on £40 a week, a stunning amount of money in those days, but inflation was running high in the UK. Britain was about to embrace decimalization, bringing us in line with our European neighbors. Goodbye to twelve pence to a shilling and twenty shillings to a pound. Goodbye to rods, perches, chains and furlongs, pecks and bushels, which at least had their own logic. Now distances were calculated on fractions of the earth's surface; a piece of wood that was four by two inches was now 101.6 by 38 mm. Companies and shop owners took advantage of the confusion over prices and sizes and inflated things overnight—suddenly forty quid didn't stretch as far as it used to.

Swarb also suggested that we stay in more expensive hotels. He reasoned that since we never made money beyond the basic wage, we might as well enjoy ourselves. We followed his advice and went from zero-star hotels to four-star ones. These usually had the advantage of a night porter who could make sandwiches and ply us with drinks into the small hours. As if he were the plaything of some particularly bored gods, gazing down from Mount Olympus, Swarb always seemed to get the worst room at any hotel. At one lodging somewhere in Scandinavia, he was assigned the last room available, which meant pulling down a flight of stairs from the ceiling and sleeping in the attic.

The economics of Fairport were always baffling, if one bothered to think about it. I don't even know if Witchseason kept books in any recognisable form, but we just assumed that we were always behind and trying to catch up, in spite of us now playing in bigger halls and filling seats. I suspect, too, that as Witchseason juggled their roster of us, Nick, Dudu and Chris, John and Bev, and the Incredible String Band, trying to pay wages across the board, they might have occasionally borrowed cash from one band's earnings to subsidize another. In all the time I was with Fairport, our income went right back into the pot. I think that was how it was for most bands, and some lived even more hand-to-mouth.

My own relationship with money was a bit abstract.

Although I was cynical about many aspects of hippie culture, other elements of it were important in my life. My reading included plenty of spiritual texts—Zen, Gurdjieff, Madame Blavatsky, the I Ching and books on astrology—and it was turning me into a kind of weekend aesthete, as I attempted to spend my evenings embodying noble human traits while at the same time getting plastered on Famous Grouse whisky, oblivious to the contradiction. I paid no attention to money; if there was some in my pocket, fine, but if not I would just make do until our next wage packet. Plus, I was earning session fees for playing on other people's records, though I would just stack the checks under the mattress and give them no attention. Many had expired by the time I finally opened a bank account at the age of twenty-two. It is possible to live irresponsibly while in a band for many years—history is littered with fine examples. At around this time, we upgraded to a new Mercedes van with reclining seats—luxury! Although we were now playing bigger venues, there was still the regular diet of bookings at the Country Club, Mothers, the Van Dike and Redcar Jazz Club. We were busy all through the first few months of 1970.

One of the shows was at the De Montfort Hall in Leicester, and a message came backstage afterwards from a local hospital that someone wanted to meet me. It was not unusual to get requests from people in wheelchairs, or with other limited ability, who wanted to come and say hello. I agreed, and two nurses accompanied a young girl. They told me that she was a mental patient, and a big fan. She wanted to meet me and show me some drawings she had done of me. She may have been eighteen, pretty, but clearly with some issues. I'm sure it was not standard medical practice, but unbelievably they left me alone with her and went outside for a smoke. She showed a drawing of me which she had copied from a photograph in a pop magazine, and then basically grabbed me, kissed me and groped me, and would have had her way with me there and then if I hadn't fought her off. I don't mean this to sound sexy in any way—it was uncomfortable and very disturbing, and more than any other feeling I felt such pity for this girl. By the time the nurses came back I was in tears, and I was a wreck when I got into the van with the band.

I pretty much forgot about this incident for many years, but these little traumas tend to bubble up eventually, and it became a song forty-six years after the fact:[*]

> All the tears in the world
> All the tears in the world
> Won't mend a Broken Doll

It haunted me that she seemed so unbroken on the surface, but was so damaged underneath. She could have been somebody's girlfriend—she could have been my girlfriend, in another reality. When I was at school, I used to play guitar and sing for "educationally subnormal" kids at a neighboring secondary school, so I'd seen some of the anger, the deep introversion, the out-of-control behavior—but this girl disturbed me deeply.

[*] See Appendix A, p. 264.

7

Just a Roll

[Belafonte] was a good teacher and looked after me.
He said, "You have such great talent, you must try not
to be a tornado—be like a submarine."

MIRIAM MAKEBA

ONE MORNING AT the Angel, we were awoken by shouting
downstairs—we had forgotten that Chris McGregor and his
band were coming to rehearse with us. Simon, Peggy and
myself had agreed to play on a recording project of South
African music, and the cream of the London-based South
African jazz community had arrived in Little Hadham. They
were all starving, but of course we had no food for them.
We scrounged some eggs from somewhere and boiled them
before heading for the rehearsal room, where Chris presided
over affairs from the harmonium. The idea was to make a
record in the sax jive style, a popular dance genre of the time.
London had a severe lack of sax jive guitarists and bass players, which is why Joe had thought to recruit us. I felt quite
intimidated playing with some truly fine jazz players—Chris,
Dudu Pukwana and Teddy Osei on tenor saxes, and Mongezi
Feza on pocket trumpet. I had seen them perform in London,
and they were as good as anyone out there. Three girls were
going to sing on the record, but they weren't present at the

rehearsal. The material was mostly drawn from an album called *Good Luck Motella*, which Joe had lent us to learn from. The rhythm was tricky—when it was played properly it really jumped, but I'm not sure we ever cracked it. It wasn't helped by Dudu wanting to play everything at about double tempo, so even the Africans sounded ragged. Once we got to the studio we had the same issues, and the beautiful smoothness of the original *Motella* recordings was never matched. Dudu was a giant of a musician and a lovely human being to boot, who could play everything from free jazz to funk, all filtered through his African sensibility. Chris was also encyclopedic in his knowledge of music, and I learned a lot from playing with them.

I was also learning a lot about traditional music from the musicians we ran into on the road, mostly introduced to us by Swarb, thanks to his folk connections—people like the High Level Ranters in Newcastle, the McPeake Family in Belfast, Cyril Tawney in the south-west and the Watersons in Hull. After our concerts in these areas, we would have a few drinks back at the hotel and sometimes a session—I remember Mike Waterson singing a beautiful unaccompanied version of "The Cuckoo" with the most delicate slides and ornaments, Cyril Tawney teaching us a sea shanty and Swarb learning a north-eastern hornpipe with an impossible time signature from the Ranters.

Mostly, though, I was learning from Swarb himself. When you introduce an alien instrument into a long musical tradition, you have to shape it to fit the modes, quirks and practices of the culture, and it was no different with the electric guitar.

People like Davey Graham and Martin Carthy had molded the acoustic guitar to fit the tradition, but the electric posed different challenges, having more of a single-stringed, horn-like approach. My part-Scottish background meant that I had always been attracted to modal music and the drone of instruments like the bagpipe, and I had incorporated some of this into my playing in Fairport. From Swarb I was learning the decorations—the subtle slides, trills, turns, hammer-ons and pull-offs of the fiddle repertoire. Swarb also had an individual style that was truly English, even when he was playing Scottish and Irish music. His bowing was incredibly fluent, and I have no idea where it came from—perhaps just his own genius.

The guitar, being tuned in fourths instead of fifths like the fiddle, made some tunes originally written for fiddle or pipes, with a lot of arpeggios, difficult or even impossible to play with any fluency, and it required ingenuity sometimes to bend the tune into submission. I always tried to avoid straight flat-picking of dance tunes, which sounded too mechanical—I preferred hammer-ons and pull-offs for the subtler sound. I could use alternate tunings on acoustic guitar, but they were fairly impractical on electric, in the context of a band.

I had swapped my Gibson Les Paul for a Fender Stratocaster, which I'd bought from Ed Carter of the New Nadir. I sold the Gibson to John Martyn, but it was stolen from him about a week later. Those were the days when I could only afford a new guitar if I sold the old one, and I regret all the guitars I've parted with, including my old Hofner from my school band days. But a lot of the players I admired were using Fenders, including James Burton, Robbie Robertson and Jimmy Bryant. Then, to cap it all, we were on a bill for a concert in Hyde Park with Fleetwood Mac, and Peter Green played a couple of songs on a vintage Strat and it sounded divine. The tone I was searching for was so crucial to expressing the voice in my head, and my insides were telling me that I should have something wirier. I stripped the finish off Ed's guitar, down to the wood—it had to be a basic, blunt instrument. It would serve me well for the next year or two.

Swarb also had a reel-to-reel tape recording of the great Northumbrian piper Billy Pigg. Northumbrian small pipes are very different from the Irish pipes or the Scottish bagpipes; the chanter has a stopped end, so it is silent when fingers are closing all the holes. This gives the playing a more staccato effect and a unique sound. Billy Pigg was a master; hearing him knocked me out and changed the way I thought about music. Here was an English musician with incredible soul—in his own way as much as Otis Redding or Muddy Waters—making up these extraordinary variations that sounded like a folk version of Mozart.

In 1970 we played a live session for John Peel's *Top Gear* program. This was in one of the smaller BBC theatres in London, with an audience of a couple of hundred. Opening for us was Mott the Hoople, a band that were little known to us at that point. They hailed from Herefordshire and seemed to have brought half the county with them to the show. For some reason, the auditorium was stuffed with Hoople fans and devoid of Fairport fans. Hoople went on first, to a storming reception. In the interval, we wondered what the best tactic would be to win over this alien crowd, but nothing came to mind. "Let's just get hammered," I suggested, which was met with all-round approval. We played an atrocious, drunken set and verbally abused the audience—they hated our guts anyway, and booed us throughout. At one point, Simon offered to take on the whole crowd one at a time, and they nearly took him up on it. And all this was on the radio. Peel was deeply upset—he later said it was like finding out your sister was a whore. We felt bad.

We began to wonder if there was something lacking in our stagecraft. I thought we were pretty lively on stage, but Hoople had made us feel old and of a previous generation (I was twenty-one at the time). Why not ham it up a bit, do some of those corny moves Hoople had done, rubbing the guitar necks together, doing synchronized steps, shaking our long hair in feigned ecstasy? And to top it all, why not get some of those motorcycle boots they all wore?

Well, we got some boots. At our next gig, we did the moves, hamming it up totally and trying not to laugh too much. It went down an absolute storm. The crowd response was immediate, with cheers for every dumb cliché. It had the effect of making us quite depressed. It really was that easy, but was that who we wanted to be? Could we go through life in this fraudulent manner, knowing that we were stooping to conquer? We dropped the whole idea and resigned ourselves to a lifetime of smaller but more discriminating audiences. And no boots.

We didn't have too much time off in 1970, but we recorded at Sound Techniques whenever we could. We never replaced Sandy—we didn't think she was replaceable—but without her we were rather lacking in the vocal department. We decided to share out the singing; no one was willing to step forward and be the voice of the band, though Swarb was a little less reluctant than the rest of us. We recorded the songs he and I had been writing and mixed in some traditional numbers. "Dirty Linen" was a medley—a jig, a reel, a slip jig and another reel. A lot of it was played in unison, normal practice in many traditional circles, but the bass was also playing the melody, an octave or two octaves lower. This required a musician of superlative skill, and Peggy was—and still is—just about the only person who could pull that feat off. The song "Walk Awhile" was a sort of introduction to the band, with everyone singing a verse each—it was an ideal album and set opener. The lyrics are obscure, a result of too much time spent reading William Hazlitt's 1870 *Faiths and Folklore of the British Isles*, as are the liner notes to the record, which mention a series of archaic games. I felt liner notes should not yield relevant information on a first reading; rather, they should puzzle and confuse, and continue to yield next to nothing over a period of years. "Doctor of Physick," another song I co-wrote with Swarb, is a traditional-sounding parody of a cautionary tale for young girls. I had been reading other nineteenth-century classics, such as Mary Shelley's *Frankenstein* and James Hogg's *Private Memoirs and Confessions of a Justified Sinner*, and was here expressing some late Gothic ideas. Swarb's melody is clearly based on traditional tunes, but it has modern twists that take it to unexpected places, both melodically and rhythmically. "Sloth" now clocked in at a considerable nine minutes—still about half the length of the live version—with an added instrumental section that was designed to give the illusion of a musical spiral: every time the chord sequence comes round, it appears to lift to another level. "Flatback Caper" is a mandolin tour de force, with Peggy and Swarb playing in unison and harmony over a traditional medley that finished with "Carolan's Concerto," the blind Irish harper Turlough O'Carolan's supposed response to hearing Vivaldi. "The Flowers of the Forest" is a lament that was written after the Battle of Flodden in 1513. Swarb recalled that a version of the lyric was quoted at the end of Lewis Grassic Gibbon's *A Scots Quair*, his 1930s trilogy of novels about life in north-east Scotland. We had to order the book and wait for it to be delivered before we could rehearse the song. We had played "Sir Patrick Spens" with Sandy, set to the tune of another ballad, "Hugh the Graeme," so it was a matter of changing the key and sharing out the vocals. "Poor Will and the Jolly Hangman" was a solo composition of mine and probably a response to what I felt was unfair treatment of Harvey Bramham by the courts. When I came to re-record the vocals at Vanguard Studios in New York, I was disappointed with my inability to sing it, thanks particularly to an unforgiving top note. I asked that it be taken off the record, which was a stupid idea. I could have persevered, double-tracked the voice, warmed up for longer—anything. It was a good track, and the record was lacking without it. When the album was re-released, the track was restored with a more confident vocal, and it has stayed there ever since.

In an obvious move for promoters, we frequently found ourselves sharing a stage with Sandy's new band, Fotheringay,

and Iain's new band, Matthews Southern Comfort. Fairport
had always been a bit like that; in spite of painful splits and
"musical differences," everyone generally remained friends,
went to each other's gigs and even collaborated on projects
here and there. I had just worked with Iain as arranger on
his first solo record, which took him towards country rock.
I remained friends with Sandy. Her flat on Chipstead Street in
Fulham was frequently my weekend crash pad when Fairport
weren't working. Walking into her living room was like step-
ping back in time: William Morris wallpaper, beaded lamps
and paisley shawls. Laudanum would have been appropriate,
given the setting, but marijuana brought it into the twentieth
century.

Watching Fotheringay play live, it was good to see Sandy
adding keyboard on stage. She was writing much more on
piano by now and had a small Steinway in the flat, and Trevor
saw to it that a grand piano was provided at all their shows.
I felt bad that this had never happened in Fairport, but we
had largely been unaware of Sandy's skill as a pianist, and I
don't think she was writing for piano much in those days.
Trevor, a no-expense-spared kind of guy, also wanted the best
sound system, so they travelled with something that gained
the nickname "Stonehenge." Each custom-made cabinet was
the size of a sarsen stone, weighed a ton and took about six
people to lift. There would be two cabinets on each side of the
stage, with a third laid across the top—hence the nickname.
However, they had failed to realize that the basic requirement
of a PA system was to throw the sound as far as the back of the
room; despite its size, Stonehenge threw sound only to about

the second row. The rest of us satisfied ourselves with the famous Watkins WEM column speakers, each of which could handle about a hundred watts of vocals and, if you were brave, the bass drum as well. All other sound came from the amps on stage. Today everything goes through the PA and is much more controllable and more evenly dispersed; back then, the bigger a band got, the more WEM columns they added. There are photographs from the late 1960s of the National Jazz and Blues Festival in Reading that show about fifty of them precariously bungeed together on each side of the stage. With Fairport, we generally ended up with about five on each side, and it always felt like adding houses to your favorite property in a game of Monopoly. I don't think the vocals were ever quite loud enough, but having each of the music's elements coming from a different source probably sounded pretty good, depending on where you were in the crowd. PA technology in the US was far more advanced, as we were soon to find out.

8

Yankee Hopscotch

Perhaps, after all, America never has been discovered.
I myself would say that it had merely been detected.
OSCAR WILDE

AT LAST IT was time for our first American tour. The accident had delayed us by a year, so it felt long overdue. Since the Beatles had conquered all before them, there had been a cachet in coming from Britain, but we were late to the game. We weren't as sexy as the Stones, or as goofy and lovable as Herman's Hermits or Freddie and the Dreamers. And most importantly, we weren't recycling recognizable American styles—if audiences there were going to like us, they'd have to take a step in our direction.

American music had been creeping across the Atlantic ever since Stephen Foster, in the mid-nineteenth century. His songs romanticizing the South, like "Camptown Races" and "I Dream of Jeannie with the Light Brown Hair," were sung in middle-class homes in Britain at a time when pianos were becoming affordable to many. With the appearance of the gramophone, American place names—"Carolina Moon," "My Old Kentucky Home"—and ways of life became romantic and mythic. Jazz, swing, blues, country and rock and roll were irresistible, and we had looked to the States for cultural innovation and excitement for decades. British music was sometimes derided as corny and non-essential by comparison. Folk music had retreated underground, with people mocking the morris dance and the finger-in-the-ear seriousness of the revivalists; the rare English folk song that crossed into the pop charts was dismissed as a novelty.

As a kid, even though I grew up singing the old folk songs at home and at school, the music that I found most exciting was either American or imitation American: rock and roll. Its infectious rhythm pushed all the essential teenage buttons and spoke of a seductive lifestyle that was beyond the means of the British, impoverished by the war and just coming off rationing. I knew nothing about the Everly Brothers other than their music, but they conjured a perfect world of big cars and kids with licenses to drive them, soda shops, record hops and sweet girls who would love you forever. In the world of Jerry Lee or Gene Vincent, it was all edgier and more dangerous, a world of speed and kicks, and sweet girls who would probably go all the way and then love you forever, even after the fatal motorcycle crash.

The "British Invasion" took American styles like blues and R&B, mixed them with some European sensibilities and made them whiter and more digestible, before taking them back to America. In Fairport we loved the response to the Beatles by bands such as the Byrds, the Left Banke and the Lovin' Spoonful. The great singer-songwriters, like Dylan, Cohen, Ochs and Mitchell, were our true inspiration, as were the Band, with their blend of roots styles that were so familiar to us from records. All around the world, people had grown cynical about American politics, but they loved American music—especially the blues and country music of the Southern poor and the tougher, electrified sounds of the urban disillusioned and disenfranchised. We loved it all but had reached a cultural saturation point—it was time to give them back rock music, but with a very British twist.

Our American record label, A&M Records, provided two limousines to greet us at the airport. This was the life! It was only several years later that we noticed every possible expense had been added to our bill, to be deducted from our earnings—even the times when they were clearly taking *us* out to dinner. One such meal was a lunch at the Brown Derby in Los Angeles, with half a dozen record executives. It was still a novelty for us to get anything free, and after we had indulged in the restaurant's famous steak Sinatra and Cobb salad, the drinks flowed freely. The meal ended in a table-vaulting contest—how many tables could we jump over in one leap? The execs looked on in horror at their latest British signing, as did the rest of the diners.

For some reason lost to me now, we took all our backline gear to the States with us—four Fender Dual Showman amps, two cabinets each, and drums—as well as instruments. The amps had no cases, the drums were only in fiber cases. It would have been easier to rent it all. We bribed the skycap a princely $20, and everything went on the plane with no extra charge. As our jumbo jet was struggling to get up to speed for take-off, we prayed that our extra ton of excess baggage was on the manifest. This seems completely nuts, yet somehow almost nothing was broken. We lost one speaker cabinet that fell off the loading ramp onto the tarmac, and that was all.

We played a week of shows at the Troubadour in Los Angeles, and one of the first people to welcome us to the city was Linda Ronstadt, who generously invited us to her house in Beachwood Canyon for lunch. At the end of our tenure at the Troubadour, rather than getting our fee of $1,000, we found out that we owed $1,500 for the bar bill. Although I have no memory of it, it is said that one night I swung onto the stage on a rope, dressed as "Henry the Human Fly"—what an entrance that must have been! As a result, the 1970 generation of Fairport still call me Henry. The club was a favorite hangout for musicians; Peter Wolf and Gene Clark were there most days, propping up the bar. We opened for Rick Nelson, who was far more interesting than his clean-cut teen idol image had led me to believe. He was moving away from rockabilly towards his own brand of LA country rock and seemed to appreciate the rootsiness of our style.

While spending a week in LA, I got reacquainted with Liz Gordon. We'd first met at the Rome Pop Festival two years earlier, and then at Phil Ochs's party. To say this was a sporadic relationship would be putting it mildly, but we hung out for the week, and she planned to come over to the UK that summer. Liz was ten years older than me and tended to steer the course of things. She asked me if I wanted to father a baby, no strings attached, and said she was quite prepared to be a single parent. This was not untypical of the thinking of the times. I was still having trouble saying no to most things, and with a hippie-esque shrug of the shoulders, I said, "Yeah, okay," with little thought for the responsibility and consequences, which were considerable. I had still not figured out that the future would finally arrive—that an action *here* has a result over *here*. Liz flattered me a bit, saying that she wanted my genes in the mix, but she was taking advantage of an easily swayed youth with ten years less experience of life. I, on the other hand, was opportunistically satisfying my short-term needs. Liz duly got pregnant and kept me up to date by letter in the ensuing months, while I was in the UK or on the road.

Despite all I'd heard before our arrival, San Francisco in 1970 never quite felt like a cultural epicenter—perhaps I was moving in the wrong circles. At City Lights Books, I stocked up on the works of Thomas Pynchon, Jack Kerouac, Henry Miller and Richard Brautigan, who always sat, like a landmark, in the same cafe every day. We played multiple nights at the Fillmore West, opening for Jethro Tull. That was about as close to an epicenter as we got, but it felt as though the cultural impact of that scene was a couple of years in the past. Audiences sat on the floor, as they did sometimes in the UK, but the reaction to us seemed a bit too laid-back. The dance tunes that had caused such a physical response back home were greeted with stoned indifference here. I liked the way musicians were treated by the promoter Bill Graham's organization, though—there was food backstage, a clean dressing room, and crew to help load and unload. In the UK, by contrast, we finally had a rider: ten rounds of sandwiches and a crate of Newcastle Brown Ale.

Then we went on to New York, where we played the Fillmore East, opening for Traffic. When we came off stage,

Bill Graham was waiting for us. "That was amazing," he said. We felt flattered. "I've never seen a band go on stage and not know what the second number was going to be." Not so flattered. We criss-crossed the country by plane, playing outdoors on college campuses and indoors at cattle markets and in clubs. We were booked for a week at the Emergency in Washington, DC, but only lasted three shows. The attendance on the first night was thirty-four, on the second night it was thirty-three and on the third it was thirty-two. The promoter spotted a trend and cut his losses. Perhaps our style of British roots rock was a step too far?

One afternoon, we were somewhere in the Midwest and I was taking a nap, trying to catch up on sleep after some long days of travel. Something was dragging me out of the deepest sleep, a knocking sound on my hotel room door. At the third knock, I cursed, got to my feet and went groggily to the door. It was Swarb. "How are you?" he asked. "Fine," I replied, just wanting to crawl back to bed. He kept shoving his face close to mine. "Okay? Everything good?" I couldn't see the point of this line of questioning and told him to piss off, but he wouldn't. I resorted to Shakespearean insults—I'd been practicing them, and there are no easy comebacks to them. I called him "a moth-bearded, putrescent slime-goblin," "a fuzzy-tongued, widow-humping corpse-lingerer" and "a backcombed, Cistercian womb-shaker." Fearing for my sanity, he backed off and gloomily retreated down the hall, and I returned to bed. When I saw him an hour later in the lobby, I got it. He had shaved off exactly half of his beard and moustache, which is why he'd been shoving his chin in my face. He was mortified that I had been too drowsy to even notice and he'd wasted a good joke.

We had a day off in New York, and I drove with Robin and his girlfriend Jilly on a pilgrimage to Woodstock in a car we had borrowed from our agent. Maria Muldaur, who had jammed with us at the Troubadour, had invited us to visit if we were ever passing. A year after the festival, Woodstock had become something of a tourist town, and the presence of Dylan as a resident was a major magnet. We wandered around for a bit and then went to Geoff and Maria's. They had been heroes of ours since the Jim Kweskin Jug Band, so to say we were thrilled and intimidated to spend time with them would be putting it mildly. Geoff took us to the recently built Bearsville Studio, where he was finishing a record, and then we went on a bar crawl with Amos Garrett and Paul Butterfield. They were serious drinkers, and it was hard to keep up; I ended up passed out on Geoff and Maria's bathroom floor.

When we got a few days off, we holed up in Ann Arbor, Michigan, but played every night at a small bar downtown in exchange for free drinks. Joe Boyd had arrived in town with the test pressings of *Full House*, the album we'd recorded before we left. We found a friendly audiophile with a good sound system and repaired to his house to listen to it. It sounded much as we had intended, but in those days of vinyl you had to check for tracking and skipping—too much bass would flip the needle out of the groove.

When we got round to compiling a live album from the recent LA shows (*Live at the LA Troubadour*), compared to the studio recordings from a month or two earlier (*Full*

House) the live tempos are insanely fast. This was punk folk, long before the Pogues. One of the reasons it all got so accelerated was Swarb's dietary regime—he had decided he needed to lose weight. He was skinny as a rake but had developed a large gut, and in profile resembled a robin redbreast on a Christmas card. He began taking diet pills (essentially amphetamines), so he was jacked up for the entire tour. DM and I agreed recently that we could never again play that fast, and had no idea how we did it back then.

We were touring a country that seemed divided, geographically and politically, but also generationally. The youth of America were having an enormous impact on US foreign policy, forcing the government to rethink its strategy in Vietnam. If you had long hair, as we did, you represented something political, not just cultural. I'd never really seen anybody snarl before, but we got that reaction a lot from the "straights" and "suits." Some code of behavior, inherited from the Pilgrim Fathers perhaps, forced them to be civil and to utter polite words, like "Have a nice day," but it was often between gritted teeth, as if their tongue and their lips were having an argument with each other. We were routinely hated for our appearance and what that represented. Pleading that we were British and really didn't think about Vietnam all that much, that it wasn't our problem, just made matters worse.

One afternoon I was riding with Liz in her VW Beetle. She lived down on the beach in Venice, but we were close to downtown Los Angeles when she did an illegal U-turn, driving in and out of a petrol station without stopping. When the cops pulled her over, she tried to turn on the charm for about three seconds; when that didn't work, she started calling them fascists and pigs. They put the cuffs on her and asked me for ID. I pulled out my UK passport, which for some reason they found highly amusing—maybe it was the shorter-haired me in the passport photo. Although they were laughing, it felt sinister. "How long have you been in the States, sir?" The "sir" was added with deep reluctance and a bit of good old snarl.

"A fortnight," I said.

"Which is?"

"A fortnight."

"Which is?"

"You know—a fortnight."

I was panicking. What part of the word "fortnight" did they not understand? It suddenly occurred to me that the term might not be used in the States.

"Two weeks?" I ventured, stuttering a bit. The tension was ramping up. The cop handed me back my passport.

"So how do you like our country?" he asked, which was about the last question I was expecting.

"I liked it very much, up until a few minutes ago," I said.

He looked concerned. "Your girlfriend here did an illegal U-turn, and has twenty unpaid parking tickets. We're taking her to the Eighty-seventh Precinct. You have to make your own way there. Here's the address."

And off they sped, making an illegal U-turn in the process. I couldn't drive Liz's car—I couldn't drive any car—so I found a cab company in the phone book. When the taxi came, the driver took one look at me and drove off again. Was I that scary? Me, a pacifist and a vegetarian? I called a different

company, and that one didn't show up at all. Finally I hailed
a passing cab. An hour and a half later, I got to the precinct
as a fearsome-looking Policewoman Sanchez was finishing a
cavity search on Liz, who was swearing like a sailor. I had just
enough cash left to pay off her parking fines. The cops were
alternately insulting me and hitting on Liz, and there was a
bit more snarling. Finally we got the hell out of there, after
another "Have a nice day."

The signs of a cultural divide in the States were everywhere.
We were in Detroit airport before a flight, having lunch in the
brown-Naugahyde-upholstered coffee shop, and as we sat eating our scrambled eggs, we heard voices from the next booth:

"Goddamn hippies!"

"Hey girlie—git yer hair cut!"

"Oh, don't she look purdy!"

The booths were high, so you couldn't see over. I leaned
around. There were six fellows in cowboy hats, western shirts
and boots. It took a moment, but there was no mistaking them.
I had one of their albums at home. It was Buck Owens and
the Buckaroos! The great pioneers of the Bakersfield sound in
country music, fabulous musicians and singers, and Buck was
a wonderful songwriter. This was disturbing, being insulted
by someone whom I admired greatly. They kept up the tirade
of rather pathetic comments until we grabbed the bill and got
up to head to our gate. I could not leave it there. As the band
headed to the plane, I made a bathroom excuse and doubled
back. I pulled out some paper and a pen.

"Excuse me, Mr. Owens, but I'm a huge fan of yours from
England. Could I have your autograph?"

He looked confused, to say the least. I was amazed at myself—I didn't know where I got the balls from. "Well . . . er . . . I . . . well . . . sure." He asked my name and signed.

"And you must be Tom Brumley? I love your pedal steel work." Now they were all looking confused. There had been a photo on the back of the album I had.

"And you must be Don Rich? I love your guitar-playing, man." They all signed, still looking deeply uncomfortable.

"You know, son, you seem like a nice kid," Buck eventually said. "You'd do a lot better with a haircut and some decent clothes." Still feeling like I was play-acting, which in a sense I was, because the real me would never have had the nerve, I said, "There is an old saying, Mr. Owens, which I'm sure you know—you can't judge a book by its cover." Without waiting for a reply, I made a dramatic exit. I lost the signatures somewhere soon afterwards, but that wasn't really the point.

9

Tuppenny Bangers and Damp Squibs

If you don't know where you are going,
any road will take you there.
GEORGE HARRISON

WE CAME BACK to England, after six weeks away, to a beautiful June morning. The foliage was bright parrot green, the hedgerows were bursting with white hawthorn blossom. The old country had never looked more lovely, and although it wasn't always the case, it was good, for once, to be back to the privations of life at the Angel.

A week later, on 27 June 1970, we played at the Bath Festival, possibly the biggest in the UK up to that point, with about a hundred thousand attendees. The logistics were terrible, so we missed seeing Led Zeppelin, Jefferson Airplane, Pink Floyd and Santana. The single- track country lanes were jammed solid, and the only access in and out for band and gear was on the back of a Hells Angels motorcycle. A greaser who looked like Baby Face Nelson insisted I wear his leather jacket on stage, and I didn't want to disappoint him in any way.

The next day, we were playing at a folk festival in Rotterdam. To get there, we decided it was quicker to fly, and at that time there existed the wonderful British Air Ferries. From the tiny,

Biggles-esque airport of Lydd, they would fly you across the Channel in a bulbous, marginally airworthy twin-prop plane. It could hold our van and two other vehicles, and a dozen passengers. It seemed to stretch the bounds of credulity that the thing would actually get into the air; the managers of the airline had foreseen this skepticism, and plied passengers with a few rounds of stiff drinks before take-off. To giggle hysterically was our way of expressing deep fear. There was no public address system—the flight attendant shouted as loudly as possible over the deafening turboprops. We lumbered down the runway, agonizingly straining to achieve altitude. We got to about a hundred feet—and stayed there, with ear-splitting fragility, all the way across the Channel. Landing was a very short drop back to good old terra firma. We played the festival with Fotheringay, then took the train to Hamburg. Anthea from the Witchseason office was acting as tour manager, and somehow we contrived to take the wrong train twice. We spent about twenty hours on various trains all over Europe, it seemed. The German customs officers were very interested in a small bag of white powder in my luggage, and were disappointed when it turned out to be laundry soap.

We played the famous Star Club, which had lost some of its glitter—if it ever had any. Of course, we had to go to the Reeperbahn, the long, straight street once used for laying ropes for the sailing ships. A different kind of "laying" was now available—women of varying degrees of comeliness were sitting in windows, in garter belts and bustiers, advertising for business, all government-run and legal. Fortified with the best German lager, some of us—I don't think all of us—decided

to sample the goods. My own experience was like visiting a
social worker with a "happy ending." She wanted to know all
about me, mothered me a bit, needs were fulfilled and I felt a
bit hollow afterwards. It took me about twenty years to process my feelings about it, but finally it turned into a song—not
literally the truth, but a fictional extension:[*]

> *How many boys, one-night stands,*
> *How many lips, how many hands, have held you*
> *Like I'm holding you tonight?*

A week after that was the Maidstone Fiesta, which we played
with Matthews Southern Comfort. The concert was fairly
representative of our performances that year—instrumentally
strong and vocally adequate. Our biggest drawback was the
fact that we had four baritones in the band. Our harmoniz-
ing tended to be thick in the low midrange, so there would
always be a scramble for the easiest parts, with latecomers left
to hit falsetto. The audience were not particularly engaged, and
they also seemed disturbingly straight—there was not much
long hair about, with most of them looking like extras from *A
Hard Day's Night* five years earlier, which was a bit of a shock.
It turned out that another world existed in parallel to our own,
where nothing of the old ways had changed—people behaved
responsibly, had real jobs and paid off their mortgages. I suppose most of our audiences for the last three years had been
students and hippies, so we had been insulated. Even in the US,

* See Appendix A, p. 270.

we had never ventured into the South, where cultural change moved more slowly.

On 26 July we took time out of our touring schedule to do a co-bill with the Incredible String Band at the London Palladium. It was a strange feeling, performing on a stage that had been used for a famous Sunday-night TV show since 1958, and backstage the presenter Norman Vaughan was arranging tickets for his daughter. These boards had been trodden by Buddy Holly, Cliff Richard and the Shadows, Ray Charles, Peter, Paul and Mary (long ago I'd been in the audience to see Gerry and the Pacemakers), and now the long-hairs were taking it over, if only for one night.

"The Increds," as they were known to all, were formed in Edinburgh in 1966, and had by this point recorded several albums with Joe Boyd. They were a wonderful mixture of ethnic elements, playing "world music" before the term was coined and drawing on influences from many corners of the globe. Mike Heron and Robin Williamson were both very good guitarists; Robin could also play fine ballad harp, fiddle, percussion and keyboard—anything, really. Mike played everything too, and if additional sound was needed, their girl-friends could play whatever else was required, in a charmingly amateurish way. Rose Simpson, who mostly played bass, went on to be Lady Mayoress of Aberystwyth—quite the career path. Licorice McKechnie, Robin's girlfriend, disappeared for about thirty-five years, having been last seen hitch-hiking across the Arizona desert, and only turned up in 2019. On stage, the Increds would change instruments after every song, with who played what sometimes varying from performance to performance. Then everything had to be miked, which meant that it could take an hour to get through three songs— but I loved all of it. Their first three albums still slay me with the originality of their songwriting. As they became more involved with Scientology, some of the charm wore off their music, and I got tired of all the proselytising, well-meaning though it was. I was still researching various spiritual paths, and they saw in me a seeker after—something. It was a time when many of us were looking for a different path to religious experience, the Age of Aquarius, and all that. I took most of it with large pinches of salt, but it did enter my dream life.* The drugs had opened the door a crack, and that generation was looking for answers. Lady Betjeman once described drugs like LSD as "trying to gatecrash heaven," but gatecrashing could be risky, and there were casualties.

IN EARLY AUGUST 1970, we played the National Jazz and Blues Festival, held on Plumpton Racecourse in Sussex. This was an area very familiar to me. My Uncle Frank and Aunt Audrey lived in Plumpton Green, and the view from their cottage took in the racecourse and the railway station and stretched away to the hills of the South Downs. As a child I had spent many happy days playing in their garden, and for a big-town kid it seemed idyllic, even if I was marshalling my army of toy soldiers on top of the septic tank. I had not visited for a while. In the intervening time, houses had been built all the way down to the racecourse and beyond. Little

* See Appendix B, p. 280.

Plumpton was now a town, and the sleepy village of my youth existed only as a memory—the walks up to the Downs, the quiet lanes devoid of cars, kids allowed to run free of adult supervision.

Later that August, we had a drastically different experience when we found ourselves playing at a festival in the middle of the Yorkshire moors. It might have been the height of summer, but it was still wildly optimistic to expect blue skies and no wind. The moors roll dramatically across the north of England, rising to well over a thousand feet, with a few gnarled trees and low stone walls as windbreaks. In the winter, the roads are frequently closed due to snow. Yet there we were at the Yorkshire Folk, Blues and Jazz Festival at Krumlin. We arrived on the Saturday and learned that the Friday had been chaotic; bands had played but had not been paid, because the expected revenue from the crowd had not materialized. A large number of forged tickets were circulating, and there was also a hole in the fence. Everything was running late, Pink Floyd were stuck somewhere in France and the wind was picking up. There was a queue of disgruntled managers in the promoter's Portakabin, and we decided that we didn't want to go on until we got paid.

We repaired to the artists' bar, which was thankfully fully stocked, and joined Pentangle, Fotheringay and Ralph McTell in whiling away the afternoon. By the time Fairport got on stage, we were well and truly out of it. The wind was increasing, the rain was stinging and the stage was beginning to lose some of its structural integrity—the plastic tarpaulin that had been keeping out the worst of the weather was adrift and fluttering like a loose topsail in a gale. Simon was more out of it than the rest of us and kicked off our set with a long and rambling announcement that was somewhere between a documentary voiceover and the first three chapters of his autobiography. He was gently led away from the mic, and a guitar was strapped onto him.

We played the opening number, "Walk Awhile," but Simon was in his own world. By the time we got to "The Bonny Bunch of Roses," in the key of A, he was sitting cross-legged in front of his amp, playing a raga in the key of D. We turned his amp off, and he didn't seem to notice. In the middle of the set, Swarb wanted to relieve himself. All the portable toilets had blown down, so there was nowhere backstage, but he noticed a hole in the plastic sheeting at the side of the stage and stuck his hampton through there, and let rip. Unfortunately, that was the press enclosure. If we were expecting a great review, we weren't going to get one now. The rain became horizontal, the wind was gale force and the audience was huddled under plastic bin liners. Mountain rescue teams started working their way down through the crowd, carrying away people suffering from exposure. I think Fairport were the last act to play, and the rest of Saturday and all of Sunday were cancelled. It looked like a refugee camp, and the rest of the wet, miserable attendees had to trudge back ten miles to Huddersfield or wait for their cars to be towed out of the quagmire that was once a car park. The only person who I know for certain got paid was Ralph McTell, because he had the most intimidating manager. I resolved never to consider Krumlin for my summer holidays.

We had a few days' break, and Liz Gordon and I went over to Paris. She was thoroughly immersed in the culture, had degrees in French literature and was also a French cinema buff, so we soaked up a lot of Jean Gabin and Jeanne Moreau. She also seemed to get a thrill from petty larceny, and her habit of shoplifting totally threw my Presbyterian morals for a loop. I got bumped off the flight home. I scrambled onto a later flight, but knew I was in trouble: we had a show that night in Dagenham, and I paid the taxi driver at Heathrow about a week's wages to try and get me there in time. We hurtled around the North Circular but were never going to make it. I arrived as the last notes of the set were being played. It was strange to watch Fairport from the audience. The band were not overjoyed to see me, and it took a day or two to thaw out. I made more conservative travel plans after that.

Sandy asked me if I wanted to join her and Trevor on a short trip to Ireland. The plan was to visit an old Australian mate of Trevor's, Brian Mooney, who had relocated to Galway. I agreed and dragged along a girlfriend, and we all piled into Trevor's Vanden Plas. (Trevor would have liked a Rolls, but at least it had a Rolls-Royce engine.) We took the ferry overnight to Dublin, across a very choppy Irish Sea, visited Luke Kelly and other friends there, then drove across to Mooney's place. Mooney lived in a big old grey rectory, freezing and damp (I was well used to that), on the outskirts of Galway. We had some wonderful music sessions at the local pub, where it was required that everyone do a "turn." They all loved Sandy, who sang, on one occasion, "The Dowie Dens of Yarrow," and on another, "Banks of the Nile." I heard the best whistler on planet Earth there, the Paganini of whistlers. He would whistle a tune full of slides and grace notes and intersperse it with bird calls. His control and range were staggering.

While there, we were invited to a wedding reception, where everyone, working around the room, would perform something, and that was some of the most extraordinary music I ever heard—I wish I had a tape of that! We visited a neighbor of Brian's who lived a few miles away in the most rickety habitation I have ever entered. The walls were made of quarter-inch plywood, the roof the same, and I don't understand how the thing stood up when the wind blew, which it did most of that night. Inside was one tiny room, with about fifteen people crammed into it. The body heat was a benefit. The music was again marvelous, as was the storytelling. Brian Mooney himself was a good singer and guitarist, a fine visual artist and a lovely man. Before we left, someone generously gave me a bottle of poteen to take home to England—it had a taste, and indeed an effect, somewhere between floor polish and paint stripper. Somehow I managed to get through most of it and still have an intestine.

In late August of that year, we embarked on a second US tour. This one was only three weeks. We played at the Fillmores again, as well as another week at the LA Troubadour. One night, Led Zeppelin turned up, and one by one joined in with us on stage. John Bonham sat at DM's kit and went through the head of the snare drum in thirty seconds, before just about destroying the rest of the kit, all to the horror of an ashen-faced DM in the front row of the crowd. Robert Plant sang a song or two, including "Hey Joe." At one point I was the lone Fairporter left on stage with the Zep. All this to a barrage of expletives and gesticulations from Peter Grant, Zeppelin's manager, who was seated front and center. It was either this night or another night during our time there that Peggy, Bonham and Janis Joplin went drinking down the road in Barney's Beanery on Santa Monica Boulevard. None of them were exactly slouches when it came to consumption, but Janis was the first to drop out and Peggy was the last man standing. He had a considerable capacity for alcohol, though I never saw him play badly, or indeed let playing interfere with drinking—he could hammer on notes with the left hand, while downing a pint with his right. Bonham missed his flight to Hawaii the next day and was eventually found lying next to the pool at the Tropicana Motel, naked and unconscious.

The jam with Zeppelin was recorded, as was the rest of that week. The basic Fairport set was released on the album *Live at the LA Troubadour*, but the Zep portion of the tapes disappeared from the A&M vaults at some point, never to be seen again—I'd still love to hear them one day. While we were in LA, we also did some recording at Gold Star Studios, on the strength of its connection with Phil Spector and the great sound of his records. We cut a few tracks, including "Banks of the Sweet Primroses" and "The Bonny Bunch of Roses"— and kept them with a mind to including them on the next album, though that was still some way off. John Wood loved working with Doc Siegel, Spector's characterful old recording engineer, and the tracks seemed to jump out of the speakers.

But the main reason we'd gone back stateside so soon was for the Philadelphia Folk Festival. The weather was sweltering and humid, and we had a good performance slot fairly near the end of the day. We finished with a medley of dance tunes, and here at last we found our target American audience—it seemed the entire crowd of about ten thousand was dancing. It was an amazing sight. This was probably our best response in the US. We'd had this reaction in the UK, and had been fearful at venues like Sheffield Town Hall that the balcony would collapse from the stomping and dancing. At the Philly Folk Festival, it was policy that no one did encores, in keeping with the egalitarian spirit that Pete Seeger and others had instilled in us. But we absolutely had to do an encore, so we played more of the same, and the scale of the reaction was staggering. We felt very welcome.

During that tour, our driver, Walter Gundy, needed to pick something up from his house in upstate New York, and I went with him. There were two units in his rental, and he mentioned that John Cage lived in the other half, when he wasn't staying in the city. Did I want to say hello? Cage had been one of my heroes since about the age of seventeen, when I read his book *Silence* and first heard his music while working with Hans Unger, so I was keen to meet him. Sadly he wasn't there, but his apartment was interesting—there was rush matting on the floor, a simple single mattress in a corner, plain white walls and a small bookshelf with musical scores and books on Zen. After that, I decided to go minimalist myself. I got the basic, barebones look down quite well, although there would always be a cupboard somewhere stuffed with junk, tangled cables and cast-offs. I saw this as a metaphor for my own life at that point: outwardly calm and ordered, but inwardly tangled and chaotic.

Back in the UK, we went to see one of our favorite bands, the Band, playing at the Albert Hall. That had always been a tricky venue in terms of sound. It's a good room to hear the 1812 Overture, though anything smaller can get lost, but the Band sounded brilliant. We did have the best seats, right opposite the stage, but they played so well and sounded like the best band in America. There were no weaknesses—three great singers, fabulous rhythm section, fine guitarist and keyboardists and perfect songs. We staggered out of there shaking our heads.

Back at the Angel, the nights were drawing in. That damp chill in the air was pricking our nostrils and reminding us of an approaching seasonal ritual. Robin Gee had pyromaniacal tendencies, and had befriended a man behind the fireworks counter at Gamages department store on High Holborn who said he could get him anything he wanted, right up to military grade. The band were excited, had a whip-round and amassed a healthy £400. With this we bought hundreds and hundreds of fireworks, including things you sank into the ground with large safety warnings on the side. By 5 November, we had sent out the word to friends that a party was in the offing at the Angel. A large contingent of Peggy's mates came down from Birmingham, and my friend the singer-songwriter Gary Farr drove up from London with a whole gang. The drink flowed, the kitchen was stuffed with revelers and every plate in the house was broken by people who insisted on dancing on the table. We had built a huge bonfire in the back, using whatever came to hand for fuel, including some of the landlord's flea-ridden furniture. We started at about 8 P.M., but then we had a lot of fireworks to get through. A sulphurous fog hung over the rear of the house, so it was hard to tell how many people were actually there. It looked like something out of a Charlie Chan movie. Visibility was down to about five yards, but the sky was clear, pierced by brilliant flashes. Some of the bigger components were mortars that shot their fireworks out of tubes in the ground with a terrifying *whoomp.*

The phone rang for hours, but nobody bothered to answer it—we wouldn't have been able to hear the other party anyway. At about 2 A.M., a couple of uniformed shapes appeared through the mist and approached the kitchen door. "Sorry to trouble you, lads," they said, "but we've had over three hundred complaints. Think it might be time to knock it on the head?" The police, who were of course our friends and protectors, had done well to allow the revelry to go on this long. We were out of fireworks anyway. My penultimate memory of the party was of the landlord, Mr. Hodgkinson, dragging his tatty old chairs off the bonfire at about 5 A.M. My ultimate memory was around dawn. In the rising mist of the November morning, there was Gary Farr, sitting in one of the rescued armchairs, which was half charred and still smoldering, fast asleep by the dying embers of the bonfire.

IN LATE 1970, Joe Boyd was offered the job of head of music at Warner Brothers Films in Los Angeles, and he accepted. He was clearly feeling frustrated at Witchseason; his roster were increasingly flexing their independence, ignoring his advice and generally acting like snotty, ungrateful kids. It was a big change for us; Joe had been there from almost the very start of Fairport and had given us a great amount of free rein, as well as excellent musical advice, putting us in the best situations to further our careers. We consoled ourselves by thinking that we had outgrown him, but in truth we felt the loss of our mentor.

We played a lot of shows that autumn, thirty in October and November, the length and breadth of Britain, and something was beginning to get to me. I was getting irritated by the tempos. Swarb had not significantly slowed down since the US tour. We were still taking dance tunes insanely fast—and, let's face it, it was going down amazingly well—but I was feeling increasingly unsatisfied. Where was the nuance, where was the swing? When Swarb was playing with Martin Carthy, there was a great subtlety to the interplay between them, it was well-rounded musical expression, and it was one of the high points of the folk revival. Now Swarb was wiggling his arse like Doug Kershaw. He was clearly excited by the possibilities of electric music, by the power it had and by the audience it reached. I found it hard to play anything meaningful at those tempos. I would work out solos that were stretching the limits of my technical ability and repeat them mechanically every night. It was not rewarding. The subtlety and interplay we had instinctively achieved in one take on "A Sailor's Life" felt a long way behind us. I was an improviser of the school of '67, and I was not finding ways of playing to my strengths. The accelerated jigs and reels were strangling me.

I felt this especially as we started to work on a Cyril Tawney song. Cyril was a merchant seaman, singer, folk song collector and very fine songwriter from the West Country.

His song "Sally Free and Easy" was covered by many artists in the 1960s, from Bert Jansch to Marianne Faithfull. The Silly Sisters did a wonderful version of "The Grey Funnel Line." Cyril had sent Fairport a few of his own songs, and a couple of traditional songs that he thought would work well in a band context. One of these was "Adieu, Adieu," also known as "Willow Day." To me, it is one of the most beautiful songs surviving in the folk canon. It has all the virtues—concise, poetical language, a stately tune and a lovable rogue as its subject. I even like the folk process that has probably turned a cry of resignation, "Well-a-day," into "Willow Day." I was excited to sit down at rehearsal and start working on the song, but I was dismayed at the tempo the band was proposing. I suggested something more processional, but the tempos merely inched back by a couple of beats per minute. I felt the majesty inherent in the song was being thrown away.

A few days before, the band had gone into Island Records to see Chris Blackwell. Chris had inherited us all—Nick, John and Bev, the Increds—when Joe brought his production company to Island, and Joe had now sold Witchseason to Island too. It was time to make a new recording contract. Chris was offering us an advance—we had never seen one of those before—on re-signing. This would mean Peggy could put a deposit down on a house in Birmingham, and the others with families could look to follow suit. But as I sat in the meeting, I knew that I couldn't keep going, that something in me had unravelled. I sat there in an agony of confusion, knowing that mentally I had already left the band, but practically that was not an option, and I did not want to leave my friends.

If I left there and then, would that jeopardize the advance and betray the band, messing up everyone's future? I would have to remain in the band and swallow my feelings. We signed, and because I didn't have a bank account, I told them to leave my portion of the advance in Fairport's account.

Back at rehearsal, I said, "Chaps, I can't do this any more." They all looked stunned. I was stunned myself. The words seemed to be coming out in spite of myself. "I think I have to leave." Silence. "I'll make you all a cup of tea, and you can talk about it." I went to the kitchen and made the tea. I delivered the tea ten minutes later, and then went off for a long walk. I mulled over the "what-ifs," but it was done, and I wasn't going back.

I had locked horns with Swarb on a regular basis—a couple of Aries butting heads together was not a way to run a band. We were definitely seeing things differently, and the last two songs we had co-written lacked some cohesion, lacked some of the unity of purpose you need in a songwriting team. I was never a horn-locking kind of Aries anyway—I'd always back down, kind of a beta-Aries.

We could have fired Swarb, found ourselves another fiddler, added a singer, but he was such a part of the appeal of the band I doubted the others would have gone for it, and the public might have finally lost patience with us. I didn't have the heart to suggest it anyway. These people were my family. I loved Swarb, in spite of his occasional annoying habits, and I couldn't stand the thought of disrupting other people's lives and causing new resentments. I was operating on gut feelings. I wanted to slink away quietly, hoping no one would notice, leaving as few ripples as possible. The issues I had with the band were my issues, no one else's. I was also looking at the horizon and seeing different possibilities. I was writing songs on my own, and they were weird. Perhaps now was the time to stop thinking of writing in a band context and start expressing all that was coming out.

Joe was concerned that his leaving had made me lose faith in Fairport. True, it was different not having him there to sound ideas off, but I said no, it had not. He asked if the band should fire Swarb and I should carry on. I said no, that was a bad idea.

It seems bizarre to me now, but I stayed on at the Angel. I kept good relations with everyone, even as they went off on tour and I stayed behind. Our tenure was about to be disrupted anyway.

10

For Hire

*You work that you may keep pace with the earth
and the soul of the earth.*
KAHLIL GIBRAN

ONE WEEKEND IN early 1971, I went into London to do a session at CBS and stayed overnight at Sandy and Trevor's flat. As usual, I took the train back on Monday morning to Bishop's Stortford, then took the bus to Little Hadham. As I got off the bus, a familiar world had turned topsy-turvy. I could see blue lights flashing from the direction of the Angel. As I came closer, there were police and fire engines, and a small knot of bystanders. The road was closed because of all the rubble. The rubble turned out to be the front wall of the Angel. There was a hole where Swarb's room had been, and where my room had been above it.

In the small hours of the morning, a lorry driver bound for Harwich had fallen asleep at the wheel and had missed the bend. He had ploughed straight into the Angel and been killed instantly. Swarb had just moved his bed into the corner of the room to accommodate some antique furniture he had bought, and the move had saved his life. He woke up as the lorry came to a halt right next to him. The antiques were matchwood. By the time I arrived, the ambulance had already departed and the lorry was being hauled away. My room had part-collapsed on top of Swarb's. I sifted through the rubble in search of records and books. My bottle of poteen had miraculously survived the fall and was bringing comfort to Swarb, who was white as a sheet. Other band members wandered around in a daze.

That was the end of the Angel. We stayed in what was left of the building for another week or so, long enough to find new accommodation. The band dispersed to sensible, real houses, dotted around what became known as the "folk rock belt"—Oxfordshire and Northamptonshire, commutable to both London and Birmingham. Robin and I moved back to London.

Now I was unemployed, and not entirely certain about how I was to earn a living. I was hoping Iain, Ashley or Sandy would hire me as a guitarist and I could get by on that, but I didn't have a plan. Ever the optimist, I thought something would turn up. Thank heavens the phone started ringing with offers of session work. I had been recording with other artists when Fairport's heavy work schedule allowed, but now it became my prime source of income. I had to buy my first diary since school to keep track. A lot of the studio jobs came from Fairport alumni like Sandy and Iain, and a steady amount came from the folk rock and singer-songwriter worlds. Occasionally I crossed over to find myself on a pop or heavy metal session. I was habitually at Sound Techniques but visited most of the London studios at one point or another. I did a lot of recording without knowing who the artist was. If a particular producer liked me, I would tend to work with other

acts on their roster. Most sessions did not require the ability
to read music fluently, which was just as well. Songs could be
picked up by ear, or we wrote chord charts. For the most part
it was enjoyable, and only occasionally felt like a job, something you gritted your teeth to get through. Artists could be
temperamental or underprepared, producers could be clueless, and you quickly learned when to keep your head down
and when it was appropriate to chip in with an opinion. For
the folk rock stuff, I found myself repeatedly on the same sessions as Pat Donaldson on bass and Gerry Conway on drums.

Pat Donaldson would never reveal his true age, but he was
about eight or nine years older than me, was a true rocker
and had hung out at the home of British rock and roll, the
2i's Coffee Bar in Soho, back in the 1950s. Something of the
Teddy boy never left him, and fluorescent pink or green socks
complemented whatever else he was wearing, which could
be any eccentric combination of styles and colors, frequently
including a kilt. The fifties sideburns were always a feature.
In a restaurant, he was perhaps the loudest person I have ever
dined with, and one lobster was never enough to satisfy his
epicurean curiosity. He had been in a group with Albert Lee
called Poet and the One Man Band, had played with Zoot
Money, and when I met him was playing in Fotheringay.

Gerry Conway was with Trevor Lucas in Eclection, and
then spent many years playing with Cat Stevens. His highly
distinctive drumming helped to add originality and musi-
cality to all Cat's early albums. He was also in Fotheringay.
Gerry's time-keeping was metronomic, and for true hi-fi fans,
he was always mumbling the words along with the track—you

can just hear it occasionally if the drum tracks are exposed. I also worked a lot with DM and Peggy as the "other" rhythm section, so often it was a case of "Who is it today? Oh, it's you lot again."

There are tricks to playing on sessions, especially if you're asked to just play a solo or "express yourself." It's amazing how good a solo you can play without remembering any of the chords, or even on running the track down for the first time. I have played many sessions where the run-through was the take that they kept. Uncharitable producers would describe something they called the "Thompson Curve"—great run-through, good first take, quite good second take, mediocre takes three to ten, and then really strong takes eleven, twelve and thirteen. I became known as a "run-through or take thirteen" kind of guitarist.

I got together with Sandy in early 1971 to discuss her next recording project. She wanted me to produce, along with herself and John Wood, and I was happy to be involved. She had just broken up Fotheringay, following a certain amount of pressure. Chris Blackwell was one of many people who saw her as a solo artist rather than as a band member who would share vocals and songwriting with others. They all wanted it to be democratic as far as possible, but Sandy always appeared to be the dominant force when they were on stage, and she was clearly the main singer and songwriter. But now she was officially solo, and the next record would be important. She wanted to bring musicians she was comfortable with into the studio, including Pat and Gerry; even though Fotheringay didn't exist, half of it was still on board! It was a strange situation, but there did not seem to be any animosity—I think everyone knew that Sandy had been destined for a solo career sooner or later.

Here at last was Sandy composing at the piano. She had a beautiful touch, and her voicings and harmonic sense were unique. I think a lot of that came from composers like Delius, whom we all grew up listening to. Perhaps some of the other English romantics were in there too—Elgar, Bliss and Vaughan Williams. It amused me to think of common musical threads from our childhoods, and one of the main ones, not always obvious, was probably Fats Waller. Ashley's father played piano in a Fats-style trio, my family listened to Fats and so did Sandy's. She did "do" Fats on a later record.

One of the challenges of working with Sandy was to find some variations in tempo. Left to her own devices, she kept to a medium-slow pace, in common or waltz time, that rarely varied. In that situation, one could admit defeat and say, "Well, that's the way it is, the songs are great, and the listener will have to adjust their expectations and accept a one-paced album." One idea I had was to call it a suite, or otherwise label it as a single piece of music, but even that didn't really resolve the issue—suites have slow and fast movements. What we did, which I felt conflicted about, was to throw in up-tempo cover songs for a bit of variety, but they never sounded part of the whole. As a co-producer, I regretted not finding a solution. Trevor bought Sandy a metronome to practice to and even write to, set at faster tempos. Not much came of that.

Another thing that I now regret about the production on Sandy's material was the way the strings were used. We all

loved Harry Robinson, who had done the beautiful arrangement for "River Man" by Nick Drake. Harry had been musical
director for Tommy Steele, formed Lord Rockingham's XI
in the late 1950s and had scored dozens of horror films for
Hammer. He could turn his hand to just about anything.
John Wood loved the big, lush sound he could create, and it
seemed a good fit for Sandy's music. What jarred a bit for me
was the mixing of the strings against the rhythm section: in
order to get the sweep of the strings, they needed to be louder
than the bass and the drums, and there were times when the
cellos came into the guitar and bass range and clouded the
harmonies, in some cases clashing with bass notes. A smaller
string section, even something the size of a double quartet,
would have dominated less and kept out of the bass register; a
large section might have played higher parts; or we could have
ditched the rhythm section altogether, leaving piano, Sandy's
voice and strings. This third option might have been the best
way to go; indeed, it was the approach we took on some later
tracks that used a full string section.

I think the string arrangement on "River Man" is the greatest in popular music, better than "Eleanor Rigby," "Kashmir"
or any other contender. It was all recorded live, with Nick
singing and playing in the middle of a mere twelve string
musicians, though it sounds huge.

I love the story of Harry Robinson, whose real name was
Harry Robertson, receiving a check made out to "Robinson"
from the BBC, and realising that it was easier just to open
a bank account in that name than to get the check reissued!
My great-grandfather, John Templeton Thomson, once had

a similar predicament. He ordered a brass nameplate for his front door, and when it arrived the sign-makers had spelled the name "Thompson"—with a "p." They swore that was the spelling he had given them. A true Scotsman, he figured that it was cheaper to change the family surname by deed poll than to pay for another nameplate!

Sandy was a great procrastinator in the studio. She would float through vocals, making a beautiful sound but not committing emotionally to the songs. It was often in the mixing session, at literally the last minute, when Sandy would say, "Oh, that vocal's a bit expressionless, isn't it?" John would say, "Well, go out there and do it properly," and then she would nail it.

But she was really hitting her stride as a composer. Her songs were melodically unlike anyone else's, and although you can hear her roots in traditional music, these are songs of their time and a fine statement by a complete artist, with a quality that endures. Were there enough hooks in the lyrics, enough variations in tempo, to attract a wider listenership? Could she stand shoulder to shoulder in the charts with the likes of Elton John, T. Rex and Marmalade? More relevantly, could she become an iconic album artist like Joni Mitchell or Jackson Browne? Like many artists from the Witchseason stable, she found it a struggle to cross over into wider acceptability. Nick Drake was under-exposed in his lifetime, as was John Martyn, and Sandy the same; and the danger with this is that you begin to second-guess yourself. Instead of sticking to your guns, retaining all the artistic qualities that made you unique in the first place and waiting for the audience to

find you (if they ever do), you think that you have to drift
over towards the mainstream a little. Nick never lived long
enough to do that, but I think John did, and Sandy did on
later records. Sometimes it is managers, sweethearts or record
executives who will encourage you in this direction, and commercially it may work—there are examples—but artistically it
rarely does. You make four or five albums that don't sell, and
you begin to wonder. I did the same thing myself from time
to time. My biggest-selling records were where there was real
belief in me from the record label, and they spent money on
promotion. The content wasn't that different.

Sandy's first solo record was called *The North Star
Grassman and the Ravens*. Not a title to trip off the tongue,
but acceptably obscure for the 1970s. Her lyrics were cryptic.
She would tell me that "The Pond and the Stream" was about
Anne Briggs, or that "Crazy Lady Blues" was about Linda
Peters, but a lot she kept to herself. Only years later did I find
out that Jackson C. Frank was in there, alongside other figures
she loved or loathed. Interpreting Sandy was like doing the
crossword puzzle.

Gerry was working with Cat Stevens, so we took Sandy's
new material on the road with a different drummer. I think
I first ran into Timi Donald when he was working on an Iain
Matthews record. He had been playing drums in Glasgow
bands like Trash and Blue, kept great time and was very influenced by the drumming of Levon Helm and Richard Manuel
on albums by the Band. He seemed a good fit for Sandy, and
we all got along well. That made us Donald, Donaldson,
Denny and Thompson, one Scot and three half-Scots—it was

all getting a bit Caledonian. You get to know people well on the road, as you are with them for weeks or months on end. You might grab a quick shopping trip before a sound check or find time for a walk, but otherwise you are together from the time you check out of a hotel in the morning to when you are dropped back at the next hotel after the show. It was like being in the army, where you could spend large chunks of your life with people you didn't get on with; but fortunately this was a happy band, and we filled any downtime with humor, tall stories and games of Scrabble.

Off the road, and back in the studio, I worked on the Gary Farr album *Strange Fruit*. We had shared many a stage with Gary, and he became a good friend. I had first seen him at the Marquee Club, fronting Gary Farr and the T-Bones, playing R&B, when I was at school. He was the son of the boxer Tommy Farr, who became British heavyweight champion, and brother of Ricki Farr, who used to run the Flamingo Club and the Isle of Wight Festival. Ricki was less beloved, a bit shady, and not very widely trusted as a promoter. Coming from a Welsh choral background, Gary had a sweet, powerful voice, and was moving away from R&B towards the singer-songwriter niche. The rest of the band on the album were from Mighty Baby, whom Fairport had shared bills with at Middle Earth: Roger Powell on drums, Mike Evans on bass and Ian Whiteman on keyboards. I thought the tracks went well, and we recorded fairly quickly, with a jam band kind of feel to everything. From that point on, I ran into Roger and Ian on other sessions, and booked them on a few. They became rhythm section number three.

I did two albums with Iain Matthews in 1971: *If You Saw Thro' My Eyes* and *Tigers Will Survive*. Both records saw Iain continuing along the path he had carved out on the *Matthews' Southern Comfort* record—a mix of his own songs and covers, in his own country rock style. We also did a few radio shows in the early half of the year as a trio with the guitarist and singer-songwriter Andy Roberts.

In August of that year, I went on a tour of the States with Iain. On balance, it might have been the most disorganized, ill-fated tour I've ever been a part of, and it wasn't really Iain's fault. The band consisted of Iain, myself and Andy playing acoustic guitar and singing, and Bob Ronga playing bass.

New York was fine. The two girls from the agency who drove us around for the first few days doing promotion would crank up the soul station on the radio and harmonize with everything, and I mean everything, every second of every trip, complete with dance moves, as far as it was possible while sitting and driving. It was thoroughly entertaining. I don't know if they ever had careers, but they were a great double act. Perhaps they were auditioning for our jobs in Iain's band? So New York wasn't too bad. It was when we got to other towns that things went awry. Boston, always a confusing city to navigate, swallowed us completely for hours on end. Bob was our driver, and it became apparent after a day or two that he:

    a) had no map
    b) had no sense of direction
    c) was drinking like a fish
    d) was having a nervous breakdown.

We went round and round and round.

I forget which town it was, but after another show Bob was driving us back to the hotel and was weaving all over the freeway, considerably the worse for wear. We pulled over and put him in the back seat, where he gurgled and argued with invisible demons. This left us with something of a dilemma. No one could drive. None of us had a license or had even taken lessons. We decided to drive by committee. "D" seemed to be the right position for the transmission. One of us steered while another worked the pedals. The third checked the mirrors. Thankfully there wasn't too much traffic around. We crawled along the freeway at about fifteen miles an hour, happily did not meet any cops, and managed to get back to the hotel at about 2 A.M. Bob was back driving us the next day, which was not very reassuring.

Compounding these small matters was the fact that we were booked in the wrong venues, on the wrong bills. In Los Angeles, we were booked to play at the Troubadour for a week, in fact not a bad venue, as I knew from Fairport days, just the wrong crowd for us. We were opening for Donny Hathaway, a fine, smooth jazz-funk act, and the audience was mostly black. Four white men slipped nervously on stage and performed Iain's heartfelt and beautiful songs, in his distinctive voice. It wasn't that the audience objected—they just didn't notice . . . or if they did, they gave it about two seconds of their time, and then went back to talking to their friends and drinking. We would finish a song to zero reaction—no hostility, no applause, just nothing. Buskers on the London Underground got more attention. On the first night I took a solo, and as is sometimes my habit, I closed my eyes to concentrate. I finished my sixteen bars, and, still with my eyes closed, noticed that Iain had missed his vocal re-entry. I opened my eyes and looked in his direction, but he wasn't there. I carefully counted the bodies on stage—three. Iain had walked off, leaving the rest of us to, presumably, finish the set. Finish we certainly didn't. We lasted one night of a six-night run.

On all those American tours—apart from one with Sandy, when we stayed at the posher Chateau Marmont—when we were in LA, we stayed at the infamous Tropicana Motel, a few doors down from the Troubadour. It was colorful, to say the least, and though it was basic, a lot of bands would stay there if they were playing in Hollywood. It was nice to fraternize with other musicians, but there were also some dodgy characters there, including drug dealers and hookers. You never quite knew who you were going to run into. One night the police decided to beat some guy up against the door of my room at about 3 A.M. They were slamming him so hard against the door that I expected it to give way and all of them to tumble into the room like the Keystone Kops.

The Tropicana had a reasonable pool, and a very good coffee shop called Duke's, where one would sometimes run into other musicians. One such was a tall, denim-clad, thin-faced guy with shoulder-length hair parted in the middle. He introduced himself as Glenn Frey and invited us to hear his band rehearsing.

We followed him to a garage, which had been set up as a rehearsal space. He explained that they played as Linda Ronstadt's backing band but were about to make their own record as the Eagles. They played "Peaceful Easy Feeling" and sounded fabulous, with vocal harmonies that were to die for. They asked us to play a song, and we gave them something of Iain's, but it sounded a bit puny in comparison. I got to jam with them on a song, borrowing Glenn's electric guitar, but the strings were like steel cables on a suspension bridge, so I'm not sure I did myself justice. Linda's manager asked me if I'd like to join her new band, but I had a lot of work coming up with Sandy and thought she would kill me if I jumped ship. There has been a rumor that I was asked to join the Eagles—maybe something went through channels, but I don't remember being directly approached. Another rumor exists that I was asked to join Traffic; again, I don't remember hearing it except third-hand. I was, however, asked to join the Animals and the Band, both in later incarnations, when they were past their creative peak. The reality was that the last thing I wanted to do was to join a band playing American styles. I felt I was on a mission, pioneering a new form of music, writing songs based on the traditions of the British Isles. Playing for hire with Iain or Sandy left me free to write and explore, and maybe I would make my own record some day.

We played four nights at the Poison Apple in Detroit. This was after the race riots of 1967 had left the center of town a burned-out shell. The club was on a short block that consisted of a convenience store, a British pub and the club itself. There was nothing else around but wasteland for what seemed like miles. It felt a little scary. We stayed in a flat above the gig, and figured we could survive for our tenure with food from the 7-11 and a few beers from the pub. A British pub! A beacon, a veritable embassy in this blighted landscape. Enthusiastically, we popped next door upon arrival and strode confidently inside. It was like one of those Westerns, where the piano player stops in mid-tune, the cowboy about to play the ace freezes in mid-air and all heads swivel towards the strangers who have dared to venture through the swinging doors. We suddenly felt long-haired and wrongly dressed—we weren't wearing Carhartt check work shirts and Cat hats, we didn't have disillusion in our eyes and three days' growth of beard. We hadn't spent the best part of our lives on the Ford production line. At least our lovable Limey accents will get them, we thought.

"Four pints of Bass please, bartender!"

"Say what?"

"Four pints of Bass ale, if you could."

"I didn't get the first thing . . . you want—pies?"

This is usually the part in the movie when the crowd finally relaxes and goes back to talking, drinking and gambling. Not so here. They kept staring. Hostile is the way I would describe that look. We got our beers. We drank them promptly. We left. We didn't go back to the British pub. In fact, we spent the next three days between the flat and the venue, and the flat turned out to be the better option. The first night about twenty people turned up for the show. The next night about fifteen. The third night we got ten. The fourth . . . word was obviously getting around. The audience in the club also stared at us. Hostile is the way I'd describe that look, too.

We played a club in Gastown in Vancouver, Canada. Gastown today is all frou-frou boutiques and restaurants, and is a very pleasant place to wander around. But in 1971 it was run-down and scary. We happened to be playing on the weekend, when the lumberjacks came into town. As with the Donny Hathaway experience, we were under-amplified and not really what they wanted to hear. They were far more into the disco, and they would grab girls and whoop it up, rather like Pythonesque caricatures of lumberjacks, all plaid flannel shirts and braces. Several times during the dancing, men would jump off the balcony straight onto the dance floor, a good fifteen feet down, with a hearty "Yee-haw!" I swore I'd get out of the habit of playing with my eyes shut, because once again there I was being all sensitive and creative, and I came out of my reverie to find Iain missing again. I can't remember if we finished that run or not.

There were some high points. We did a week at the Bitter End in New York's Greenwich Village, opening for Dion DiMucci. He was a lovely guy—totally unpretentious, a fine songwriter and a wonderful singer. In true New York style, he would sit on the front steps of the club between sets, strumming. He asked me to play on an upcoming recording, and it was a great regret that I had to leave town before that could happen. Between sets, we would watch the Mahavishnu Orchestra or the Blues Project at a club across the street.

There was—and still is—a shop in Greenwich Village called the Music Inn, selling exotic instruments from around the world. In those days they also stocked a few vintage gems. I bought a 1966 Martin 000-18 for just $150, which I used both on stage and on record for years. On the next tour with Sandy, I went back to the shop and bought a Gibson A2 mandolin,

which recorded like a dream. I regretted not forking out a
mere $700 for an amazing 1947 Martin D-18, but that was
several weeks' wages at the time.

While we were in New York we had fun hanging out with
Paul Nelson, probably the most significant blues critic of his
generation. He was working as an A&R executive at Mercury
Records, and he got them interested in signing me. I went into
Mercury Studios and cut a few demos, with a lot of help from
Iain and Andy. The next day I received a phone call from the
president of the company expressing enthusiasm, and then a
contract turned up at my hotel. It was about a thousand pages
long, and full of that strange legalese that bears little rela-
tion to real life. I promised to look at the document but got
stuck around page one, where it described records as "78 rpm
discs or the equivalent." I intended to get professional help,
but never quite got round to it—perhaps the head of Mercury
sounding like James Cagney on the phone had put me off.
I put it all on the back burner—I don't know what happened
to the demos, but the songs ended up being recorded when I
got back to London.

I FIRST MET Linda Peters at Sound Techniques on the
Liege & Lief sessions, and we sat next to each other in the restaurant when the gang went out for dinner on the King's Road
afterwards. I thought she was pretty cute—dark-haired with
strong cheekbones, shapely and dressed in a miniskirt with
thigh-length boots. By all accounts she was less impressed
with me, thinking I was all peace, love and vegetarian.
I subsequently used to run into her at Sandy's flat a lot—they

were great pals—and I became aware that there was chemistry between us. We became friends, but there was a spark too. By 1971, we were going out. She was far more worldly and experienced than me, and I once again felt that in most ways—except musically—I was the junior partner in our relationship. I didn't mind that—I was flattered that she liked me enough to date me.

Linda was living with her friend Philippa Clare in Marble Arch, in a flat that was another great meeting place of the folk scene. Philippa was the daughter of a diplomat, had an elder sister who wrote cookbooks, and at one point managed Fairport. She usually had a couple of spare rooms for rent, and at various times Robin and Barry Dransfield, Dave Swarbrick, Leapy Lee and John Wood lived there; it felt like you could run into just about anyone from the folk world in the kitchen. Linda had been engaged to Joe Boyd and had been living with him in LA for a while, but it hadn't worked out and she was now back in London. We got on well, sharing a love of Scottish culture, music and the arts. She had been in a folk duo with Paul McNeill and was working on a more pop-oriented career, and surviving by singing on commercials. I was away touring a fair bit, so in the beginning our relationship was stop–start. Eventually she moved in with me in Hampstead, which gave us a bit more time together. We saw a lot of films up at the Everyman cinema, ate in a lot of restaurants, bought our health food from Steve Howe's shop across the road and walked a lot on the Heath.

One evening, Linda and I were having dinner in the Witches' Cauldron in Belsize Park with Martin Carthy, and he mentioned that Lal and Mike Waterson had begun writing songs. He quoted some lines from their song "The Scarecrow":

> *As I roved out one winter's day,*
> *I saw an old man hanging from a pole in a field*
>   *of clay.*
> *His coat was gone and his head hung low,*
> *Till the wind flung it up to look, wrung its neck*
>   *and let it go.*
>
> *How could you lay me down and love me?*
> *How could you lay me down and love me now?*
> *For you're only a bag of bones in an overall*
> *That the wind blows and the kids throw stones at*
>   *the thing on the pole.*

It was powerful stuff, coming right out of the English tradition, but with a surreal Waterson twist. Lal, to my mind, was one of the great songwriters to come from this country, and even though Hull isn't exactly out on the Yorkshire moors, there was a touch of Emily Brontë about her writing—dark, romantic, idiosyncratic and always windswept. When her style moved a little to bridge that space between traditional and popular music, it was towards the sad, Northern mood of the likes of "Eleanor Rigby." Mike had a unique kind of musical genius, which I'm still coming to terms with. His choices of notes as a harmony singer were completely unpredictable and were a major component of the Watersons' sound. As a solo singer he could shape a ballad into something completely his own, through his use of slides and grace notes, and he never seemed to breathe when he sang. He was untrained, as far as I know, but his musical instincts were unlike anyone else's—naive yet sophisticated. It makes no sense, but that's as near as I can describe it.

My appetite had been whetted by Martin, and I was keen to hear more of the songs. I was delighted to be invited to play on Mike and Lal's record. It also offered a challenge. Martin is quite an orchestral player—that is, he covers most of the possibilities of accompaniment, so to be a second guitar in there means not treading on toes, and looking for counter-melodies and spaces that won't be intrusive.

We recorded at Cecil Sharp House in Camden Town, with the wonderful Bill Leader producing. Bill had recorded just about every traditional singer and revivalist, all on a shoe-string budget. Everything was done on a two-track recorder. I had the flu for the whole recording. To make matters worse, the studio had installed new baffles to improve the acoustics but had yet to cover them in cloth, so I was breathing in glass fiber, which made me feel like I was drowning. Despite this, the music was divine. We had DM and Ashley playing on some tracks, but most songs were just the two guitars, which fitted their starkness. For the track "The Magical Man" I found a soft electric guitar tone, which sounded like a fairground organ in the mix. Another example of the dark, macabre tone of the songs is illustrated by the lyric to "Winifer Odd":

> *Waiting for God*
> *She bent down to pick up a glittering thing*
> *And was knocked over by a car*
> *It was a lucky star*

Lal's sister, the inimitable Norma Waterson, sang on a number of tracks, owning them as she does everything she sings. The album, *Bright Phoebus*, was well received in some folk circles, but it's taken forty-odd years for it to be rightfully acclaimed as a classic. I am very proud to have been a part of it.

As well as being in Iain's band, I was also playing in Sandy's touring band, a natural extension from playing on her album. It was probably my favorite time working with her; though she would constantly complain about missing Trevor when either of them was touring, she was not drinking too much at the time and seemed balanced and happy. Rehearsals were enjoyable, taken at Sandy's usual reluctant pace—a break to change a string or make a cup of tea always seemed better than actual work. We did a long tour of the UK, playing mostly concert halls, before heading off to conquer the US.

In January we played the Bitter End in New York, with twenty-three-year-old Jackson Browne opening. He was obviously something special, with amazing maturity of voice and songwriting, and a genial human being. Between sets, we would repair next door to Nobody's Bar, sawdust on the floor and *Tapestry* on the jukebox. One night, the guy on the door at the club told us that Bob Dylan was in the house. If there was one sure way of ruining Sandy's set, it had just happened. I'd never seen her so nervous, self-conscious and clumsy on stage. Bob slipped away before the set ended.

On a night off, Pat, Timi and I decided to go out for a drink. It wasn't exactly a contest, but it was agreed that each man would not shirk from his duty. We were drinking some draught German lager, and round after round was summarily

consumed. We got to round sixteen and called it quits. The
bartender then brought us one more on the house. I was seriously incapacitated. The others cabbed back to the hotel, but
I was engrossed by the TV behind the bar, which was showing a documentary about the First World War. I proceeded
to lecture the remaining patrons on the demerits of Generals
French and Haig, until I was thrown out, like in the movies,
face first into a pile of snow. For some reason, I was wearing sandals in weather about twenty below. Well, I know the
reason. We had just come from California, and a friend had
suggested I buy these buffalo-hide sandals—you wear them
wet and they mold to your feet. I'd found them so comfortable I didn't want to take them off, and so I wore them for the
entire tour, rain, snow, ice, whatever. My feet were freezing,
of course. My life was full of such disconnects. I got back to
the hotel, was sick all over the bed, sick all over the bathroom,
and felt ill for days. I thought I could hold it, but Dave Pegg or
John Bonham I was not.

Back in the UK, more studio work beckoned. It was
Trevor's idea to do a rock and roll record featuring the folk
rock community. This seemed a redundant exercise from the
outset and I voiced concerns, but there was no damping his
enthusiasm—everyone else was on board, and I didn't want to
be left out. He booked the Manor for a week. This was Richard
Branson's studio out in Oxfordshire, and it was one of the first
fully staffed and catered studios in Britain, where everyone
could stay, be fed regularly and get concentrated amounts
of work done. Trevor wanted to get Jerry Lee Lewis over to
guest, but his asking fee was about double the record budget.

Although he was a hero of mine, I could see him being tough to work with and was relieved he didn't make it. The studio was not entirely to John Wood's liking, and he was hanging blankets against bare surfaces to soak up some of the "honk." Sandy, Linda, Trevor and I sang, Ian Whiteman played keyboard, Gerry Conway, Roger Powell and DM played drums, Pat Donaldson and Ashley played bass, we had a horn section—the whole scene was there. Recording took a week. It was fairly easy, as everyone knew the songs, and we would work from around noon into the night, recording tracks and overdubbing with a revolving cast of players. We would break for a communal dinner around the large dining table. The food was excellent, and Richard Branson would sometimes preside and steer the conversation. I rarely remember politics being discussed over this or any dinner—music was 90 percent the topic, with the occasional diversion into house prices, clothes, family. Hardly anyone had children at that point. When the meal was just men or just women, the opposite sex would become a bigger topic. Typical of most people in their early to mid-twenties, we were all upbeat about our prospects of continuing employment in music.

The results of our labors became the album *Rock On*. There was nothing new to be found in the material or the interpretations, for the most part. Sandy sang beautifully, as did Linda, and their performances were the highlights for me. Their duet on "When Will I Be Loved" was the outstanding track. But all in all, a project of small consequence. It was a nice time socially, it was fun to play songs that had formed the soundtrack of our youth, but nothing moved forward.

I DECIDED TO upgrade my electric guitar, and asked Sid Bishop in Roka's in Denmark Street to look out for a vintage Stratocaster. "Vintage" seems a barely appropriate term for an instrument ten or fifteen years old, but there had been a sharp decline in quality in that short time, and the earlier models became sought after. A few days later, they had a 1959 sunburst model in the shop, which I purchased. I also grabbed a 1952 Telecaster. The prices were very reasonable; it was just before the market in vintage instruments went crazy. I got a couple of older Fender studio amps, a 1964 Deluxe Reverb and a 1956 Deluxe, both of which I still use. I was happy to get closer to that one tone in my head that meant I was no longer fighting the equipment, that I could think a musical thought, my fingers could respond, and the sound would *be* the thought. It will still be a good painting if the artist's technique is good, but better if he's not fighting inferior paint and canvas.

We started a second album with Sandy, this time with Trevor producing. The formula was similar to the previous record, in that Sandy was writing great songs, and covers were thrown in to add variety. She did a version of Bob Dylan's "Tomorrow Is a Long Time," with Sneaky Pete playing pedal steel, which was a much more successful cover, adding tempo variation and a more straightforward narrative. Pat and Timi were the rhythm section. On "Listen, Listen" I overdubbed about six mandolins to be a "section," and bathed in echo, it's quite convincing. I had my usual gripes about the string arrangement climbing down into the electric bass, but otherwise I think it stands up as a fine album, one of Sandy's best.

I did so many recording sessions in 1971 that memories of them blur and overlap, or seem to form one long, confused hallucination that mutates a little every time I remember: my amp catching fire on a Mick Softley session at CBS—at Island Studios with the ever-cheerful Mike Heron, whose songs were way more complex than they sounded, and playing while basically asleep after a hard night's partying—trying to overdub a fast wah-wah guitar part at Sound Techniques for Stefan Grossman and nearly breaking my ankle—all night in Olympic doing sixty-five takes of a Badfinger song—Françoise Hardy teaching me the correct way to peel an orange—being so fed up on a session at IBC Studios that I got drunk and incapable, and wasn't asked back—playing three sessions back to back at Olympic: 2 to 8 P.M., 9 P.M. to 8 A.M. and then 10 A.M. to 1 P.M. the next day. Shelagh McDonald was a sweet young girl, a really good singer-songwriter, but soon after the sessions I did with her she disappeared, and it was rumoured that she had been working for the CIA but her cover had been blown. She emerged recently to say that she had had a bad drug experience, which had caused her to become something of a recluse, and her voice had also been affected. I still prefer to believe the CIA story. Why would the CIA be interested in the British folk scene? It was a hotbed of left-wing politics—indeed, many singers could be categorized as communists—and they may have been concerned about the influence of music on young minds. The CIA rarely give you credit for thinking for yourself.

It was always good to play with John Martyn, whose voice and guitar style were unmistakable. We were neighbors for a while in Hampstead and would often jam and play each other our latest finds from the record bins. I played on *Bless the Weather* and *The Road to Ruin*, both great records in my opinion. I regret seeing a lot less of John during the rest of the 1970s, after he moved to Hastings. Like many artists from the Witchseason stable, it's taken a long time for people to realize his genius. Now everyone quotes him as an influence.

Marc Ellington was from Eugene, Oregon, had grown up with Tim Hardin and Richard Fariña, among others, and had come to the UK in 1967 to avoid the Vietnam draft. He and his wife Karen had bought a castle in Aberdeenshire as a ruin and restored it to habitability, winning prizes in the process. I had met Marc in 1968, at which time he was every inch the slightly madcap, very funny singer-songwriter. He opened for Fairport many times, and he and I became firm friends. I worked on two or three of Marc's records, which featured the usual gang, plus some visitors to our shores like Sneaky Pete and Chris Hillman. The budgets were small, recording mostly done on four-track, but these records of Marc's are now collector's items. He had sung a cameo on Fairport's *Unhalfbricking* back in 1969.

In December, Ashley's wife Shirley Collins found herself with three bookings in the West Country and no plan to fulfill them. Ashley put together a scratch band of himself on bass, me on electric guitar, John Kirkpatrick on accordion and Royston Wood on vocals and behind the steering wheel. Rehearsal was minimal, thanks in large part to the fine musicianship of Kirkpatrick, who reeled off tasteful melodic and countermelodic accompaniment with seeming ease. The gigs were in arts centers and pubs, and showed me, if I didn't already know, that Shirley was one of the unique voices of the folk revival, pure, understated and invested with a musicologist's knowledge. The enjoyment of it all was aided by someone plying us with Mahogany, a drink I had last heard about in Boswell's *Life of Dr. Johnson*, but which was still current in the West. It consisted of gin and molasses, heated, so that the alcohol gets to the brain in double-quick time. I still think of it as the Mahogany Tour. We laughed a lot, and occupied the stage a little unsteadily.

That year, I went home to my parents for Christmas, perhaps the only time in the year I would see them. My father had taken early retirement from the Metropolitan Police, and they had relocated to Southerness, down on the Kirkcudbright coast in south-west Scotland. This was near where my father had grown up. They'd had a house built right next to the beach that also backed onto the golf course, so Dad could indulge his love of the ocean and his love of golf, and also run the bar at the nineteenth hole. It was a beautiful, desolate spot, not as desolate as I remembered from my youth, when there were fewer caravans and campers coming down for "Glasgow Fortnight," but in winter it was empty and isolated. A mile's walk along the beach brought you to Paul Jones's Cave, where the American naval hero John Paul Jones would land his goods in his earlier incarnation as a smuggler. There were curlews and oystercatchers on the beach, and far in the distance, across the Solway Firth, was the hazy outline of Sellafield nuclear power station. A neighbor would routinely check the beach with a Geiger counter, but the count was low.

I lasted a day, or two at the most, before I felt the familiar suffocation of home and wanted to flee. No reflection on my parents, who were doing their best. We went through the rituals of exchanging presents and Christmas dinner, but I frequently disappeared on long walks. I wasn't at the point where it was comfortable to be around them. I thought I knew about life better than they did. I was still growing emotionally, had no need of whatever they had to offer as parents, and could not accept them as just flawed human beings who tried hard. The arrogance of youth. My father had worked long hours with the police, and when he wasn't working he was drinking with his mates, so he was a distant figure to me. He tried hard to make it up to me—he took me to my first football match, and we went to see *Zulu!* and *Mutiny on the Bounty* on birthdays—but the bond was never there. My mother was closer, a real mum, but I found being mothered was something I didn't need too much of. I loved her, but didn't get home very often. There was a connection there, though—when I was going to visit, I rarely bothered to call, because my mum would know when I was coming, usually to the hour. She would have baked my favorite things in anticipation. She was always a bit "fey."

1971 HAD BEEN a fragmented year, but typical in the life of a working musician. It was particularly nice to have a couple of projects with Ashley. I had been working a lot with Fairport alumni, which I think was an indication of two things. Firstly, Fairport was a friendly band. We started out as a group of musically minded friends, and didn't add anyone to the band who was self-obsessed, dysfunctional or tough to work with. Secondly, British folk rock was a small scene. Many players were drafted into the core bands over the years, but the small number who stayed the distance had to be musically flexible, with a good understanding of both the folk and the rock side. The musicians whom everyone wanted to work with boiled down to about three drummers, three bass players, three fiddlers, two squeeze box players, three guitarists and a handful of singers. It was inevitable that those musicians would go from band to band, session to session and project to project.

In the summer of 1971 I played on *No Roses*, an album by Shirley Collins that featured, under the umbrella of the Albion Country Band, the usual faces, as well as some peripheral players like Roger Powell and Tim Renwick. Ashley, having formed Fairport and founded Steeleye Span, was becoming aware that traditional English music had so far been neglected in the latest electric revival—Fairport's music had been a blend of Irish, Scottish and English. Shirley had grown up in the Sussex folk tradition and was the perfect interpreter of Ashley's vision. The sessions were a lot of fun to play on, and we unearthed some fine songs like "The Murder of Maria Marten" and "The White Hare of Howden."

On the heels of that project came *Morris On*, an album of rocked-up morris dance tunes, with a core band of Ashley, Dave Mattacks on drums, Barry Dransfield on fiddle, John Kirkpatrick on accordion and me on twelve-string guitar. Various guests helped out, including Shirley. The Chingford Morris Men came and danced in the studio, which for me was a high point—all the bells they wore on their ankles sounded great in stereo. The record turned out really well, and I think helped to move the public perception of morris dancing music from being something faintly ridiculous to a vital and even hip tradition going back to pre-Christian paganism. Britain lost many traditions in the first half of the twentieth century, preferring imported to home-grown. At the end of the First World War, there were only three morris sides left in England; now there are around six hundred.

Between it all I found time to write and develop the strange, surreal songs I was collecting in my notebooks. I'm glad I spent years in a band, and I'm glad I spent a year or two playing in other people's bands and being for hire on records, because when I became a bandleader I knew the feeling of being employed, and never put myself above those I was employing. The music world is full of arseholes—absolute, arrogant, self-serving dickheads who imagine it all revolves around them. I've met plenty, and there's plenty more I avoid. To work for these people can be painful, and usually an unmusical, unrewarding experience. Many of them are talented, many are adored by the public, who are happy to see self-confidence and egotism up there on stage, manifesting as showmanship. Give me a folk club with thirty people who treat you as nothing special. And that was approximately the world I was about to enter.

11

Return of the Fly

Be secret and exult,
Because of all things known
That is most difficult.

W. B. YEATS

I TOLD JOHN Wood to book me some time at Sound Techniques and to bill it to Island Records, where I was nominally still an artist. This was without asking Island if they wanted me to make a record. I was hoping they wouldn't notice until it was too late. I worked cheap anyway. I had slowly accumulated a pile of songs over the past year—from approximately my last six months in Fairport—and now seemed the time to collect them together into an album. I saw these songs as a kind of statement of intent: this was the way I thought British songs should sound from this point forward. As in Fairport, I was almost imagining that Britain had never totally succumbed to American influence, the tradition had never been broken and we had all grown up singing and playing this way.

In reality, it was an artificial construct. Songs could rock out, but they had to bestride the two worlds of rock and tra-ditional. I didn't really understand these songs; as is often the case, I knew the songs came out of me, but didn't know why. Why these eccentric subjects? Was I just being a channel for music that hovers out there somewhere, until it picks you as the medium to bring it into the world? I felt that by recording them, and putting them together on a concrete object like an LP, I could gain some perspective. I could hold it in my hands, see all those song titles written on the sleeve, listen to them back to back, and maybe understand what the hell I was doing, get some overview. Just as the ancient Greeks didn't like to leave spaces between words, I wanted these songs to be brothers and sisters to each other, to exist cheek by jowl.

I recruited Pat Donaldson and Timi Donald as the rhythm section, and the three of us laid down backing tracks. Our work together on so many projects gave us a good familiarity with each other's playing, and we managed to put the tracks down in three days. Island did, of course, notice the bills, but agreed to pay.

If the album was a statement of intent, then the opening track was the distillation of the statement. "Roll Over Vaughan Williams" is telling the listener that the music they are about to hear must not be prejudged—preconceptions must be set aside. The chorus "Live in fear" meant, as far as I was concerned, being fearful of finding yourself in the wrong critical camp—a mortal sin. I put a tank commander's microphone onto an accordion, plugged it through the console and overdrove it to get the distorted sound that features on the track. I double-tracked electric guitar, panned them hard left and right, and played a couple of reels I had written for the piece in unison as the instrumental breaks.

"Nobody's Wedding" was inspired by seeing a Romany wedding, where the bride and the groom both pee into a wooden bowl, their urine intermingles and lo!—they are hitched. The song describes an even more surreal nuptial, not intended to make too much sense. John Kirkpatrick plays some Jimmy Shand-style accordion on a strathspey in the middle, and on "Mairi's Wedding" at the fadeout. Timi remembered some of the pipe band snare drumming from his youth.

The New Zealand jazz harpist David Snell played on "Twisted" and "The Old Changing Way." He was a joy to work with, such an accomplished musician, and forgiving of my musical naivete. On the tracks "Mary and Joseph" and "The New St. George," we used the horns from the Barry Martyn Jazz Band, one of the more authentic New Orleans-style bands in the UK. It was well outside of their usual musical territory, but they responded with patience, good humor and an accompaniment somewhere between Mardi Gras and the Salvation Army.

The track "Wheely Down" was inspired by a road sign I'd spotted on our way back from the Bath Festival the previous year. It's too good a place name not to have a song written about it. I used a trick learned from a David Bedford classical piece that Ashley and I had seen a few years before, "18 Bricks Left on April 21st." This is a piece for two electric guitars, and at one point the guitars are laid flat on the floor and a milk bottle is gently rocked back and forth over the pickups. This gives a surprisingly wide range of random notes and noises.

"The Angels Took My Racehorse Away" is one of the songs I demoed for Mercury—and they still wanted to sign me! They must have thought I was raving mad, or at least raving eccentric. The song featured an exotic blend of Chuck Berry-style guitar riffs and melodies from a Highland reel. Linda and Sandy sang some nice back-ups. The songwriting process started with the name of one of the oldest sporting trophies in Britain, the Lanark Silver Bell, and fantasized on from there.

It may have been Ashley who got me into reading Thomas Hardy's novels. I had read a couple at school as set books, and that can sometimes prejudice you against almost anything, but I picked up where I left off and now read the rest. They began to seep into my dream life and songwriting. The theme of "The Poor Ditching Boy" might fail to make sense unless seen in that context, although melodically it's very Scottish. The dulcimer of Andy Roberts and the fiddle of Sue Draheim add drone and lilt.

So many of these songs had traditional roots, with a tougher rhythm applied, and more contemporary references. I was happy with the songs and happy with the style, but as a singer, I wasn't there yet. I had a thin tone, no nuance to my voice, and should have sought out a vocal coach back in 1967. But on the theory that the author always has an amount of credibility when singing his own work, I figured I might get away with it. Randy Newman, Noël Coward, Hoagy Carmichael, Ry Cooder, Leonard Cohen—I liked them all as singers, even though they might not be considered A-list by critics or public.

Something I forgot to do was to play more electric guitar on this record. If I had to do it over again, I would have it on nearly every track. I was concentrating so much on the songs, and on the album as a song statement, that it barely crossed my mind.

For the cover, Annie Sullivan, the Island art director, considered the title and thought that she had the ideal setting. We went out to Pampisford Hall near Cambridge, a beautiful old stately home fallen on hard times—hard enough that they would rent it out to hippie musicians for photo shoots. I reincarnated as Henry the Human Fly, surrounded by bizarre antiques and hand-me-downs from the extensive collection of continental ceramics and furniture. The house had a stunning arboretum, and the lord of the manor was slinking about, looking like the weight of the house was resting on his shoulders. The eccentricity of the cover matches the eccentricity of the music and the surrealism of the liner notes, leading me to believe that . . . perhaps I was eccentric? Better that than boring, I suppose. Apart from something lacking in the vocal department, I was quite proud of my first solo foray. I was interested to see what people would make of it.

Henry the Human Fly was released to universal indifference. You never know how a record will be received. I had spent a year preparing, through writing, arranging and recording, and of course had hopes that people would "get" it, whatever the "it" was, though I didn't really know that myself. I thought I was making a record of contemporary songs based on the British tradition, and I knew that was still a leap for some listeners, who preferred their music from America, or distilled through American-sounding Brits. I could understand that the vocals would put people off, but there were stylistic issues as well, which still kept me on the margins of popular music. I was happy to live with that because I thought what I was doing was original. I wanted to be successful, but if I wasn't, I could find perverse comfort in that. I could say my music was too good for the masses, and have something to complain about.

Linda and I had moved in together, sharing a flat on Thurlow Road, Hampstead, with Robin Gee and his girl-friend, Pamela. When it became available, we moved one floor down to the middle flat and remained there for a good few years. The rent was controlled, it was surprisingly quiet and it was handy for the bottom of the M1 motorway and the Tube into Central London. In Hampstead, you could see Peter O'Toole striding down to the Tube station or run into Judi Dench in the greengrocer's. I often saw Peter Cook buying his paper at the newsagent's. He would routinely ask, "Who the hell are you, then?" To which I would mumble my name, and some excuse for living, and say how much I enjoyed his work. "Never heard of you!" he would say dismissively, and disappear down the high street. This happened many times, and he never remembered a previous meeting. After a pleasant night drinking at the Spaniards Inn, the haunt of highway-men, I even dreamed of Hampstead.*

I WAS WORKING a lot with Sandy and Iain, and Linda was doing demos and planning a more commercial musical career. It was a wrench to spend time apart, sometimes for months. It occurred to us that we would see more of each other if we worked together, and one place where we could work and earn a living at that point was the folk clubs. Linda had done

* See Appendix B, p. 277.

all that already with Paul McNeill, so she wasn't thrilled at the prospect, but it did make sense, and it didn't necessarily jeopardize any other career plans—it just put them on hold for a while. I was fairly unimpressed with Linda's manager at the time, who was a lovely guy but seemed clueless and inexperienced. I thought she was being wasted on pie-in-the-sky dreams, with people trying to mold her into a pop singer, and if I could drag her away from that, I might be doing her a favor—or so I thought in my idealistic way.

I gave in my notice to Sandy, who screamed at me for five minutes, upset that I would leave her and work for her best friend, and in her mind perhaps rival, but a week later she was fine and all was friendly. We had no manager, but took on an agent, Jean Davenport, the ex-wife of traditional singer Bob Davenport. Jean would phone most days with offers of bookings, our diary filled up, and in June 1972, off we went around Britain.

British folk clubs evolved into what they were in the 1970s through an historical succession of circumstances. The first major revival of traditional music had happened at the turn of the twentieth century, with figures like Cecil Sharp and Lucy Broadwood, and composers like Ralph Vaughan Williams and Percy Grainger, going out into the countryside and noting down, or recording on cylinder, folk songs from working people. This they considered a matter of some urgency, as they feared that industrialization would be the death of the old traditions. They were as interested in dance as they were in song, and paid little attention to music from urban or industrial areas. This led to the establishment of archives of folk song, English folk music being taught in schools and English composers using folk themes in a classical setting. In true Victorian fashion, they did clean it all up, leaving out the bawdy and risqué.

The second revival came off the back of the skiffle craze in the 1950s, a uniquely British phenomenon, home-made music that could be rendered with a guitar, a washboard and a tea-chest bass—a mixture of jug band and American folk and blues singers like Leadbelly and Woody Guthrie. Skiffle was a big influence on British rock and roll and the beat boom, and clubs emerged as venues in which to hear and play the music. Ewan MacColl and Bert Lloyd formed the Ballad and Blues Club in the mid-fifties, and soon were trying to encourage more home-grown music as a way of counterbalancing the American influence. They promoted British folk songs, and at some point created a policy that in their club you could only sing songs from your own culture, in your own accent. Many more clubs sprang up, with widely varying ideas of what should or should not be played, and by the 1960s there were around three hundred in the UK. Many of them booked guests. This was to be our bread and butter for the next year.

Most clubs were weekly, and met in the function room of a pub. There were exceptions, but by and large folk clubs stuck to a formula. The resident singer, often also the club organizer, would kick things off with a song or two, followed by "floor singers"—anyone in the audience who wanted to perform, usually by prior arrangement. The main guest would then do half an hour. After an interval, perhaps the resident would sing again, more singers from the floor, then the raffle—usually an LP as the prize—and the profits from that would help pay for club expenses. Then the headliner for another half-hour. Encores were permitted in some clubs, while others thought it a bit bourgeois. A typically blunt pre-encore announcement might be: "All right, stop that clapping, you lot! If you promise to return your glasses to the bar downstairs, you can have another one. Right . . . here he is."

The formula works really well. Headliners are never allowed to get too big for their boots; amateur singers of all levels, old hands to beginners, get a chance to play in front of an audience, in many cases gaining vital experience, and everyone gets to sing on choruses. Some clubs in 1972 had PAs, some did not, so you had to reach the back of the room somehow, which was more valuable experience for me.

After years of playing on stage, I was still very self-conscious, but this was where shyness had to come to a full, dead stop. Confidence finally enveloped me, and it was playing in folk clubs that did it, because there was no hiding at the back—there was no back, there was no front, there was barely a stage, and if there was one, it was about three inches high. You were an equal with the audience, no more. They might be a foot from your face. No place here for shyness, or arrogance or pretension, because you would be found out and judged. It was all very socialist.

We travelled to our first couple of clubs by train. If Martin Carthy did it, why couldn't we? It was difficult, changing trains, being picked up by the promoter; it took hours. So then Linda drove, and we did that for a while, but it was a strain having one driver, and at the late age of twenty-three I took a driving test. It was fun, having always been in bands, to feel independent, playing music and getting paid cash in hand, driving ourselves around and getting a great response from audiences. At the end of the day, though, there was no one to complain to about the inevitable small setbacks and disappointments except each other, and so on days off we would try to create some space and see other friends.

Linda's parents lived in Glasgow. Her mum, Betty, was a salt-of-the-earth type from the Gorbals, and at one point had been a dancer. She never lost her love of show business, and would embarrass everyone except herself by hailing a celebrity if she chanced upon one in the street. Her influence on her children must have been considerable, because Linda and her brother Brian were both childhood actors, who appeared on TV in the adaptation of A. J. Cronin's *Dr. Finlay's Casebook*. Brian Pettifer has had a long and successful career as a character actor, recently completing the circle by playing senior partner Dr. Cameron in the radio adaptation of *Dr. Finlay*.

Linda's father, Harry, was from humble East End of London origins, and described bouncing his neighbors the Kray twins on his knee when they were babies. Harry dealt in used cars, and his disclosures to the purchaser may not always have been scrupulously honest. He insisted that if we were doing a lot of touring, we get a "proper" motor. He found a Mercedes 220 at auction, and this was to be our chariot for the next year. It was a bit grand for pulling up to a folk club. The bodywork would notoriously rust on these cars, and after a month or so the paintwork on ours bubbled, revealing a lot of body filler. The engine became noisy, and was on its last lap, but it was fun while it lasted. We bought more cars from Harry over the years, usually sourced from dodgy auctions, and they were fine for six months, before they fell to bits.

We played two or three clubs a week, sometimes more. Having some reputation from the Fairport days, we had good crowds from the outset. We would sing our own compositions and a mixture of covers, some traditional, some country or rock. We harmonized a cappella on "Napoleon's Dream," a song we had learned from a recording by Sam Larner. We covered "The Wild Side of Life" by Hank Thompson (perhaps a distant relative?), and I wrote songs like "Dragging the River," which was very music hall-influenced. It went down well, we almost always got rebooked, and in some cases we were back at the same club three months later. We were getting paid about £50 a night, and that sometimes went up to £100. Petrol was about 30p a gallon. We rarely stayed in hotels, usually crashing in the promoter's spare room or that of a fellow musician. Our expenses were minimal, our rent was small—in comparative terms, I'm not sure I've ever felt as wealthy.

We met some real characters on the folk scene, many of whom became friends, and a few, like Billy Connolly, went on to greater things. Alistair Anderson, the great Northumbrian piper and concertina player, was a born teacher, and would sit patiently but firmly teaching me dance tunes. Luke Kelly from the Dubliners was living in London at the time, and it was wonderful to get to know him better—he was such a warm, gifted, loving and unpretentious human being who left his mark on so many people. The Glaswegian Alex Campbell was another extraordinary person who impressed me endlessly with his compassion and humanity. He and Luke always encouraged me musically, and they felt like big brothers to me—fellows who would stand up and fight for you in the playground.

If there was a negative to the whole scene, it was the back-stabbing. Having come from the very supportive environment of the London underground, where people would rarely say a bad thing about another act, I was shocked at the bitchiness in the folk world, and often it seemed rooted in jealousy. Sometimes a performer, often a comedian, would get a break and move on to a bigger audience and a more commercially successful career—like Jasper Carrott and Billy Connolly. Barbara Dickson and Isla St. Clair also started out in folk clubs. They could be treated like Judases, betrayers of some ideal, some egalitarian principle. In some people's minds, the clubs were exclusively for working-class music, and there were many interpretations of what that might be. In truth, after the early 1960s, they were venues for entertainment, where traditional music was a strong element, but you would also find singer-songwriters of every description, and people to make you laugh. Connolly started out as a funny banjo player, but evolved into a comedian who played a bit of banjo on the side. In spite of the formulaic program, there were many types of clubs, and a club in Kew, on the outskirts of London, was very different in intent from a club in Hull, in Yorkshire.

Speaking of Kew, if we were playing there, or in nearby Richmond, we would often be heckled by a familiar plummy voice: "Dear boy! How wonderful to see you! I brought my ukulele with me—do you mind if I sit in?" And from the back of the room, the eccentric form of Vivian Stanshall would appear. I knew Vivian from his days in the Bonzo Dog Doo-Dah Band, one of the funniest acts I ever saw. We shared many a bill with them, and I got to know Vivian through Andy Roberts and through Robin Gee's former girlfriend Pamela, who would marry Viv in 1980. He did countless voiceovers for ads on British TV, having total mastery of the "posh" version of English, so people knew him even if they didn't know him. I once went round to his house in East Finchley, and on opening the fridge to get some milk for the tea, found a dead terrapin. This had been his son Rupert's pet, but when it died, Vivian couldn't bring himself to break the news, so he kept it refrigerated and brought it out for "playtime." This speaks of both Viv's extreme sensitivity and his inability to deal with the world.

At our shows, Viv would jump up on stage, dressed like a psychedelicized Victorian gentleman in smoking jacket and fez, and sing and play the ukulele. That would be the end of the show as far as we were concerned. The evening would dissolve in wave after wave of hysterical laughter, and once he started, there was no getting him off stage again, not that we would have wanted to. He lived on a houseboat moored on the Thames. When he moved to Bristol, he lived on a converted minesweeper, a suitably eccentric berth.

Between touring, I enjoyed getting to know Linda's family.

They seemed a lively and tight-knit bunch, and I would go to working men's clubs with them in London, and casinos in Glasgow. When her parents moved down to London, we would stay with Linda's Uncle George down on the Pollokshaws Road in Glasgow. George worked on the docks, but was someone I could talk to about my inquiries into spiritual matters, as he had similar interests himself. We would have long discussions about all things esoteric, and I would regale him with my latest occult discoveries at Watkins Books, whether Ouspensky, the Kabala, Rosicrucianism or Subud, most of which he was well familiar with already.

We spent a lot of time in Glasgow that year, and I got to know and love it, appreciating the architecture of Charles Rennie Mackintosh, visiting the Citizens Theatre and the fine snooker hall on Sauchiehall Street, and treating it like a second home. My own family was from there a couple of generations back.

On a fine October morning, Linda and I got married in Hampstead Town Hall. She was resplendent in white. Robin as best man wore top hat and tails. I got most of it right. I rented the outfit from Moss Bros, but forgot about the shoes. Come the morning of the wedding, and after an alcoholic stag night, I was having trouble finding a pair of black shoes—I couldn't get married in sneakers. The only black footwear in the cupboard was Lancashire clogs, good for working in the mill or indeed in a restaurant, but not first choice for weddings. I clattered my way in and out of the registry office. We had the reception in a local Italian restaurant, mostly for family—there were few friends. I realized that I was more used to seeing Linda's family than my own. As usual, I was embarrassed to be the center of attention, and had probably talked the whole event down to the bare minimum of ceremonies, but I was proud to be musically and romantically entwined with Linda, and I was building another pile of songs that needed an outlet. We began to think about recording again.

12

Bright Lights

*There are times in life to play it safe. I'm sure you can
think of several. Music is not one of them.*

DEKE SHARON

AFTER A YEAR of playing folk clubs and thoroughly enjoying the experience, Linda and I were realizing that our career
was going round in circles, instead of going in a more desir-
able upward spiral. There was a cultural and numerical gap
between a folk club and a theatre that was not easily leapt. We
looked at options. The logical move was to take on a manager,
but there were very few choices. The name that kept coming
up, indeed had been coming up since Joe Boyd had made the
suggestion as a potential alternative to himself back in 1968,
was Jo Lustig.

Jo had a reputation as a hard-nosed American, screaming down the phone at agents and record companies, not
well loved, but respected for making a difference and getting
the job done. Fairport's hesitation then, and our hesitation
now, was all about this image. Was this how we wanted to
be represented to the world? We were unimpressed with the
alternatives, who all seemed flawed one way or the other, and
we took Jo on.

Jo was from Brooklyn and had grown up with John Cassavetes and Mel Brooks, whose films he distributed in the UK. He had worked for George Wein, who ran the Newport folk and jazz festivals in the US and had been a tour manager with some impressive jazz names, including Miles Davis. He came to England with Nat King Cole, met his future wife Dee, a former Miss Cambridge, and decided to stay in the UK and go into management. He had a lot of success with Julie Felix, Pentangle and then Steeleye Span, and several other luminaries of the folk world passed through his hands. Dee handled the day-to-day running of the office. People's opinions of Jo were not misplaced, but there was a softer side to him as well. Beneath the tough, utterly unforgiving exterior, there was the odd glimpse of the Brooklyn kid who had fallen in love with music.

Jo gradually took us out of the folk scene and into bigger theatres and clubs. The leap of faith in bridging that gap was one that Jo was happy to make—as he had made it for others before us. Our next phase would include touring with an electric band and making a new album.

During the mixing sessions for *Henry the Human Fly*, I had jotted down a couple of pages of song titles. Every song on our next record had started with the title first, inspired by that list. We now had an album's worth of songs ready to record. I think I wrote all of them sitting on the floor at the bottom of the bed in the flat on Thurlow Road. Sometimes you just find a spot that works for you. A couple of pillows to cushion the coccyx, a window to gaze out of blankly from time to time, several cold cups of tea lying around all made for a creative environment, apparently. Parents, partners and friends rarely understand that staring blankly out of the window is an important part of the creative process, and only occasionally an excuse for doing nothing. I had been listening to a lot of the field recordings that Alan Lomax made in Britain and Ireland in the 1950s; they were my driving music to and from gigs—it drove Linda to distraction but they helped me gain a deeper understanding of the tradition and were a big influence on my writing.

I was losing count of the number of projects I had been a part of at Sound Techniques studio. I did five with Fairport, then the solo record, and many other albums and sessions. The good thing about that was that, like Motown or Muscle Shoals, a lot of the sound was already dialed in. You knew roughly what the drums and bass would sound like, you knew where to place every instrument for optimum results, where to put the vocalist. This saved hours of preparation and freed everyone up to enjoy more creative time.

We cut basic tracks for *I Want to See the Bright Lights Tonight* with Pat and Timi in a few days in the spring of 1973. Sometimes I think you get lucky in the studio. Tracks go down in just a handful of takes, there are no major arrangement issues, the keys all work for singing and it sounds remarkably like music coming back off the tape. Sometimes you get that one track that is obstinate and wants to hold up the whole project. You leave it and come back to it, even once a day for a week, until finally you crack it or it cracks you. I've never had the budgets to indulge too much, but you hear stories of single songs taking months—but that is a different mindset to recording. The tracks went well, and the overdubs were quick.

It is also rewarding when something that you heard in your head, in your dreams, in your fantasies, comes to be a real piece of music, performed by others and down on tape, as solid as music is capable of being.

One of my favorite bands at the time was Gryphon, who combined rock music with early European music, recognizing a similarity between the styles—rhythmic, aggressive, pungent, basic. We used two members, Richard Harvey and Brian Gulland, who played crumhorns on "We Sing Hallelujah" and "When I Get to the Border." Crumhorns are double-reeded, similar to an oboe but with a lot less flexibility. It is a distinctive sound, and once heard, not easily forgotten, even if you want to.

"When I Get to the Border" opens the album, and again is a kind of statement of intent, this time not lyrically but instrumentally. There is a back-and-forth conversation at the end between the accordion, hammered dulcimer, mandolin, two crumhorns, penny whistle and electric guitar. I was trying to suggest that the electric guitar could live seamlessly in the company of the other instruments, swapping phrases, joining in unison, extemporising where possible. I was still on a mission.

All the electric guitar was overdubbed on this record, as it was on *Henry*. We had done almost everything live with Fairport, except maybe the vocals, but I played rhythm on the basic tracks, to save money more than anything. This needed to be a cheap record—in the end it cost the princely sum of £2,500 to make, a tiny budget even for the period. "The Great Valerio" was the last song recorded, and it is mostly just acoustic guitar and bass. Hammered dulcimer comes in at the end, where we tagged on an Erik Satie piece, "La balançoire," from *Sports et divertissements*. The end of an album is always interesting—do you taper off (as I often do) or keep up the energy? "Tomorrow Never Knows" is a great high-energy closer on *Revolver*. It's also opening the listener to a whole new aural experience—the first use of a looped rhythm track, backwards guitar, heavily modified vocal sound. I think our final track, "Valerio," leaves the listener dangling, which isn't a terrible thing. It is the other musical choice, the opposite of resolution, with which one would finish a symphony. It is the opposite of emphatic, in some ways the opposite of satisfying, but I see lack of resolution as almost poetic, as keeping the questions coming, as keeping the listener returning for another crack at tying the strands together.

I've always loved the sound of brass and silver bands, and we had a song that seemed to cry out for the addition of at least a brass quintet. The British tradition gained strength from around 1800 and was very much tied to the Industrial Revolution. Every major coal mine, mill or steel works would have its own band, and there would be keen competition. As a kid you would hear them on the bandstand in parks on a Sunday afternoon. The BBC had a long-running brass band program, and the sound was part of the British landscape, but it was the Northern bands that seemed to excel at that time, and the CWS Band from Manchester, in 1973, was about the hottest in the land.

We drove up to Stockport, on the edge of Manchester, where the band 10cc had their studio, and we gathered five

CWS players to overdub onto "I Want to See the Bright Lights Tonight." Why that particular song? It has the line "There's a silver band just marching up and down," so why not reinforce that idea? I nervously wrote out a horn chart—these were excellent musicians, including one of the great players of his generation on first cornet, Derek Garside, and I didn't want to make mistakes and be judged as too young, too Southern and "soft," or too incompetent.

After arriving early and fruitlessly wandering around Stockport looking for sustenance ("On a Sunday? You must be joking!"), we got down to business. The brass players were excellent, and we got what we came for, except for the introductory four bars, which would not sit in tempo. That part of the arrangement is on the cutting-room floor somewhere, and the guitar brings the track in instead.

This album shows Linda at her finest as a singer. Sandy always seemed the finished product, and you never had to question her interpretation. Linda had a simpler but no less effective style. She was more open to discussion and experimentation, and would willingly take suggestions. I found it refreshing to talk about songs—what they meant and how they could be interpreted—with the person who was going to sing them. It was real collaboration, and that was a change from the 1960s, when we were all a lot less forthcoming about our creative output. Maybe we were just young then, and not ready to open up.

The record was mixed and finished in the spring of 1973, but it took a year to release it. There was a vinyl shortage at the time, and that was the reason we were given for the delay, but other acts on Island were having their records released. If it was just a pecking order, dictated by who was selling the most records, I could have accepted that, but there was more going on. Our A&R man at the company, whom I never met, came from the world of R&B and had no interest in what we were doing. He saw no virtue in the record, didn't like "folkie" stuff and was happy not to release it. When he finally moved on and a new A&R came in, suddenly, hey presto! We had a release date a few months later. "Bright Lights" came out as a single in the UK and scraped into the bottom of the Top 40.

Folk rock in the UK was a declining force by 1973, and it would never be mainstream. When we made *Liege & Lief* in 1969, I suppose we thought it would tap into something, some race memory of the British people that had been sleeping for generations, and that at last they would recognize their own music and take it to heart. But there was a lot of prejudice to overcome. The niche remained a niche. Pentangle, Fairport, Steeleye, the Albion Band, Sandy, Five Hand Reel and a few others maintained an audience with broad-minded folkies and adventurous rockers, but styles and fashions were changing. Progressive rock was becoming the dominant force in the album market, along with early incarnations of metal, while glam rock dominated the singles charts. This was the year that Pink Floyd released *The Dark Side of the Moon*, Led Zeppelin released *Houses of the Holy* and the Who were pioneering arena rock. Steeleye Span glammed up a bit and hit the charts with traditional music, but the way it was received was disappointing. Steeleye's "All Around My Hat" speaks of a bygone era, a rural world of courting farmworkers, still relevant by the Edwardian age but lost after the First World War. It would have no resonance for the *Top of the Pops* audience, who therefore treated it as a novelty song, in there with Rolf Harris and Clive Dunn. Perhaps a grittier industrial song would have spoken more to the political unrest of the day and had a deeper effect on public taste? Mike Oldfield had a hit with a tune from John Playford's seventeenth-century collection *The English Dancing Master*, the catchy "Portsmouth," and it was bizarre to see the all-girl dance group Legs & Co. on *Top of the Pops* doing a saucy interpretation of what they thought a sailor's hornpipe should look like. It seemed like another example of British pop culture looking down on and parodying its own tradition.

There were still a lot of colleges on our date sheet, but these began to dry up as the government subsidies diminished, and in the eyes of students we became musicians of a previous generation. The economics of Britain were changing. The oil crisis caused by OPEC countries reducing their output had the effect of quadrupling the price of petrol, and petrol rationing meant queuing for an hour to get your allotted gallon—tough on many professions, including the touring musician. Inflation was insane, causing many unions to strike for pay raises. Power cuts and transport strikes were common. The three-day week was designed to conserve fuel; the lasting effect of it demonstrated that people could achieve the same output in three days as in five, which did not send the right political message. Britain's labour relations had been in a mess since the Second World War, and now, compounded by external crises, the country was caught in a class war, which would reach a climax with the miners' strike of 1984.

Despite this difficult time of transition in the music business, our career was on the up. Linda and I were working now sometimes as a trio with my old bandmate Simon Nicol, who at this point was not involved in Fairport. This gave me more flexibility as a guitarist—I could take solos without having to keep the tempo and chord structure at the same time. Jo Lustig was able to book us into bigger venues as we finished the remainder of our folk club gigs. Yet there was a familiar ache inside me that never really went away, no matter how much I distracted myself. I needed to fill the void in the pit of my stomach, and not with numbness, but with nourishment.

13

The Strangers

Abu Huraira reported: The Messenger of Allah,
peace and blessings be upon him, said:
Islam began as something strange and it will return
to being strange, so blessed are the strangers.

SINCE MY SCHOOL days, reality had been a puzzle to me, and existence a riddle that I could not decode. I had had early experiences of seeing and feeling ghosts and other unexplained phenomena. This led me to think that perhaps, rather than these being illusions, it was not a mechanistic universe, as traditional Cartesian science would have it, but something far more subtle, complex and even intelligent. It was impossible to step outside of the universe to understand its origins and purpose by direct observation, so I had to believe—either in science or in an intelligent creator. Reading about the subatomic world convinced me that the universe was a construct, a giant Meccano set—but who built it, and why? Morality seemed to be very important in this world too. Why all the duality, why all the good versus evil?

My bookshelf back at Thurlow Road was groaning with esoterica I had purchased from Watkins bookshop, alongside the usual books of ballads, dance tunes and orchestral scores, and more current reading matter—John Michell's *The View over Atlantis,* Colin Wilson's *The Outsider,* David Lindsay's reprinted *The Haunted Woman* and *A Voyage to Arcturus,* all books searching for answers in their own ways.

I had paused in my trek through the shelves of Watkins at the letter "S." The Sufis were much quoted elsewhere: Sufism as an influence on the Kabal, as being that which Rumi taught, as being a thing that certain Western groups in the US and Britain practiced, with varying degrees of authenticity. I had, over the years, read books by Pir Vilayat Khan and the Englishman Reshad Feild, who I was intrigued to find out was a former member of the Springfields vocal group, alongside Dusty. I was also reading stories about Nasruddin, a kind of Middle Eastern folk hero. Much of the content of these books struck me as Zen-like—cryptic as poetry is cryptic, hinting at something greater where words fail. I learned that the real Sufis were spread throughout the Islamic world and fell into various sects. I wanted to find out more about them, but it remained a thought only. At the same time, I was developing a love for things Middle Eastern, as I romanticized the world described by Gurdjieff and Ouspensky, Richard Burton and T. E. Lawrence.

I was becoming an orientalist. I filled our flat in Hampstead with Indian and Egyptian furniture bought cheaply from Portobello Road market. A friend of my sister's, Leon Norell, had an oriental carpet warehouse in Kentish Town, and he gave me great prices on rugs. At one point I asked him if he had any Belouch kilims, and he dug out a bale that had never been opened, dating from about 1880. I bought two of the exquisite, pristine rugs from that bale, and it set something

off in me. I had a hankering to become a carpet dealer, travel-
ling the Middle East looking for what was fast becoming a lost
world, the world before the fall of the Ottoman Empire. I was
drawn to photographs and paintings of mosques, souks, bath
houses, port scenes, pilgrims, Berber encampments. I found
it romantic, as Burton and Lawrence had found it romantic,
but there was a nobility there, and a pre-industrial, pre-West-
ernized quality of life and of being that was discernible in the
images. This was all in my head. Practically, I did nothing
except acquire furniture and more books, and continue my
life as a working musician.

As can happen in life—if one is fortunate—what I was
looking for, but was too distracted to seek out, came to me.
In *Time Out* magazine, there was an ad for a Sufi meeting in
a church hall in Belsize Park. I was not working that night. I
went along to watch. It was three hundred yards from my flat.

The thirty-odd participants, men and women, were singing
what was clearly a work of devotion, in unison, without accompaniment. A couple of followers were passing round cups of
mint tea. It was intense but loose, and in no way precious. As
I sat on the outer fringes, I began to recognize faces. There
was Ian Whiteman, Roger Powell and Mike Evans, all from
Mighty Baby, whom I had played many sessions with. There
was Peter Sanders, who had taken many live photographs of
Fairport. They smiled in recognition. As the intensity built,
the whole assembly got to their feet and performed a kind of
dance in a circle, in which the intense, rhythmic breathing
seemed to be important.

Afterwards, we sat and chatted and drank more tea,

and caught up. I told them about all that had led me to that meeting—reading Reshad Feild, Pir Vilayat Khan, tales of Nasruddin—but they looked blankly at me, as if unfamiliar with anything I was referring to. They invited me for lunch the next day at their zawiyya (literally a corner—a Sufi center). The food was delicious, and the room we ate in seemed to have some magnetic force, like standing next to a meteorite.

I visited often and felt at home there. I attended more nights of dhikr (invocation). It was explained to me, and I really had not figured it out, that Sufism was the inner core of Islam. I started practicing the prayer, collectively or on a borrowed prayer mat at home, and with the first prostration realized that this was something I had wanted to do my whole life—surrender, submit, hand over to the universe my ego, my conflicts, my troubles. Someone said that water takes on the color of the glass into which it is poured; a Christian glass, a Buddhist glass, a Muslim glass—the same water, just the outside trappings and methods are different. This all seemed to me like coming home after a long journey. There was no conversion, as you would change your dollars into euros, just affirmation that this was who I had always been, and this was the relationship with the universe I had always had. Linda followed me into Islam a few months later, and I hoped it was because her heart called her to it, and not out of fear of losing me, or from being persuaded by the extraordinary women at the zawiyya.

This London group were followers of Shaykh Muhammad ibn-al Habib of Meknes in Morocco. The shaykh had recently died, and a successor had not been named. The London zawiyya had mostly English and Americans, but there were reputed to be seventy thousand adherents around the world. He traced his lineage, saint by saint, back to the Prophet Muhammad—peace and blessings on him.

I had never thought of myself as an alcoholic, but my consumption had risen as the years went by, and for a year I had been drinking solitarily and secretly. Still, at twenty-three, I thought I was indestructible. When I started praying, I gave up drinking immediately—stopped on a sixpence. I no longer felt a craving for it nor missed the camaraderie of the pub, and I didn't need it as a crutch to get me through social interaction or a musical performance. I used to drink to fill a chasm, that old empty feeling inside, which was a spiritual emptiness, and when I filled that, I had no need of anything else.

With a radical change to my worldview, many friends fell by the wayside. People would drop by Thurlow Road as they had always done, but it now felt awkward and strained—I did not know what to say. Some were bemused by the change in me and would humor or avoid me—it was too painful for them, and sometimes too painful for me, to coexist in the old way. I realized that I had only spent time with some friends while drinking. Sober, I didn't really have much in common with them. I found solace in the Sufis, who were also musicians and who understood both worlds. They tended to be down-to-earth and not sanctimonious. They also had a sense of humor. I, meanwhile, was unbalanced, thrown off-kilter by my beliefs. It would take me a year or two to realize that I was not part of a superior club, but that everyone was on a journey, everyone had struggles in life, and those that I'd considered the good guys sometimes were not, while the bad guys weren't all bad.

MEANWHILE, I WAS a musician, and there were more mouths to be fed. Linda had gone through a fairly routine pregnancy and had given birth to our daughter Muna a few months earlier, in Middlesex Hospital. I was in the room for most of the time, but I was thrown out for the last twenty minutes—I think Linda felt she couldn't let rip and scream her head off with me there. It was wonderful to start a family, but my fear all through the pregnancy had been that this would curtail our career together for the next year or two. I would have to become a guitar for hire again to pay the rent. We still had dates booked, starting in just a few months' time, and how would we manage that? Linda's mother Betty stepped into the breach. She was thrilled to be a grandmother, and was happy to help out in any way. She came with us on the road at first, and would babysit backstage during the shows. This still didn't give Linda much of a rest, so when it became more practical, we would leave the baby at home with Betty for the evening.

We were working as hard as ever, still doing both duo gigs and the trio with Simon, and for a good chunk of the year we added bass and drums. Our extensive autumn touring, which covered much of October, November and December, was compromised at the outset by the lack of a rhythm section— for some reason, those we had counted on dropped out, and we had to scramble. We were able to recruit an acolyte of DM's on drums, Willie Murray, who kept good time, although he was never as masterful as his hero. He was a very funny, like-able man and an excellent photographer who went on to work for *Playboy*. His chat-up line was second to none, as he pulled out his "*Playboy* Talent Scout" business card. Steve Borrell, the bass player, came from the progressive band Spirogyra, and used the drive from London to Dundee to learn the set, which he did admirably.

Linda and I also kept recording. Our next album, *Hokey Pokey*, straddled two worlds. I was very influenced at that time by music hall, British variety theatre, which was mostly from my grandparents' generation. Much of it was well known and loved, but I took pleasure in researching and digging out more neglected masterpieces. I think it appealed to me in the same way that traditional music appealed—it was home-grown, and it was just at the point of being culturally sidelined. Some of the stars had been captured on record at the end of their careers, some not, but there were books of sheet music and records going all the way back to the 1840s. Some acts, such as Stanley Holloway, Gracie Fields and George Formby Jr., started their careers at the end of the music hall era and went on to be film stars. A lot of the songs were still occasionally sung on radio and TV, but might perish with our grannies. When I was a teenager, part of the school's outreach program was to visit retirement homes and provide entertainment. I would take my guitar and kick off with something familiar like "The Old Bull and Bush," and then they would take over with no prompting and sing non-stop for an hour. Such was the percolation down through the generations that I rarely heard a song I did not know.

I bought a lot of Formby records from flea markets. Aside from being very funny in a cheeky, risqué way, he was also a formidable ukulele player, and had a wonderful way of syncopating his strumming hand, overlapping his thumb and first finger. People think I'm kidding when I say my right-hand technique is influenced by George Formby, but it's true. I got heavily into Gracie Fields too, and the wonderful comic recitations of Stanley Holloway, many written by Marriott Edgar, like "The Lion and Albert." All of this colored the songs we were writing and the way we arranged them.

So one foot was in the world of music hall, folk and rock that we knew well. The other was in Andalusia. Part of Sufi practice is to gather and recite the Diwan of the Shaykh—basically songs of spiritual guidance and ecstasy. These are set to (usually) older tunes, some a thousand years old, from when the Moors ruled the southern half of Spain. This is called Andalusian music, and the remnants of it make up the classical music of Morocco, Algeria and Tunisia. Remnants because some of the science has been lost—only thirteen of the twenty-four modes remain. A man called Ziryab brought a science of music from Iraq, and another, ibn Bajjah, integrated it with Western styles. The different modes, arrangements and sequences of notes were designed to have a measured effect on the human heart. There are stories of music curing the insane and elevating men to spiritual heights. This music does not sound especially oriental; it is often in scales Westerners recognize. Some scholars argue that Andalus was a considerable influence on the medieval troubadours, lyrically and musically, and in turn influenced the trouvères and the Meistersingers, and so was disseminated across Europe. Singing it daily gave me a whole new strain of musical experience to absorb, and it took time to integrate it into the styles I already knew.

Of the recording sessions, I am left with flashes of memory, punctuation between the more routine hours of studio life. Adding brass players to two tracks; the joy of writing parts and hearing them come to life; the electric guitar on "Hokey Pokey," amp turned up to ten, one take, got it! "Never Again" revisiting the loss of Martin and Jeannie, a tribute, looking over the shoulder of my younger self, still feeling the pain of it eating my stomach; fantasizing on the repair man at Sound Techniques, turning his prosthetic eye into a song of playground bullying and misery; channelling Kurt Weill into a dark outtake from *Oliver!*, "The Sun Never Shines on the Poor"—hunger and poverty, it never rains, it pours; Sidonie Goossens, classical harpist, looking forty when she was seventy, serene, unflappable and effortlessly becoming one with whatever music was thrown at her.

The end result was a record with two personalities, pre- and post-Sufi, and it was hard to invest emotionally in some songs that had been written just a few months earlier. With almost every record we made, there was no second chance, no leaving it in the can to think it over, no possibility of scrapping it and starting again. The economics were tight and the release date was set in stone to coincide with the tour that was already booked. We had been lucky on *Bright Lights* that the ducks lined up a bit better. This felt scrappier, but our attitude was, "Oh well, that's the best we can do for now—on to the next one." We appeared on radio and TV promoting the single, "Hokey Pokey," still on pop shows, but we felt ancient, being all of twenty-five.

We had definitely left the 1960s behind. My haircut was short again, maxi skirts replaced minis, and classic rock and roll was already being recycled in the charts, a mere fifteen years later, by the likes of Shakin' Stevens and T. Rex. This was probably the year I stopped watching *Top of the Pops*. It just seemed to be more of the same. Pop music was eating itself. Folk continued to be more of an inspiration, along with a diet of jazz, classical and what would be termed "world music," but I was becoming distracted. My Sufi studies left me little room to write, and what was I going to write about? I felt like a child dipping my toe in the shallow surf of an ocean. Whatever quasi-wisdom I had acquired by the age of twenty-five suddenly felt inadequate. I was in many ways back to square one, searching for another way forward.

WE WENT BACK into Sound Techniques with John Wood, Pat Donaldson, Timi Donald, Dave Mattacks and Dave Pegg. Again, our budget was small, and I was increasingly distracted. There are divided opinions about music in the world of Islam, especially about rock music. I was coming under fire for merely playing in that form, regardless of the fact that the content was far removed from the theatrical darkness of a band like Black Sabbath. I thought our songs were open to quite a spiritual interpretation, and for me, music was like breathing—an everyday, beautiful, life-affirming activity—so why be puritanical about it? Why deny joy to others because you deny it to yourself? The criticism made us stronger.

We planned the recording to be stripped down, naked, nothing percolated through production filters to get in the way of raw emotion. *Pour Down like Silver* was recorded as a three-piece, occasionally a four-piece, with almost everything cut live. We redid some of Linda's vocals—since the *Hokey Pokey* record, she had been having difficulty singing, producing the actual notes, and this had been exacerbated by pregnancy and childbirth.

There were songs of loss—"For Shame of Doing Wrong," "The Poor Boy Is Taken Away." Why is there pleasure in such a song? Perhaps it is common human experience, and to sing about it, or to hear someone else sing about it, gives release to one's feelings, and maybe some healing. There were songs of yearning—"Dimming of the Day," "Beat the Retreat" and "Night Comes In." Secular love or spiritual love? I enjoyed the ambiguity. "Streets of Paradise" speaks about nirvana the quick way, the temporary way, with consequences. The song doesn't try to judge, because it's so tempting to take that road; we all want to get out of our minds and our bodies. There was a kind of improvised strathspey duet at the end between the accordion of John Kirkpatrick and my electric guitar. John was a frequent musical fellow traveller from *Morris On* onwards; it was always a joy to play with him, and he *almost* made the accordion a sexy instrument! I never worked very much with pianists—I felt that on the whole they occupied a lot of musical space, which I preferred to fill with guitar. The accordion in John's hands was a more delicate harmonic counterpoint. Besides numerous recordings, he was also a member of my touring band. He had an innate sense of swing in everything he did, was an excellent singer and songwriter (he wrote a wonderful song in the barely used Phrygian mode) and was inarguably the outstanding accordionist of his generation.

When we had finished recording the album, it seemed even more naked than we had intended, but anything overdubbed onto it sounded mismatched, and never felt integrated with the basic track. I didn't know how to move it further along, and so it was left as it was, a stark piece of music, warts and all. As a songwriter, I was now reflecting my new life, trying to speak to the audience in a language they would understand. I felt uncomfortable to be laying myself out naked, but after the obfuscation of the 1960s, hiding myself under layers like Nick and Sandy, I accepted that this was how it had to be at this moment, up front and in your face, like Otis Redding, like Percy Sledge, or the British suburban version of that, anyway.

WE TOURED HARD behind this record, as we had always done. If a record didn't sell, it wasn't going to be because we did not promote it to the best of our abilities. We had a great band—Mattacks, Pegg and Kirkpatrick—and toured the length and breadth of Britain, and also did a long tour of the Netherlands. The audience response was good, better in venues with a standing audience, slower when they were seated—on that tour I first noticed that even a crowd in their mid-twenties would start to get comfortable and passive when seated. But the energy of the response was falling away.

Island Records, like all record companies, went through regular personnel changes. Every couple of years, there seemed to be a night of the long knives, and your buddy in the

A&R department was gone, to be rehired weeks later by a rival company, and your new A&R didn't have a clue about your music. You put your head down and waited for the next purge and a better slice of luck. If you waited long enough, your original A&R guy might be rehired, having done the complete round of every company in town. Record companies tried to be an interface between creativity and commerce, which was a thankless task. If a couple of temperamental acts failed to finish their records in time for the quarterly accounts, the whole ship might founder. I could not tell at that point if we were out of step with Island or they were out of step with us. Music was sailing off in various directions, and we seemed to be in our own small world, making statements and exploring our own backwaters, to the general disregard of the music business and the rest of the world.

As a Muslim, pilgrimage to Mecca is recommended at least once in your lifetime, and that April, a group of us— three Americans, two Brits—decided it was a good time to make the journey. The politics of the Middle East never looked very stable, and who knew what future border closures and embargos might make the trip impossible. We were mostly in our twenties and thirties, but young Hassan, from our Bristol Gardens community, was only twelve. We were part of a larger group of thirty, mainly Pakistani British. When we got to Mecca, we learned that our guide was the former state executioner. He said that in thirteen years on the job, he had never had to behead anyone, but had cut a few hands off. This was clearly not a man to mess with. We had travelled without enough money to pay for everything, and could not pay for our Meccan accommodation. Our guide kindly let us sleep on a pile of rugs and plied us with mint tea.

The Haj basically consists of circumnavigating the Kaaba, a large granite cube, seven times, walking and running between two points, Safa and Marwa, throwing stones at pillars that represent Satan, and standing on the plain of Arafat, believing that it will be the final gathering place of mankind at the end of time. It takes six days to complete the whole ritual.

The foreknowledge that the Kaaba was stage-lit for full dramatic effect did not detract from the breathtaking other-worldliness of the first sight of it. It seemed to float and shimmer and change through the spectrum. The Haj is crowded, packed tight all the time. To stumble while circum-navigating the Kaaba can lead to being trampled, and several bloody bodies bore witness. To kiss the Black Stone set in the corner of the House is to connect with Adam, the first man, and the whole of humanity, but that's not always possi-ble. Still, the intention is enough. Some speak of the crowds miraculously parting to allow one to approach it, but that was not my experience. To go around an object seven times, to run between two points, to stand for a while in one place—all simple geometry, but somehow doing this washes one clean, like a man reborn. To symbolize this rebirth, our heads were shaved at the end of the Haj. There were many volunteers on hand to dry-shave us, with razors at hand, unnervingly wedged between twigs. One of our group was suffering from heat bumps on his head, which were remorselessly sliced off in the shaving process, leaving a score of blood trails trickling down his face. There was an outbreak of cholera—there always is. There was a fire that raced through the tents at Mina—there always is. A planeload of pilgrims crashed into the mountains—it always happens. I had the feeling that the Kaaba represented my own heart, and that the Haj was a journey to find that out, to travel two thousand miles only to meet my inner self.

After a week without a bath, we took a taxi the short distance to the Red Sea, dying for a swim. As we got out and headed for the beach, a car cruised by, with four Saudis inside. They wanted to buy young Hassan for sex. They had picked on the wrong group of pilgrims. After some brief fisticuffs, they drove away in a hurry. The beach wasn't exactly at a resort—it was near the port and was a bit oily—but we were desperate. From the pavement to the water was only about ten yards, but the sand was alive with insects, mostly cockroaches, about three deep and all running very fast. We crunched our way across and into the ocean. It felt good, as long as you didn't swallow or stick your head under. After ten minutes, the bloated, headless body of a camel floated by. We moved further along the beach, only to encounter the bloated, headless body of a sheep. Time to get out.

That night, we took a bus to Medina, the town of the first Muslim community, the burial place of the Prophet, peace and blessings on him. Here was sweetness and a bed, our budget stretching to a room to ourselves. We survived on cornflakes and powdered milk, and the occasional curry. In the little pharmacy, in search of aspirin, we found thalidomide on the shelf, fifteen years after it was banned in the UK. We stayed eight days, long enough to pray forty prayers and buy dates from the Prophet's orchard.

At Jeddah airport, the queue to get on a plane was halfway down the runway. We resigned ourselves to a long wait, but a group of soldiers took us out of line and marched us away. We thought we were being arrested, and we could think of several reasons why. Instead, they escorted us onto the first plane leaving for London and left us with a crisp salute. There was no explanation.

On the train from Gatwick to Central London, the passengers seemed neurotic and distracted after time spent with a million people focused on God. Complicated life, complicated trouble. Simple life, simple trouble. Saints spoke to me in my dreams; or sometimes things were more encoded.* I had to walk down Oxford Street the next day to buy a pair of trousers. It was a Saturday and the crowd was dense—but after the Haj, nothing ever seemed crowded again.

IT WAS GETTING harder to reconcile my musical life with my spiritual life—harder, but not impossible. I was more sensitive to things that I would have ignored before, and was wondering why I put up with other people's worldview and lack of a belief system. I was getting used to the company of the likeminded, and was becoming intolerant. But it was more the nature of the music world that was discouraging me from pursuing my chosen career. Folk rock was losing ground— not that it had that much ground to begin with. From being a

* See Appendix B, p. 279.

sideshow of popular music, we were now playing to an ageing audience that consumed less and went out to concerts less. Our allies at Island Records had left one by one, and eventually they dropped us.

My own songwriting was neither one thing nor another at this time, a bit like my life. I was failing to reconcile the British thread of me with the adopted North African thread in a way that made sense, and this was reflected in the musical no-man's-land of our next two albums.

I seemed to have traveled far from the innocent ideals and musical hopes of 1967. From being a schoolboy to becoming a professional musician to making records, all at the age of eighteen; the comradeship of the road, and tragedy and loss; marriage, children and responsibilities; and the realization that life was full of distractions to divert you from the best musical intentions. My life was rich and rewarding, and not without difficulties, but my musical focus had scattered to the winds. It wasn't a bad feeling. In some ways it was a relief not to be trying to invent a way forward. I would find something else to do. I sensed myself as if running on a treadmill, but whereas before I was grinding the corn and producing an end result, now the gears were disengaged and I was just spinning fruitlessly, spinning out of habit. I slowly ground to a halt.

14

Beeswing

When I had money, money, O!
My many friends proved all untrue;
But now I have no money, O!
My friends are real, though very few.

W. H. DAVIES

IN 1976, LINDA and I were living in Suffolk, in a thatched cottage of some antiquity near the village of Hoxne, at the end of a long, winding lane. Hoxne became famous later as the site of the discovery of an amazing hoard of late Roman treasures. The house was painted in the classic Suffolk pink, had a small pond with five Aylesbury ducks and enough garden space to allow a vegetable patch with potatoes, carrots and cabbages. We kept chickens—sixty-five at one point, which meant a lot of eggs, so we would sell the surplus to the post office-cum-shop in the village. Our daughter Muna was four and our son Teddy two, and it was an idyllic, safe spot for young children, apart from Teddy contriving to fall out of the upstairs window occasionally, to little effect—upstairs was barely five feet above the raised lawn. We shared the cottage with the owner sometimes, and sometimes with another family with children of similar age. A donkey in the field next door provided further entertainment. We would drive the kids the short distance to the coast, to visit towns like Aldeburgh and Southwold, land of my mother's forebears, and to breathe in a few inspirational molecules from the exhalations of Benjamin Britten.

A tramp used to call by, infrequently but regularly, every four or five months. His name was Ted, and he was always looking for any kind of manual work, in exchange for money or food. He was a pleasant man, tall and thin, perhaps sixty years of age, his clothes shabby but not ragged, and always with a half-smile, but with some pain and anxiety etched around his eyes, perhaps from the uncertainty and hardship of his lifestyle. We would set him to work in the garden, digging up potatoes or clearing away the endless nettles. We always put him up for a couple of days, giving us a chance to feed him and wash his clothes before sending him back on the road with a few quid in his pocket.

Ted had worked as a stable boy for much of his life, around the racing world in East Anglia. At some point, he had been thrown out of his work and accommodation, and had taken to the road in search of other employment. He said it was easy to slip through society's safety net, to lose one's papers, in his case accidentally, but for others deliberately, as a way to avoid debts and bad marriages. He had been a tramp for thirty years, but his goal was to settle—he dreamed of a caravan somewhere, and a little piece of land to grow food. A more modest dream I could not imagine. His stories about his life were extraordinary: rescuing horses from stable fires, the camaraderie and the dangers of an itinerant life—some men would share their last crust with you, some would take the few things you possessed and beat you. His was also a life without marriage, without any fulfilled relationship. The girl he loved as a young man let him down badly, and he never loved again.

WHEN I WAS on the road with Sandy, there was always downtime: waiting for the gear to be set up and the room tuned before sound check, waiting for a delayed flight in an airport, having a quiet (or noisy) drink after a show. We would talk about various things: fellow musicians and our admiration of them (or the opposite), music business hassles and convolutions (we were both generally inept at that side of things, although Sandy owned her own publishing), ambitions, goals, dreams and relationships—close and distant, lovers and friends. The late-night conversations were best, lubricated with a few G&Ts.

One of the people Sandy was closest to was the traditional singer Anne Briggs. Anne was a key figure in the folk revival of the early 1960s, spending her formative years with Bert Jansch and Johnny Moynihan, and being one of Bert Lloyd's favorite song interpreters. Sandy counted her as one of her two or three best friends. She wrote the song "The Pond and the Stream" about her—Sandy was the pond, stagnating in the city, Annie was the free-flowing spirit going where the current took her. Through Sandy's stories, I built up a picture of Anne, whom I had never met, as someone wild, impetuous, impossible to chain down. I was keen to meet her as she sounded quite intriguing, but the two times I had the chance—once backstage at the Roundhouse, once at Sandy's flat on Chipstead Street—she had already fallen sound asleep.

I never saw her play live, but I took great pleasure in catching up with her recordings, and Sandy's respect for her as a singer and interpreter was not misplaced. Her influence on Sandy was clear, but I think they admired and influenced each other.

When I started writing the song "Beeswing," many years later, I was making up a story. One line led to another, and I had no idea where the tale was going. It was like being seven years old again, placing one foot in front of the other, step by step, with my head in thick fog, unable to see my hand in front of me, not too concerned if I found my way to school or not.

Songwriting is a strange business, and those who claim to understand the creative process are usually uttering bullshit of the first magnitude. Robert Burns captured it best:

My way is: I consider the poetic sentiment, correspondent to my idea of the musical expression; then chuse my theme; begin one stanza; when that is composed—which is generally the most difficult part of the business—I walk out, sit down now and then, look out for objects in nature around me that are in unison or harmony with the cogitations of my fancy and workings of my bosom; humming every now and then the air with the verses I have framed. When I feel my Muse beginning to jade, I retire to the solitary fireside of my study, and there commit my effusions to paper, swinging, at intervals, on the hind legs of my elbow chair, by way of calling forth my own critical strictures, as my pen goes.

But what worked for Burns will not make a hoot of difference for others.

Or there is this from Beethoven:

You ask me where I get my ideas. That I cannot tell you with any certainty. They come unsummoned, directly, indirectly—I could seize them with my hands—out in the open air, in the woods, while walking, in the silence of the nights, at dawn, excited by moods that are translated by the poet into words, by me into tones that sound and roar and storm about me till I have set them down in notes.

At some point in the "Beeswing" process, I felt the story was taking me towards a reflection on the 1960s and 1970s. What I took for fiction seemed to have roots in Ted's itinerant life, and in Sandy's love of the freedom of Anne Briggs—people who left society behind because they had no choice, or because they wanted to. When the Who sang "My Generation" in 1965, it was angry, defiant, urban. Just a couple of years later, the mood was more about escaping society rather than confronting it head-on. A disturbingly large number of my school friends and acquaintances did not take the road well-traveled and head off to university, the true destiny of a William Ellis boy. They dropped out, got into drugs, sought out alternative lifestyles, lived in hippie communes in Denmark, went off around the world and never came back, carved out a life selling food or leather goods at festivals, never wore a tie again in their lives, and broadly rejected the path of normality. We heard of similar trends in North America, where it was easier to relocate to somewhere warm and sustaining and practice a different way of life, inspired by religion, or philosophy, or just a desire to be self-sufficient in every respect.

People shared houses or land, or did it solo. Most of those communities burned out in a year or two.

And here were Linda and I, out in rural Suffolk. We had moved there to be close to the Sufi community, which had relocated to East Anglia with the intention of buying some land and surviving by farming. There was talk of building houses with traditional wattle and daub construction, and going wind-powered and severing ties with the National Grid. It was a steep learning curve. Our biggest shortcoming was that we knew nothing about farming, so the sheep got infected with blowfly. It is romantic to think of building walls and putting roofs on, but less romantic digging foundations and finding somewhere for the sewage to go.

Various musicians I knew, or knew of, took to the road in some form or another. Vashti Bunyan did it with a gypsy caravan and horses. Nick Drake and his friends headed down to Aix-en-Provence; Wizz Jones, Alex Campbell, Davey Graham and others to Paris or North Africa. Donovan and his sidekick Gypsy Dave undertook a bit of road life—or said they did. In Britain, the weather generally conspired against too much of a rambling life, hence the popularity of going south towards the Mediterranean.

I think we write songs for pleasure, but also to understand ourselves and to decode life. I have written songs about the Second World War in an attempt to understand my parents' generation and what they went through. I wrote a whole requiem about the First World War to go back further and try to understand the sacrifice of my grandfather. I'm also always trying to figure out why I am the way I am, and the forces that brought me to this point. "Beeswing" reflects upon a generation of dropouts, willing dropouts, and the likes of Ted, for whom it was not an option.* The song has a strong heroine, and my life has been full of strong women, starting with my sister, who showed me that a creative life was a possibility if you did not waver in your ambition. In the song, the woman is too wild to be seduced into any kind of life that has a whiff of compromise—a bit like Sandy's version of Anne Briggs, told over many nightcaps. The protagonist of the song loves her but can't hold her, and will yearn for her the rest of his days—romantically unfulfilled, like Ted the tramp, who haunts this song. It begins like this:

> *I was nineteen when I came to town*
> *They called it the Summer of Love*
> *They were burning babies, burning flags*
> *The Hawks against the Doves*
>
> *I took a job in the steamie*
> *Down on Cauldrum Street*
> *I fell in love with a laundry girl*
> *Was working next to me*
>
> *She was a rare thing*
> *Fine as a beeswing*
> *So fine a breath of wind might blow her away*
> *She was a lost child*
> *She was running wild, she said*
> *"As long as there's no price on love, I'll stay*
> *And you wouldn't want me any other way"*

* See Appendix A, p. 267.

Afterword: Continuing

Recordar é viver
BRAZILIAN SAYING

As FAR AS I remember, Linda and I played no concerts in 1976. We lived in Norwich for a while, and then at the cottage in Suffolk. The Sufi community went through something of a paroxysm; there were questions of succession and leadership, and some considered the claimants false—I did, and we left in 1977 and moved back to London. With my friend Larry I ran an antiques shop for a year, on Crawford Street. We also had a stall in Church Street Market on Saturday mornings. I'd get up at 4 A.M. and be down to Brick Lane market buying furniture—the early bird catching the worm, smoked salmon and cream cheese bagels for breakfast at 5 A.M.—and clearing houses of the recently deceased. For the time I was involved, I probably made a very modest living, perhaps broke even. Larry was a bit more ruthless than me—I was too kind to the old ladies, whom I should have been swindling out of their heirlooms. I was subsidized from 1976 onward by a publishing advance, but after a year's hiatus, I needed to get back to playing; I had been given the gift of music, and I needed to use it, unless the signals were clearly to the contrary. The mistaken thinking may have been in the kind of music I chose to play. The singles charts had been dominated by glam rock, the album charts by metal and progressive rock, none of which remotely interested me. Was there a way to play our own style of hybrid folk and rock and have an audience? I felt derailed and needed to get back on track quickly, for my own sanity. At twenty-seven I felt as if I was on the musical scrapheap, like generations of musicians before me.

1976 was a strange year, mostly remembered for a record-breaking heatwave and the longest drought since the 1720s. The IRA were bombing the crap out of London—not for the last time, I was a hundred yards from an explosion. The year began with "Bohemian Rhapsody" at number one, and "Save Your Kisses for Me" won the Eurovision Song Contest—two musical pinnacles, in their own way. The first punk singles were released by the Damned and the Sex Pistols, and here was hope. Guitar, bass, drums, attitude, two minutes. Not that different from Elvis on the *Sun Sessions*. Linda and I had to get back to basics, to the direct expression of emotion, but it was still hard to connect the ideal with the market and with the desires of managers and record companies.

That year, disco was also starting to gain ground. The whole idea of dancing to records seemed bizarre to me. It had a logical beginning in occupied Paris during the Second World War, when live music was banned, and basements and cellars became meeting places where couples could dance to records—they were called *discothèques* (record libraries) to allay suspicion. When the war ended, the discos remained popular, but only with the French. In the 1970s, there was a club in Soho called Le Kilt, and my friends and I would go there to check out the French girls, but we thought it ridiculous to be dancing to records when you could pop down the road and see a real band. One reason, of course, that disco ended up winning the battle was that it was cheaper than paying musicians. From disco come electronic music, samples and loops, all valid tools in the right hands, but brain-numbing conveniences in the hands of the unimaginative. From here comes the diminution of texture in music.

Also around this time comes the ubiquity of music, the phenomenon of the personal soundtrack to life. In early-nineteenth-century England, there was the village band, composed mostly of fiddles and cellos, with the odd clarinet or flute thrown in, playing for dances and, until organs became more affordable, in church as well. People would sing and play traditional and popular songs around the house, at work in the fields and down the pub. A military band might occasionally come through the village or play at a fair in the local town. The posh folk up in the big house would have access to more—art songs and classical music—but for most people, that would be the extent of the music they would hear. Today, music from anywhere on the globe, from any recording era, is available at all times. Many jog to music, commute to music, recreate to music. I find I have to fight it off, ignore it, not pay attention. It's all too much. I love to put on one track, crank it up, give it my full attention—and then I can be nourished for the day.

In 1977, we toured with a "Sufi" band, with Ian Whiteman, Roger Powell or Preston Hayman, Mike Evans and Paul Pickstock. This always felt undercooked as a project, and when it came to recording it, we were dissatisfied and canned it. All fine musicians, but it was rudderless.

Our next two albums, *First Light* (1978) and *Sunnyvista* (1979), came out on Chrysalis, and again I felt we weren't quite getting it right. The focus still wasn't there. We were trying to please an audience that didn't exist, trying to please a record company that seemed to like us on the label for prestige reasons, rather than because it had some idea of how to market us. Next, we did a record produced by Gerry Rafferty. He approached us with very clear ideas of the record he wanted to make and the songs he wanted on it, and we were hoping what success he had had with "Baker Street" would rub off on us. It was a claustrophobic recording process—lots of triple-tracking of instruments and voices, until there was no air left in the music. It was dense and poppy, as can be heard on the bootlegs that have snuck out, but it didn't really suit the songs or the performers. Gerry was drinking a lot—what I thought was a pint glass of healthy, bowel-stimulating apple juice at the start of the day's recording turned out to be neat whisky, and there were refills. It transpired his main motivation for doing the record was to get his hands on Linda. We felt like peripheral figures on our own record. When I turned up for the mixing sessions, no one would speak to me. By the end of the recording, we refused permission to release it.

Joe Boyd put us back on track. He heard about the aborted record, liked the songs and said that we could re-record it simply and cheaply, and release it on his label, Hannibal. This became the *Shoot Out the Lights* album, released in 1982, which gained us fans, some great reviews and a good deal of airplay on US college stations.

It was also the end of our marriage, after ten years. Our time with the Sufi community had put a tremendous strain on our relationship, and we barely survived that. We emerged as substantially different people, and I am guilty of falling out of love with Linda and wanting to end it. That was a tough time for everyone, especially our children, and the wounds are still healing.

Linda had struggled with vocal problems in the past, but she now began suffering from hysterical dysphonia as well. It was a gradual process, with mental and physical components, that reduced her ability to produce notes. For a singer, this is absolute torture, taking away the gift you have been given. It was easier to manage in the studio, in more controlled conditions, where she could lay down her own track and do multiple takes. But in live shows and singing over a band, it was much harder. Our musical partnership of ten years might not have survived much longer.

It was twelve years before I developed a relationship with Liz Gordon's son, Jesse. Linda and I had three kids—Kamila was born in 1982—and we felt overwhelmed at the time, but I should never have neglected Jesse; it was immature and irresponsible. We get on well now—as I do with all five of my talented children and six grandchildren.

AFTER SANDY MOVED to the countryside, we saw much less of her. When we did run into her, she was angry, uncomfortable with the fact that we didn't drink any more, feeling that we had somehow betrayed her. When she had her baby, Georgia, we heard worrying reports of her still drinking and doing drugs, and of neglect. She would phone Linda frequently, sometimes in the middle of the night, saying that the baby had stopped breathing or wouldn't stop crying. She had been so desperate to be a mother, but the reality of it was too much for her. That missing layer of skin that made her hypersensitive to so many aspects of life made her sick with worry about Georgia's tiniest needs. She could not handle it, just as she increasingly could not handle life in general, and chose to numb her way through it. When I heard that Trevor had taken Georgia to Australia to be looked after by his parents, alarm bells rang in my head and I had a terrible premonition that Sandy would not survive this.

I thought she might take her own life, but the fall she had looked like an accident, or the culmination of a series of accidents, and she never came out of the coma. Linda and I visited her body at the mortuary and said prayers for her. I did not get the sense that she was at peace. I hope she is at peace now, with all the love that is sent her way by those who appreciate her music. Time only adds to her stature.

Epilogue

FAIRPORT CONVENTION ARE still playing, in the style that they invented. Having their own annual festival at Cropredy has given them a higher profile than many other bands of the 1960s, and along with their sheer longevity, has made them part of the folk establishment. That was something we all would have feared back in the day, but Fairport wear it well, retain integrity, inject new songs into the repertoire, rearrange the old chestnuts from time to time. Simon and Peggy are still my friends—more like brothers really, after all the shared experiences, the laughs and tragedies of a life lived on the road. No less the other members of the Fairport family—Ashley, Iain, DM—whose paths I often cross, in a working capacity or at a festival somewhere, whose careers I admire and take a brotherly pride in. And I cannot count the number of conversations I have had in my dreams with those who have gone before—Swarb, Sandy, Martin, Judy, Robin—in which I say things I wish I had said at the time.

I was contacted recently by Jeannie Franklyn's sister. Jeannie's family had never been told the whole story of her death, and knew little about her life after she had left home. I was glad to fill in some gaps over dinner. There was healing in that for both parties.

I have been solo now for thirty-odd years. Audiences have been well trained to listen to the quiet songs, stamp their feet to the rockers and laugh at the jokes. I treasure the experience of communicating a song, and it doesn't matter if they receive it differently from how it is given. The greatest reward is for someone to come up after a show and say, "I really got that song—it spoke for me." I love to feel that I express the unexpressed for the listener, things that sometimes are even subconscious feelings. In that sense, every person in the auditorium has a part, it is a shared experience and the stage is an illusion. Yo-Yo Ma has said, "Make the music live in the hearts of others."

When I play live, the repertoire is drawn from all decades of my musical life. A painter paints a picture, sells it to a collector on the other side of the world, and never sees it again. Maybe he took a photo of it. Most creative people are tightly caught up in the present fire of creativity, too distracted to think about their work from ten, twenty or thirty years past, unless it is to hang a big retrospective, and then they might pause to reflect. A singer-songwriter may also be working on a new piece or a new album and be equally distracted, yet he has to take himself back every time he plays before an audience, to render parts of his catalogue.

Not that this isn't a pleasure, but it is strange to have this constant reminder of where you come from, and if you are writing something new, to see where it fits in with all the other stuff. You may play an old song for pleasure, or because you feel the audience would like to hear it, or indeed deserve to hear it, having stuck with you for years. I think of a set list as a balance between things I really want to play and things I think the audience wants—and of those, things I still have love for.

To play a song like "Meet on the Ledge," written fifty years ago on my bed in my tiny room in Brent, for reasons I cannot remember, with a worldview that was understandably naive, is curious. I am and I am not the same person. I have to forgive the author of the song for being youthful, but I salute some of his insights into life, which seem hard-won. I no longer share the emotions he felt at the time, so I have to see what new emotions the song arouses in me, or I cannot sing it—music without emotion is a heinous crime, after all. So I restructure my approach to this piece, invest it with a layer of old man's cod wisdom and weary insight, and it seems to work. The sprinkling of survivors from the 1960s in the audience appreciate, I think, the effort.

There are some songs—probably more than half of everything I have written—that have fallen by the wayside, and I'm happy about that. You can't get it right all the time, and sometimes, in the name of innovation, you take a risk and fall short. But the songs I sang with Fairport, the songs I wrote for Linda, are precious to me.

In Britain, it took until the late 1950s for the swollen generation of boomers to begin to have a cultural impact, and it took until after the *Lady Chatterley* trial for them to have the spending power to revolutionize music, fashion, photography, film and visual art. It took the pill to revolutionize sex. What was being dismantled was really Victorian Britain, which we saw as hidebound and inhibited. When British comedy began to make fun of anyone—judges, generals, even the royal family—it was the death knell for the establishment, and Britain finally and belatedly could catch up with the modern world. Fairport weren't at the heart of the first wave—being five years younger, we weren't hobnobbing with the Mop-Tops and the Stones—but we were in London, at the center of the next wave, part of it but always removed a degree or two. A song like "Genesis Hall" was about current events, counter-cultural events, but expressed in the language of something more ancient, and that was always our intention. Songs on *Full House* seem part of the neo-ruralist movement that was familiar in the early 1970s. Like our contemporaries, we rejected the stuffy, established new social rules, idealized new ways of existing and shaping society, generally condemned war and those who waged it, and lacked sympathy for our parents.

Do I think Fairport was an important band? We really did invent a genre of music, and not many can say that. We rattled a few windows, without actually blowing the house down. Of course, it would have been interesting to have transformed British music to the point of bringing about major stylistic change, to have altered the accents, modes and harmonies of chart acts—stranger things have happened. But the folk world is now closer to the pop world. Some barriers have been trampled, and what was once unhip is now, at least, not laughable.

Like Fairport, like so many of my contemporaries, I don't know when to stop—and hooray for that. There are still mortgages to be paid off and bills piling up, but more motivational than that, there is still an audience. It may be twenty thousand at a festival, a thousand in a theatre or ten in a retirement home, but the desire to communicate from my heart to their hearts is the strongest pull, and the sweetest feeling. That's why we tolerate delayed flights, lack of sleep, lack of food, partings from loved ones. The process is an ancient one, probably as old as the existence of towns, fairs and patrons. Although the early troubadours were noblemen, later generations, like us, were itinerant, going from castle to castle. Our patronage comes from the public rather than the nobility, and we use the stage door instead of the servants' entrance. Our circuit is less well-defined than it would have been for a band of performers in the time of King John, walking or riding from patron to patron. Geography can be short-circuited to an extent by road, rail and air travel, but the effect is similar, playing the same venues year after year—if they ask you back.

I play with my band, a trio these days, and I love it. I love the fact that band and crew (seven of us) can jump onto a tour bus for a month and play all over North America or Europe and still have an audience. Between those tours I can go out solo—just myself and tour manager/sound engineer Simon Tassano—and play acoustically. Some of the songs I play, besides "Meet on the Ledge," are having their fiftieth birthdays, which gives me pause, but they seem to hold up in more contemporary company, and the audience respond, hopefully not with just a pat on the back for a poor old troubadour. It's the best thing, playing live, richly rewarding for me, and hopefully providing something useful for the listeners. I would like to do it for as long as I am able, but if I can't, perhaps I'll be just another old geezer sitting on a park bench with his mates, telling stories about the good old days of the 1960s and 1970s, the stories getting more improbable with every telling.

The attic is empty now. It was time to throw out some old junk, but in doing so, it brought up a lot of memories, fond, tragic, regretful, loving. The arrow is arcing back towards earth now, and catching a glint of gold from the setting sun.

Acknowledgments

To WRITE A memoir about the sixties and seventies was Scott Timberg's idea, and he cajoled me gently for a couple of years before I got up the courage to embark. The premise and much of the shape of the book are Scott's. That we lost him mid-process was devastating and deeply saddening, and this book must stand as a memorial to a great writer and friend. My thoughts always with Scott's family.

My thanks to: my editors Alexa von Hirschberg, Kathy Pories, Nick Humphrey and Eleanor Rees, and all involved at Faber & Faber and Algonquin; Paul Lambden at Domino Publishing Co.; my agents David Patterson at Stuart Krichevsky Literary Agency and Daisy Parente and Jenny Hewson at Lutyens & Rubinstein; my management team at Vector, Brad Oldham, Ken Levitan, John Ingrassia and Mark Nesbitt. Huge thanks to Joe Black for images of all album covers.

A lifetime of thanks to the friends, family and musical colleagues mentioned in this book. Where I have strayed from the truth, it is imperfect memory, rather than a cheap attempt to embroider the facts to make a better story—honest!

Finally, thanks to my partner Zara Phillips, for her love, insight and support.

RT

Songs quoted in the text

WALKING THE LONG MILES HOME

Oh the last bus is gone
Or maybe I'm wrong
It just doesn't exist
And the words that flew
Between me and you
I must be crossed off your list

Chorus:
So I'm walking the long miles home
And I don't mind losing you
In fact I feel better each step of the way
In the dark I rehearse all the right things to say
I'll be home, I'll be sober by break of day
Walking the long miles home

Not a soul is around
As I put more ground
Between me and you
And the whole town's asleep
Or maybe they're deep
In the old voulez-vous

Chorus

O the party was grand
But I hadn't quite planned
On staying so long
And while you accused me
The hours confused me
And my friends had all gone

Chorus

JOSEF LOCKE

My name is Josef Locke
God bless all here and state your pleasure
If you'll refill my glass
I'll sing "Ave Maria"
I'll sing "The Old Bog Road"
Or "A Shawl of Galway Grey"
And I've been gone from you for some while
Those English taxmen they cramped my style
And if you think I'm some bold upstart
Just let my voice be my calling card
It melted hearts and royal teardrops fell
They loved me well
They loved me well

My name is Josef Locke
Ladies and gents now, on your honour
This is a damn poor show
You'll not call me a drunkard
I've sung for kings and princes
How the memories still glow:
O cessate di piagarmi
O lasciate mi morir
O lasciate mi morir
All the applause, all the cheers and cries
How many times did that curtain rise
And now you dare mock the Singing Bobby
I'll find the door, take your bullies off me
A sweeter age it was that loved me well
They loved me well

MEET ON THE LEDGE

We used to say that come the day
We'd all be making songs
Or finding better words
These ideas never lasted long

The way is up along the road
The air is growing thin
Too many friends who tried
Swept off this mountain with the wind

Chorus:
Meet on the ledge
We're gonna meet on the ledge
When my time is up
I'm going to see all my friends
Meet on the ledge
We're gonna meet on the ledge
If you really mean it
It all comes round again

And now I see I'm all alone
But that's the only way to be
You'll have your chance again
Then you can do the work for me

Chorus

BROKEN DOLL

You called for me so here I am
Not a boy and not a man
Man enough to know the odds are long
They dress you up and keep you clean
Like courtiers around a queen
Show you good from bad, right from wrong

All the tears in the world
All the tears in the world
Won't mend a Broken Doll

The little things in life escape her
Dolls are made of rags and paper
China cracks and chips so easily
Doesn't have the will, the strength
To hold the world out at arm's length
Skin's too thin, eyes too wide to see

All the tears in the world
All the tears in the world
Won't mend a Broken Doll

Wish I could give love to you
And life to you and hope to you
As you look through me to somewhere else
In your face I think I see
Twisted-up infinity
Angel soul imprisoned in a shell

All the tears in the world
All the tears in the world
Won't mend a Broken Doll

SLOTH

Chorus:
Just a roll, just a roll
Just a roll on your drum
Just a roll, just a roll
And the war has begun

Now the right thing's the wrong thing
No more excuses to come
Just one step at a time
And the war has begun

Chorus

She's run away, she's run away
And she ran so bitterly
Now call to your colours, friend
Don't you call to me

Chorus

Don't you cry, don't you cry
Don't you cry upon the sea
Don't you cry, don't you cry
For your lady and me

Chorus

BEESWING

I was nineteen when I came to town
They called it the Summer of Love
They were burning babies, burning flags
The Hawks against the Doves

I took a job in the steamie
Down on Cauldrum Street
I fell in love with a laundry girl
Was working next to me

She was a rare thing
Fine as a beeswing
So fine a breath of wind might blow her away
She was a lost child
She was running wild, she said
"As long as there's no price on love, I'll stay
And you wouldn't want me any other way"

Brown hair zig-zag around her face
And a look of half-surprise
Like a fox caught in the headlights
There was animal in her eyes

She said, "Young man, oh can't you see
I'm not the factory kind
If you don't take me out of here
I'll surely lose my mind"

Oh she was a rare thing
Fine as a beeswing
So fine that I might crush her where she lay
She was a lost child
She was running wild, she said
"As long as there's no price on love, I'll stay
And you wouldn't want me any other way"

We busked around the market towns
And picked fruit down in Kent
And we could tinker lamps and pots
And knives wherever we went
And I said that we might settle down
Get a few acres dug
Fire burning in the hearth
And babies on the rug

She said, "Oh man, you foolish man
It surely sounds like hell
You might be lord of half the world
You'll not own me as well"

Oh she was a rare thing
Fine as a beeswing
So fine a breath of wind might blow her away
She was a lost child
Oh she was running wild, she said
"As long as there's no price on love, I'll stay
And you wouldn't want me any other way"

We was camping down the Gower one time
The work was pretty good
She thought we shouldn't wait for the frost
And I thought maybe we should

We was drinking more in those days
And tempers reached a pitch
And like a fool I let her run
With the rambling itch

Oh the last I heard she's sleeping rough
Back on the Derby beat
White Horse in her hip pocket
And a wolfhound at her feet

And they say she even married once
A man named Romany Brown
But even a gypsy caravan
Was too much settling down

And they say her flower is faded now
Hard weather and hard booze
But maybe that's just the price you pay
For the chains you refuse

Oh she was a rare thing
Fine as a beeswing
And I miss her more than ever words could say
If I could just taste all of her wildness now
If I could hold her in my arms today
Well I wouldn't want her any other way

TURNING OF THE TIDE

How many boys, one night stands
How many lips, how many hands, have held you
Like I'm holding you tonight
Too many nights, staying up late,
Too much powder and too much paint
No you can't hide from the turning of the tide

Did they run their fingers up and down your
    shabby dress?
Did they find some tender moment there in your
    caress?

The boys all say, "You look so fine"
They don't come back for a second time
Oh you can't hide from the turning of the tide

Poor little sailor boy, never set eyes on a woman
    before

Did he tell you that he'd love you, darling, for
    evermore?

Pretty little shoes, cheap perfume
Creaking bed in a hotel room
Oh you can't hide from the turning of the tide

Did they run their fingers up and down your
    shabby dress?
Did they find some tender moment there in your
    caress?

The boys all say, "You look so fine"
They don't come back for a second time
Oh you can't hide from the turning of the tide

Dreams

KEITH

It is Keith Richards's birthday. I present him with a large cardboard box.

"Go ahead, open it," I say.

He opens it, and unfolds and unfolds the contents. It is a small rainforest, about fifty feet square, and about two hundred feet high.

"It's like the Tardis—bigger on the inside," I say. We both step into it, and you can't see the edges.

"Reminds me of Dartford," he says, "when I was a boy."

"Dartford? In South London? Where you and Mick come from? There's no rainforest there."

"Oh yeah, smarty pants? Have you been there?" I shake my head. "Come on then."

We jump into a gondola, complete with gondolier, and set out to cross the Thames from the north bank. As we get closer to Dartford, I see huge balsa trees, cecropias, figs. Scarlet macaws are arguing in the canopy.

"Told you," he says. "Let's visit my mum."

There is a house made of twigs in a small clearing. We go inside. Keith's mum appears to be a howler monkey. They seem glad to see each other. She lovingly grooms her son.

"*You can't play the blues unless you live in a rainforest,*"
he tells me.

"*Stands to reason,*" *I say.*

JESUS

*I am sitting on a Tube train. It's fairly full of commuters
engrossed in their newspapers, or asleep. Sitting opposite me
is Jesus. He is dressed as a tramp, but I know it's him because
this pulsing, glowing light emanates from him. He winks at me.*

"*To follow me,*" *he says,* "*you have to do without.*"

I nod. I get the idea.

"*No, you don't,*" *he says.* "*I mean everything.*" *He gives me a
big grin. He has no teeth.*

"*I have to do without teeth?*"

He nods. "*Everything . . . and gonads.*" *He unties the string
holding up his trousers, to reveal—nothing. Instead of a penis
and scrotum, there is a small drawer. He opens it, and from it
produces a piece of paper. He hands it to me.* "*Message for you.*"

I read the message. It says, "*It is only authentic if it has a
"W" stamped on the bottom.*"

*He turns around to show me his bare arse. Sure enough,
there is a "W" tattooed on his cheek.*

*All this time, the other commuters have been ignoring the whole
business. Jesus laughs.* "*I cast a spell on them,*" *he says. He lifts
up the leg of a young woman to show me the bottom of her shoe.
It has an "X" on it.* "*Not one of us,*" *he says. He turns over a man's
briefcase. It has a "W" scratched on it.* "*He's okay,*" *says Jesus.*

"So that's how you tell the good guys from the bad guys?"

He tut-tuts. "That's how you know the do-withouters. These are my people."

"And if they do without, they get to Heaven?"

For the first time, Jesus looks evasive. "Something like that . . . Heaven as a concept—it's so . . . medieval." He looks up as the train comes to a station. "This is my stop." He opens a trap door in the floor of the carriage and disappears through it. I realize I'm on the wrong train, because I don't recognize the name of the station.

"Porcupine," says the station announcement, "Porcupine. Change here for Sonny Rollins."

I get off the train and look at the map on the platform wall. It just looks like spaghetti—in fact, it is spaghetti that's been glued to the wall. The train announcement board has strange destinations. I decide to take the train to Glamour, because I can change there for Camden Town.

JONI

I am painting Joni Mitchell's portrait, but she is a very opinionated subject.

"Don't do me like Les Demoiselles d'Avignon," she says. "I don't suit being all angular. Do me a bit Frida Kahlo."

I oblige, but when I turn it around to show her, it turns into a De Kooning.

"Traitor! Bashi-bazouk!" she says. "Here, I'll do you instead." She paints furiously for a few minutes, then shows me the result.

"But it's a photograph," I say.

"Aha! Well, it is and it isn't. You have to look very very very closely."

I look very very very closely, and I see that the picture is composed of teeny tiny mice. Suddenly they all run out of the frame, leaving just a skull.

"That reminds me of a song," says Joni, and starts to sing "If Practice Makes Perfect," sounding more like Billie Holiday than Billie Holiday. "Hey—you can take a solo," she says, and I pick up a tenor saxophone. Roy Eldridge smiles at me.

THE RIVER

I am standing on Albert Bridge, leaning on the rail, looking down into the water. It's a nice old bridge, and I like standing here, as I have many times before, not really thinking about anything, just enjoying the river and the view towards the city. It's early, in the long twilight before summer sunrise. When I can't sleep, I come here or to another bridge along the Thames, to feel the city waking up.

There is something happening below, but it's out of my line of sight—men are shouting, the sound of a machine. I cross to the other side of the bridge and lean over. There is a diver coming out of the water, the old-fashioned kind, with the full suit and the metal helmet. His air line is attached to a pump. He is carrying a body. The body has stones tied to the arms and legs, which a policeman now cuts off. The diver lays the body briefly

by the side of the water, to catch his breath, on the little beach
that reveals itself every low tide. It is the body of a girl, partially
clothed. Where her flesh is revealed, it is impossibly white, and
glows in the pale light of morning. Her eyes are open and stare
up at me. She looks in her early twenties, black hair, white face,
ghostly. There are red weals around her wrists and ankles from
the ropes.

A policeman carries the girl into a small tent erected on the
beach, and I see no more of her. They remove the diver's helmet,
and he sits hunched over on the sand, shattered. They bring
him a cup of tea. An ambulance arrives. More police arrive. I
am ushered off the bridge by a friendly old copper, straight out
of central casting. "Terrible business," he says, "I hate to see it.
Third one this week."

HAMPSTEAD

I am back in Hampstead and having a pint in the upstairs
room of the Spaniards Inn with Dick Turpin, the notorious
highwayman—except he looks a lot like Michael Caine. He is
dressed in the typical three-cornered hat and frock coat. His
feet are shod in a fine pair of black boots, which are resting on a
second chair. A brace of pistols lie on the table.

"I thought you'd be darker complexioned," I say.

"They're always painting me darker than I really am," he
replies. "How many people have I killed? I'll tell you—none.
Wounded—yes. Killed—no."

"Rob the rich and give to the poor?"

"Nah! That's all bollocks—I keep the lot. I am my
own favourite charity." He lowers his voice and leans in,
conspiratorially. "You keep watch out of the window ahind me,
and I'll do the same ahind you."

I look to the window. There's a queue of cars waiting to
squeeze through the single-lane road between the pub and the
toll house.

"I don't think the troops are coming," I say.

"I can't get on with the modern world," he says. "The rules
have changed. This used to be open country clear away to
Somers Town. I could slip into the woods in a jiffy. Now it's all
plain-clothes coppers and such, sneaking up on a man when
he's in the warm embrace of a barmaid—or two." He chuckles.
"You don't like it either, do you? You hanker after a simpler
life? I can see it in yer eyes. Come back with me to the good
old days, and I can show yer a good time. No fucking traffic,
no sodding M25, food that tastes of something . . ." He spits
out a mouthful of chicken tikka masala. "And all the crumpet
you can handle. You can be my assistant—I was going to say
muscle, but you haven't got any."

"No dentistry, no credit cards, no John Lewis—it's a big
trade-off," I say.

"You can always go back a bit further." Turpin is now
dressed as Elizabeth I, with an unconvincing wig.

"Still, the dentistry—that's a big one," I say. Elizabeth I
is now looking like Judi Dench, and she gives me a big grin,
revealing a fine array of black stumps.

"Being queen has its perks though," she says.

"*Like executing your cousin?*

"*That's one of them.*"

THE WELL

I am lying at the bottom of a well. I don't know how I got here. I stare up at the tiny circle of light above. There is no water in the well, but as my eyes adjust to the dark, I realize it is full of animals—there is a deer, a raccoon, a small bear the size of a dog and lots of mice. The animals, of course, can talk.

"*Don't even think about it," says the deer.*

"*I've been trying to get out for centuries," says the raccoon, "and believe me, I know how to climb.*"

"*But I'm a human," I say. "I've got brains. What if we all stand on each other's backs? That might work.*"

"*Tried it," says the raccoon. "You just have to accept that it's life, and only life. Life is a dingy pit, and we're always reaching for the light. You think getting up there will solve everything, but you'll still be the same person up there, with all your hang-ups and dilemmas. You have to find another way.*"

"*Inward," says a mouse. "Look inward.*"

"*I'm not taking advice from a fucking mouse," I say. "This is all getting too Disney.*"

"*The mouse is right," says the little bear. "Everything you want is right there within you. Relax and go with the flow.*"

The well begins to fill with water.

BUS TO HEAVEN

*I am on a bus, all the way at the back. It's a yellow American
school bus, but I know we're in the Middle East somewhere.
The bus is jammed solid, and has been sitting for some time
in the heat. I appear to be the only one sweating. I ask my
neighbor in Arabic where we are going.*

"Heaven, with a bit of luck," he says.

*A soldier comes down the bus collecting passports. Mine is
a different color and twice the size of everyone else's. He checks
my face against the passport photo.*

"You. Come with me."

I wait in a tiny, roasting office for an hour. He comes back.

"I'm not supposed to let you in," he says. "Wrong visa."

*"Look," I say, "I have to be on that bus, as far as I know,
but I think I've had some memory loss—I can't remember
where exactly I'm supposed to be going."*

*"That's the bus to Heaven. There'll be another along
tomorrow, but all the seats are taken. I can fix your visa, but
that was your assigned bus—it left ten minutes ago."*

"What's the alternative? I see other buses—where do they go?"

*"You don't want to know. Shitholes, for the most part.
There are stories . . . but no one ever comes back. Look, I'd like
to help, but . . . why don't you go back where you came from
and reapply for a proper visa? Then they'll assign you a seat,
and off you go—to a nicer destination."*

*I go outside and look for some shade. It's over a hundred
degrees. I wait at the bus stop marked "Earth." I wait for a
long time.*

MOUNTAINS

I'm having that same dream again. I'm sitting on top of a mountain, but it's a mountain of rubbish, of garbage. It's too steep to climb down. Every object on this trash mountain— the old washing machine, the doll without a head, the sofa with the stuffing hanging out—has a label on it, and the label is the name of a song. Although I recognize none of these song titles— "The Winter Coat," "Birds That Sing to Me," "Hawthorns and Heartaches"—I know they are my songs, and I am sitting on a mountain of my own music. I look over, and there is another mountain not too far away, and there is a guy in a cowboy hat on top of that one. He touches the brim of his hat, and I nod back. In fact, all the way to the horizon, on all sides, are mountains of rubbish, with songwriters perched on top, all unable to climb down, all prisoners of their own creativity. The man in the cowboy hat has taken up his guitar and is singing gently to himself. I smile over at him and do the same.

Lyrics Credits

Richard Thompson and Elvis Costello:
A CONVERSATION

On 8 April 2021, Elvis Costello interviewed Richard Thompson as part of the Montclair Literary Festival. This is an edited transcript of their conversation.

Elvis Costello: I was thinking that we're a couple of years apart, and we came into this world that you describe so beautifully in your book, which was a world defined by the short licensing hours and the Light Programme and post-war austerity and music hall. Can you tell me what drew you to write about that?

Richard Thompson: To some extent it's scene-setting, but it's also what I love. I'm probably fonder of the 1950s than any other decade, however bleak it might have been, just because of that childhood thing, where things happen to you for the first time. Bomb sites seemed kind of glamorous and were wonderful places to play, and your sweets were coming off rationing—it was an unbelievable event, and we stuffed our faces for the next ten years. So although the 1950s were very grey—it was austere, it was very black and white—I sort of love them as well. Hopefully, in the book, the scene is set sufficiently for those who weren't there to get some of that feel.

EC: It certainly feels that way. Obviously, you focus quite quickly on discovering the guitar. Can you tell me about that feeling of opening that case, knowing it was going to be your companion?

RT: In the book I mention this very brief thing when I'm very young, about three years old, and my father opens a guitar up in the attic, and it's like this magical instrument. I kind of fell in love then, probably. But it wasn't until a guitar appeared in the house, when I was about ten, that I thought, "This is for me, this wonderful object. The Shadows play one of these"— you know, the great British instrumental band—"Elvis has a guy who plays one of these."

EC: Well, the horn-rimmed glasses, which I happen to have a pair of here, people say, "Oh, Buddy Holly glasses." Well, for my generation, they were Hank Marvin [of the Shadows] glasses.

RT: Yeah. I think Buddy Holly came slightly before Hank, but Buddy gave the glasses-wearers permission to be cool. If Buddy Holly was cool, then Hank Marvin could be cool, in his slightly ironic way—and Elvis Costello could be cool.

EC: Let's not get carried away!

In the book you mention some experiences that seem to be quite defining. Seeing Segovia, that was an amazing thing. Did it ever make you think, "Well, I want to dedicate myself"? And you mention Ida Presti, whom I had to look up—a wonderful French classical guitarist whom I was listening to last night playing Scarlatti with her husband.

RT: Yeah, extraordinary. As a duo, I don't think they've ever been equalled in classical guitar-playing. She had a wonderful spirit to her playing, incredibly emotional; almost like the Jacqueline du Pré of the guitar, I always think.

EC: That came across immediately. She happened to be playing my favourite Scarlatti sonata with her husband, and when it began, you couldn't believe it wasn't accompanied by other instruments. The touch and the delicacy, and this is a very miniature piece: it's only three minutes long, it's not a large sonata by any means—one movement. And I have to thank you—another great introduction!—you mention the name Bert Weedon and educated me that he actually played with the Hot band in Paris.

RT: The Hot Club de Paris, yes.

EC: He was seen as kind of a square player to a lot of kids who learned from his books. Did you know then that he had that history?

RT: Back then, I didn't know. It was only more recently that I found out that he followed Django Reinhardt into the Hot Club, which is in some ways staggering if you'd heard Bert Weedon on a programme like *Workers' Playtime*, playing something very, very square. He did really corny stuff; it was not very exciting. He'd say, "Okay, I'm now going to play a thousand notes in a minute." And you'd think, "Gosh, Bert, that's incredible." And then he'd just do a sort of really easy thing, "Diddly, diddly, diddly, diddly." It was so corny!

But he wrote the great instruction manual of the time. I'm sure a better one has superseded it by now, but he wrote this thing called *Play in a Day*. I'm sure Jimmy Page and Jeff Beck, everybody started on this book, and you could play in a day, you could get three chords learned in one day. That's a kind of genius thing. I mean, really, he had this wonderful, wonderful way of progressing you through the earliest stages of guitar-playing.

EC: It's one of the terrible secrets, isn't it, of the guitar, that you can actually gather enough chords to play simple songs in a very short time. It's where your curiosity takes you afterwards that's the difference. Maybe people just know the party trick of one song they like to play at Christmas or something, but I suppose that is a liberation. And when you mention Jimmy Page, you're talking about near contemporaries of yours, aren't you?

RT: I think we were really the next generation after. I used to go and see the Yardbirds at the Marquee Club. Fridays with the Yardbirds, Tuesdays was the Who, Gary Farr and the T-Bones was another night, the Nice had a residency then, and the Spencer Davis Group had one too. So a lot of those guys are a little bit older than me. I think they're mostly five years older, and five years is a crucial difference.

EC: That's the crucial difference in age between you and me, too. I lived on the bend in the river around from Eel Pie Island, and although I was much too young to go and hear the Who or the Yardbirds, or go to the Station Hotel to hear the Rolling Stones, I've romantically thought in later years that maybe I heard the sound of the guitar on the breeze, you know, coming round the bend in the river, because we were literally fifty yards from the Thames there.

You were very young when you started playing in bands, but reading your book I discovered that you could have actually been in a punk band with Andy Summers and Hugh Cornwell. Cornwell, from the Stranglers, was a school friend of yours, which really surprises me. I suppose you have to go to school somewhere, and you have no way of knowing what you're going to be doing later. I knew a few people who went on to be doctors and lawyers and bank robbers and all sorts of things. You never know that when you're all twelve, but it's strange to think that you crossed paths with such people. Maybe the world was a little smaller then.

RT: I think it was. You could say that the music profession was probably a tenth of the size it is now, maybe even smaller, so you did know everybody—certainly in London. If you read *Melody Maker*—you know, the great weekly British music paper—you knew about every band in Liverpool, every band in New York, every band in Los Angeles, probably every band in Chicago. It was a great education, plus you also knew about who was who in jazz, who was who in folk music. It was a smaller scene and much easier to wrap your head around, really.

EC: I think that's true. You had writers like—I think you mention him in your book—Max Jones, a great advocate of jazz, who wrote for *Melody Maker* and befriended the artists. Maybe the speed with which they wrote and communicated on a weekly basis meant that they had more time to think about what they were saying; they weren't as glib and as quick. With the instant access to everything we get tired a bit quicker now, we have a shorter attention span. Back then we had those experiences of, yes, the excitement of a club, but also the contemplation of a concert hall or the efficacy of one player.

One player I'm curious to know if he reached you in that time, maybe from a record, is Eddie Lang. Did you ever listen to him?

RT: A little bit later. My father had Django Reinhardt and Les Paul in his collection, and also some Lonnie Johnson, which was pretty amazing to hear as a very young child. But Eddie Lang I probably found at seventeen, eighteen years old, when I started to explore. In fact, I must have heard Lang because my father had Bix Beiderbecke records, so he's surely on some of those. And what an incredible guitar player, extraordinary.

EC: Incredible. I was wondering about that, the way in which we sometimes find a great song on the B-side of a single, almost hidden away, but that's actually where the bands were able to experiment sometimes. In describing the record collection in your house—and I'm sure all of us had far fewer records, and we didn't have access the way we do now—you talk about music hall records as well, and this influence from Scotland. It isn't so much the Scottish folk songs you're speaking about; you're talking about Scottish music hall songs, Jimmy Shand and show band songs. How did they feature in your development as a musician?

RT: Well, it was something that was always in the background. Probably my first real musical memory is of a Scottish dance band playing in the little village that we used to go to in the summer in the Scottish borders, and it would be an accordion, a piano and a drummer. That memory was always on the back burner, because it didn't seem relevant at any point. You know, Buddy Holly seemed relevant and exciting, and the Who and the Byrds seemed relevant, and all this other stuff, and all my father's old music seemed slightly old hat in comparison. And you'd think, "Gosh. Django, what an extraordinary guitar player, but how do I apply that?"

EC: Don't you feel it got in your bones somewhere? It sort of made an appearance, not just in obvious references like Jimmy Shand, but it came back to you, as if it's almost another form of folk music. All of us used to listen to—you might say suffer—the *White Heather Club* of a Sunday evening, which was a stylised form of Scottish folk music that the BBC fed us, with Kenneth McKellar and Andy Stewart, of course, who was responsible for the wonderful "Donald Where's Your Troosers," which is a song we all love. You love that song, I know you do, because it breaks into rock and roll halfway through. It's like a blueprint for your life!

RT: It has the greatest Presley impersonation in the middle.

EC: Incredible. I wish we could play it for people now. They'll have to seek it out.

So, the "Losing My Way" of the book's subtitle [in the US edition]: do you feel as if that was initially losing your way and casting off some of this post-war stuff that you speak about with affection but is still quite contained? Or did you feel it was wading into that freedom, and the bands that you were talking about—the Who, and later on you played on bills with the [Pink] Floyd? This was the early Floyd that I actually like myself. I'm not a big fan of their later stuff, but I love those early psychedelic records.

RT: Yeah, me too.

EC: Did you feel a freedom in that, or was it just something you were doing? Was it part of the late teenage years?

RT: It was a wonderful world to get caught up in. Myself, Ashley [Hutchings] and Simon [Nicol] formed this kind of proto-Fairport, and it was just a joy to play music, and we thought, "Well, we've got to get some gigs. Wouldn't that be wonderful?" So then we started playing out, and that was great, and then Joe Boyd signed us and we started making records. Then we signed with an agency, and such were the times that you would find yourself on a bill with Pink Floyd and the Crazy World of Arthur Brown and Blossom Toes and the Social Deviants and Ivor Cutler and Duster

Bennett, all these amazing characters, and this would happen regularly.

We suddenly found ourselves working all the time, four or five nights a week. We played lots of universities, which had an entertainment budget at that time, and they'd book four or five, sometimes ten bands a night, and you'd find yourself at Manchester University playing at three in the morning, sandwiched between the Bonzo Dog Doo-Dah Band and the Hollies or something—something just ridiculous. And even in the course of our first year on the road we'd be on bills with Joe Cocker and the Animals and the Small Faces and the Moody Blues—all these incredible people. It was a real education, and fantastic for us as young musicians to watch and learn from other bands as well.

EC: That's what I hear in listening again, because obviously I know all these records that you played on, and I know Fairport's records, but I listened to them with different ears as I read the book—it's something that it makes you want to do.

One thing that is obviously going to stand out for people all around the world is the casual mention that you were playing . . . I forget, the Speakeasy or one of the clubs in London, and Jimi Hendrix came and sat in with you. I mean, of course it stands out, but did it stand out at the time? Because he was just another person managed by the bass player in the Animals and he wasn't famous in America—he came over here to make his name initially—were you immediately aware he was something "other"? Or did you think, "Here's another young guy who plays the guitar great"?

RT: I think he was immediately exceptional, and he really intimidated the other guitarists around the London scene. Eric [Clapton] and Jeff [Beck] and all of them, Pete Townshend, they were all kind of intimidated by Jimi because he was so good. And you couldn't upstage Hendrix because he'd have another trick: he'd play behind his back, he'd play with his teeth, he'd have sex with his guitar—you couldn't compete. If you could compete as a player, he'd upstage you as a showman.

EC: You've taken all of that stagecraft into your own act over the years, haven't you? I've seen you do all of those things! Do you think you had the benefit of being seventeen or eighteen, just that bit younger, so that you still felt like you had a road ahead? Those guys probably thought, "This guy [Hendrix] is going to take us out of the picture entirely," because they were exact contemporaries. You were all very young.

RT: And also blues-based players, as Hendrix was as well. He was a superb blues player above all else, but then he layered the psychedelic and weird stuff on top of that. I always tried to play a little bit differently. I tried not to be blues-based and really tried to bring other influences into the thing. And especially playing with people like Hendrix, I thought, "Well, I can't compete, so I'm going to jump sideways. I'm going to have a different style so that I don't get pigeonholed with all these other British blues guitarists."

And he jumped in with us a few times; it wasn't just once. At least three times he had a few drinks and jumped up onstage. This was in a club called the Speakeasy, which was really an after-hours drinking and eating club, so bands would roll in after midnight after a show in Birmingham or Manchester or something and get something to eat, and then have a few drinks until three, four in the morning. I think our second set was usually about 3 a.m.—or our third set in some cases—and Jimi was always there. It was just very intimidating for him to suddenly say, "Mind if I sit in?" Oops, that's Jimi Hendrix!

EC: It's a clubhouse environment that we probably can't imagine now, because bands arrive in an entourage and for the most part they're on larger stages. Even in the late 1960s, when I first went to America, I remember going to a bar in New York, and there were members of the Ramones sitting along from members of the Talking Heads, members of Blondie, and it seemed as though it would have been much more like the gunfight at the OK Corral if you'd had that same scene with the London bands. So it's really nice to know that there was a sense of camaraderie among the players, because as a young teenager, I did actually see Fairport several times. I may be misremembering this, but I think I saw Fairport Convention, Fotheringay and Matthews Southern Comfort all on the same bill, so it was quite possible.

RT: That happened many times. Many times.

EC: And I also saw you at the wonderful Lincoln Folk Festival, too, where you were playing with Sandy Denny. Now, that's in the period when you're both on the edge of leaving Fairport, but you're on a bill with the Byrds and James Taylor, and also Sonny Terry and Brownie McGhee and Ralph McTell and Steeleye Span, and I have a memory of there perhaps being a little bit of a rock and roll encore in one of those sets. My memory doesn't stretch to saying whether it was in Sandy's set or Steeleye Span's, but I believe there was almost an impromptu the Bunch—the rock and roll outfit you all contributed to— which as a member of the audience seemed really shocking, because I didn't think of you playing Buddy Holly songs. But, of course, when you explained how much that meant to you, it makes much more sense now than it did sitting in a field in Lincoln, where we had come to hear folk music and suddenly saw electric guitars being wielded.

RT: In retrospect, I'm thinking, "Why would we do that?" But I suppose there was almost like a rediscovery of American rock and roll, for us, in the 1960s. There were so many records that you couldn't get in the 1950s, and then suddenly the import shops would have these Sun Records compilations and things that no one had ever heard. No one had heard the *Sun Sessions* by Elvis. We were probably feeding off that a little bit. I think it's probably not a great idea to play it at a folk festival, but who knows what we were thinking at the time.

EC: Over a whole afternoon, variation. People would come out and something would be more dance-based, somebody would be playing reels, somebody would be playing very introspective music that's hard to put over in a field. As a member of the audience, I loved everything, all day. It was spectacular.

And at all of those events—and I caught the tail end of those multiple-band bills—there was a sense of something very beautiful going on. When I listened again, particularly to *Unhalfbricking*, I was struck by how influenced by the Byrds you were over those two—the second and third—records, and I hadn't really noticed that at the time because I didn't make the connection.

Your own voice as a songwriter is coming to the fore in those Fairport records, and you're writing some of the most enduring songs of that repertoire. They aren't strictly traditional, but they're in traditional form. It occurred to me listening to "Genesis Hall," which is on the same record as "Dear Landlord": do you think Bob Dylan was reading your mail? Because it's sort of about the same topic, isn't it, when you think of it: it speaks of dispossession and people being taken advantage of in a bleak way, and also does so without necessarily pointing a direct finger, trying to see two sides. There's something very beautiful about the evenness of your song, particularly, and I hear it in many of your songs over the years, that ability to take the other perspective rather than the easy one—wave the flag and the easy slogan. It doesn't seem like that's you. Were you aware of that when you were writing those songs? Or was it like, "I must produce songs for the band"?

RT: Well, the beginning of a song can be almost anything. It can be as mercenary as saying, "We need more songs. Gosh, wouldn't it be great to have something in 3/4?" That's a starting point, and then you think, "Okay, from there I'd love to write about this topic." Or you start writing a verse, and you aren't quite sure why you've written this verse, but it seems quite good. And then you write another verse and you think, "I don't know where this is taking me," and then the song drags you somewhere you didn't even intend to go. Then you look at it afterwards and say, "Well, actually, that's about me. I didn't really think about it; it just kind of came out." You may have had a similar experience, I don't know.

EC: It's something that struck me while listening to these songs again with the benefit of reading your text: the way in which songs sometimes almost predict or suggest the world that we're about to move into. Obviously, one of most moving and traumatic passages in your book—it's something you couldn't go around—was the terrible accident that the Fairports were involved in, and you lost your drummer, you lost your then girlfriend. And then listening to songs from that record, like "Who Knows Where the Time Goes?" and also a very specific verse in "Percy's Song," I really don't know how, as young people, you could stand the pain of listening to yourselves singing that, assuming it was recorded before the accident, and because it came out shortly after. I wonder if there was any ability to edit or think, "What are we saying? Are we revealing too much?"

I had the same experience at seventeen, of losing a friend right in front of me in a stupid road accident, and it completely changed my path in life. I realised how brief time was. Sandy's song affected me today much more than it has done for many years, having accepted that it is now a standard, almost, such a beautiful song, and to think now that an incredible song like that in a short life should also have a poignancy to the other short lives that were taken right as you were making this. And how very young you all were, and how you picked up.

I have to compliment you. I don't wish for you to enter the sorrow of it again so much as I just wanted to compliment you on how sensitively you wrote about it, how honestly. It's a very difficult thing to imagine. Loss late in life is difficult, but loss of young life is particularly intolerable.

RT: It is hard. I mean, after *Unhalfbricking*, we had the accident right there, at the end of when we were recording that record, and after the accident we didn't want to play that repertoire anymore; we really couldn't bear to play the songs that we'd played with Martin. And we drew a line. We said, "That's it, the next record is going forward from there." And on the next record you have songs that seem almost like requiems for Martin and Jeannie, and I think that was our way of dealing with the grief, that was our way of mourning, to put it into music. We didn't have therapy. Nobody thought of sending you to a counsellor in those days for trauma, for mourning, for stress, for grief, so we dealt with it musically. That was our way of paying tribute to those who'd gone before, and it was our road forward, and for better or for worse that's what we did. It might have been better if we'd shared a lot more of that grief, but we were British and a bit shy about showing our emotion, I think.

EC: I don't think there's anything restrained, but the way it's expressed is maybe different, and certainly different to the modern era, where people would have the benefit of help in other ways. But it could also become part of the act, if you know what I mean: the grief could become part of the act, and yet it doesn't feel indulged at all.

There's an awful lot of dying in the songs, there's a lot of sudden death, there's a lot of early death in the songs that became more of the repertoire in the next years, and as that big change came, and with the move towards a folk form, you got even further away from American influences and more into the depths of it. Were you uniform in this interest? Because you yourself had exposure to it—as you explained, you're part Scottish—but there were others, like Dave Swarbrick, who were more from a traditional form of it and had not played rock and roll before. Was there ever a sense of, "Okay, this song has got twenty-seven verses; could we get to the middle eight?" Was there anything you carried over from your sense of song from before that, or did you joyfully go with it?

RT: I think we were always looking for balance. There are some songs which we tackled that were multi-verse, strophic songs that you just had to edit down. There are songs with any number of verses: fifteen, thirty, forty, if you want to go that way. So we were thinking, "Let's make it five minutes, six minutes, seven minutes, at the outside. It's enough for a modern audience to deal with." So some songs, like "Sir Patrick Spens," ended up being probably six or seven verses, and we were very happy with that, because we felt we told the story and didn't leave anything out. "Tam Lin" is another song that has as many verses as you want to sing, and we cut it down to maybe fifteen or something, but it's still only five minutes long.

EC: You also had the benefit of percussion and electric instruments to create tension. I mean, there are wonderful recitations of these songs at full length, but they wouldn't be put over to the same audience, they wouldn't be shared with such a wide audience, so you did something. And there's also a very deep sense of the carnal side to those songs, like "Tam Lin." There's a lot of sex and death all wound up together in them, isn't there? They're not two separate occupations.

RT: Absolutely. Folk song generally can be quite dark: there's a lot of death, there's a lot of the supernatural in traditional music, and you can take that as you want. But there's a lot of unrequited love, a lot of lovers being torn apart; often there are murder stories that become ballads. Like with something more recent like "Tom Dooley," which is from the 1920s, it was an actual murder case that became this Appalachian mountain ballad, which then became a hit with the Kingston Trio and was kind of common currency. But it is a murder ballad.

EC: I was shocked when I heard the Doc Watson version, which is closer to the account of the time, and how brutal it is—"I rolled the cold clay over her and I tramped it with my feet"—and very specific, in more than just killing her: "I'm going to make sure she doesn't even get up." It's so horrible and it's not even reported with any emotion, any drama—or melodrama, anyway, as it is very dramatic, but only in the sense of the coldness of it.

RT: This was the news. This is how the news was conveyed before television, before newspapers. If you lived in the Appalachians, you had a radio, maybe, so you'd get some stuff from that, but entertainment could be a murder ballad, something local or something distant. And going back to Britain, entertainment could be a song like "Matty Groves," where you're talking about the rich people up in the castle, who are always interesting. They're always up to something, so it's the toffs having the debauchery and the murders and the dramas. It was entertainment, and through entertainment you found out the news at the same time.

EC: One thing I'm curious about is that there's a balance. You had these members of the Fairport lineup, like Ian Matthews, who seemed to have an ear for American styles at least as much as you did early on. I'm very, very fond of a record he made, produced by Michael Nesmith, called *Valley Hi*, where he sings your beautiful song "Shady Lies," and it sounds for all the world like you could have made a career as a Nashville songwriter. Did it ever occur to you, Denmark Street or Brill Building? Did you ever think, "Maybe I should be writing a few more of these and sending them out"? I know that your songs have been picked up over the years—and so they should be—but at that exact moment there was definitely a pound note in writing certain types of country-style song, and you do it incredibly well. It's a really, really beautiful song, and Ian sings it exquisitely, and all the wonderful West Coast players are playing on it. Did it ever cross your mind that there might be a secondary career?

RT: Nah, not really! I was also on a mission. I'm still on a mission: to find music that satisfies my soul and not necessarily anybody else's. I want this hybridised kind of British traditional meets rock and roll thing, and there's so much to explore in that area. There's so much that hasn't been done yet that it keeps me interested. If I'd been hard up, maybe I could have been a staff songwriter or something. But yeah, it's more satisfying.

EC: It seems to me you've written a lot of songs. You've been prolific.

RT: I'm busy. I've got a tennis match at three and I've got to see my accountant at five! I don't know. I mean, I love and admire country music, and I'm very influenced by the great country music writers, but I try to shift it to a UK perspective if I can, and I try to pretend that someone as inspirational as Hank Williams is kind of very Scottish, certainly in his melodies, and often in his themes as well, so I try and do something that satisfies my soul a bit more.

EC: Now this is a guitar-player question, really: you moved towards the fuller tone, say, of a Strat-type guitar, but many of the things that you do come from banjo technique, or so it seems to me—hammer-ons and roll-offs and things like that, which you hear a lot in Telecaster players. Did you have an ear for Telecaster players and just decide, "That's all taken up over there, the Telecaster players have got all the angles covered. I'll stay with this"?

Because I never heard the blues influence, obviously, but many others, the broader understanding of other modes and music from across the world, feed in. I'm always most thrilled when you seem to get to the edge of the known map and go a little further; that's where I love your playing most of all. You know the sort of playing I'm talking about, where the intensity carries you out of known forms completely. Did you ever think, "Have I got the ideal instrument?" I know acoustically you've gone towards luthier-built instruments, but you found that voice. I'm sure you don't have just one guitar; I'm sure you have many, like I do, but I need a little more help than you do.

RT: I have two.

EC: You only have two?

RT: I have two guitars. Sorry, only two.

EC: One acoustic, one electric?

RT: No, I'm joking, I'm kidding. I've got hundreds! I've got dozens of guitars, dozens. The answer, I suppose, is you're always looking for that tone that satisfies your soul. If you're Miles Davis, you're going for that choked emotion; if you're John

Coltrane, you're looking for that sound that will kind of take you to another dimension. Being a session player in the early 1970s, I really studied all the styles, and when I was playing with Ian Matthews, for instance, I had to figure out all this country stuff so that I could play pedal-steel licks on the guitar. I wasn't necessarily listening to other guitar players, listening to pedal-steel players.

EC: Did you ever use a B-bender, like Clarence White did? They're very difficult to use. I had one for a brief time.

RT: I never did. I mean, Clarence was an extraordinary guitar player, a wonderful acoustic guitar player, just staggeringly good. But I thought his electric playing became mechanical, and even with other people I've heard using the B-bender it becomes this kind of mechanical thing, slightly unemotional, almost. It's kind of too easy, somehow.

EC: It's a little bit like doing the Charleston with your feet and the tango with the upper part of your body; coordination is incredibly difficult with this counter-intuitive thing. For people who don't understand what it is, it's a device that bends the second string of the guitar from the guitar strap, similar to a steel pedal.

RT: The Nashville guys, all through the 1950s and 1960s, were experimenting with this kind of idea on the guitar. There was one guy who had all six strings wired up to different parts of his body, so he twitches his elbow and that's the third string, and he taps his left foot and that's the sixth string. And Grady Martin, a wonderful session player, had these kinds of levers on his Gibson 335 for all the different strings. I never quite figured out what his process was there.

So, playing sessions, I just figured I had to be able to play everything, including the blues if I had to. I mean, when I was fifteen, I could play the blues, and then I just figured I didn't want to do that anymore; I wanted to do something else. So all those things, all the stuff you listen to, it all becomes part of your technique, so all the Coltrane stuff that I used to listen to, all the Shostakovich, all the weird stuff, it all kind of goes in there and hopefully you can bring it out when it's time, when you need to.

EC: And how about the English music, like Dowland? Do you listen to Dowland?

RT: Oh, absolutely, yeah.

EC: And what about the twentieth century—Vaughan Williams and Delius?

RT: All the British ones. I mean, that speaks to my soul. Delius, Vaughan Williams, Elgar, all that stuff absolutely speaks to my British soul, and I love it. And Benjamin Britten, one of my favourite writers as well. So, all that stuff, you listen to it, and it goes in there and becomes part of your musical vocabulary. Someone like Dowland, he was the absolute superstar of his time, a great songwriter—my God, such a great songwriter—and apparently a great singer, and also a wonderful lutenist. Really, an all-round incredible musician, definitely the Hendrix of the 1580s, or whenever it was.

EC: You often speak about the spiritual and the soul, instruments speaking to you, composers speaking to you. It seems to me that you mention a very specific location, a bookshop where, little by little, texts that might have seemed obscure or may not have been in your initial education suddenly became open to you, and they took you down paths in terms of philosophy, and eventually in terms of theology and belief and your conversion to Islam. People always assume when people are converted or particularly observant to whatever degree that it kind of colours every single thing and somehow takes away their identity, your Englishness in this case. But I'm not getting that from this book at all. Do you find a balance in expressing these things on the page?

RT: I think my view of it is that I didn't change, that the more I found out about various spiritual paths, the more clearly I saw who I was, really, and when I ran into the Sufis, I thought, "Well, that's me—they're like me. But they've got a few extra things that I don't have. I feel a real kinship with these people, but I could learn from them. I can become a better person if I hang out with these people"—because you tend to be like the people you hang out with. And I thought, "If I'm smart, I'll hang out with these people, because these people know more than I do and I can enrich myself in their company." That's it. But I didn't feel different. You can't change your spots. I mean, if I'm English, I'm English, and that's it, basically. I'm not going to change in that way.

EC: It's curious, though, because around this time it was as if you had distilled a lot of that Englishness. You'd struck out on your own and made *Henry the Human Fly*, and then, as you gradually developed your partnership with Linda, *Bright Lights*, which obviously contains many of the things that you'd been speaking about in some of the songs that you wrote for the Fairports, but it's in a much stronger brew, as a songwriter, anyway. You know the way I feel about those songs. I've sung two songs from that record in concert and recorded one of them.

RT: Bless you, thank you.

EC: To this day they seem to me to stand outside of time, which is an odd thing, because you've had the experience of having written—as a very young man—a song which became anthemic for the Fairports in "Now Be Thankful," which is a beautiful sentiment. I was looking again at an absolutely beatific version of it at some open-air festival in 1970, and then you singing it maybe ten years ago at the Fairports' festival, and I realised you are your own folk music. There's a tradition, there's a life, embodied in one song, to be sung in a beatific, youthful, optimistic way, and sung again, so many years later, so beautifully, with people that you had probably fallen in and out of love with over the years, I'm sure, like all band members, but they were all standing together, playing. That's a beautiful, beautiful thing.

RT: It's weird. I think I express in the book somewhere the strangeness of being a singer-songwriter and singing songs from your whole career. I might ask you about that: how does that feel, to sing a song you wrote when you were much younger that you resurrect from time to time? Do you have the same emotional connection to it? Do you have to reinvent the way you think about it?

EC: For myself, it's really just a question of creeping up on yourself and suddenly being surprised to feel that you're moved and it's new again. You can't do it every night, but if you place the song somewhere unexpected in the show or do a slight recontextualisation—maybe the arrangement is changed or the dynamics, such as singing a loud song very quietly or bringing some more force to bear on a ballad—you can hear that other meaning that was always embedded in there. But I don't have a relationship with folk music, except to clobber it over the head occasionally, so I'm not as informed about it. I'm writing songs end on end, and the next one, I hope, is the next good one I write. That's all I'm hoping for. I'm not part of some other thing—that I know of, anyway. It's lonely, but I'll take it.

RT: But you become your own tradition, as you were saying.

EC: That's the point I was making. You embody it in these two very contrasting performances. One is beatific—and I don't use that word lightly. It's from 1970, and you can look it up on YouTube. You're in the open air, and it's as if everybody in the band knows how beautiful this is as you're doing it. It's unusual to play that well live, in the open air, where the sound can be floating around, and it's very well balanced. And then there's a kind of strength and I won't say weariness but a gravity to that second version, where you're leading, and I was just very moved by that, particularly as you've written the song with such grace and great love, but inevitably acknowledging people who weren't always kind to themselves or didn't stay long enough to maybe do some of the work we'd hoped to hear from them—Sandy Denny, obviously. You wrote a song evoking a kind of spirit that tries to embody something we imagine Anne Briggs to be, somebody who seems to be uncontrollable, but when she's singing, so incredibly vivid. She's somebody who you really could stand to listen to sing twenty-seven verses of anything, because it's just like an extraordinary gift she had. And yet, as you say, you never really managed to have a conversation with her, because she was always off somewhere tearing it up, which is some people's way of getting through the day.

There is another question that I would ask: would you consider, having written this, covering the years that followed to bring a different sort of perspective? Or do you feel that the songs you wrote then now speak for themselves? Would you write a sequel?

RT: I don't know. I don't really want to, because 1975 to 1981 doesn't seem very interesting to me. I don't think I made good records. I made three, I think fairly bad, records. Everybody wants to know about the tour from hell, where our marriage was breaking up but we went on tour anyway. Nick Hornby was interested in making a feature film of that tour, which I think is quite an amusing idea.

EC: Who would play you, Richard?

RT: I think Jude Law would be a good me, actually.

I didn't want to cover that period. I get bored with rock biographies like Keith Richards's and Pete Townshend's and Paul McCartney's. About two-thirds of the way through I kind of give up, because it becomes repetitive and it's all about award shows and "Here we are, playing Scranton for the twentieth time." What are you going to say after you've been round and round and round some shows so many times? When you do something for the first time, it's a lot more exciting, and I wanted to write about that period where things happen when you're young and they make a deep impression. So if I write something else, I'd rather do something not related to memoir, about music or something.

EC: I would love to read that book. I would buy that. Sign me up for that book from you! I totally agree with your decision. I respect it. You know, I wrote a pretty long book myself a couple of years ago, and it's not chronological, because I wasn't really writing about the story of my career—you can read all that on Wikipedia. I wanted the emotional reason for why I arrived at things.

That Bob Dylan, he must be reading your mail, Richard, because his book, *Chronicles*, stops exactly when most people would say, "Well, that's the period, 1966, that's the one we want to know about," and he doesn't reveal anything about it. He leads you up to the door and then picks up after coming back from all of that turmoil. And I completely understand, particularly when I see you all together and see your family playing together: why should you, for other people's delectation, speak about those painful times? By the way, I saw the tour from hell, as it's sometimes referred to, and you played brilliant music despite the tortured circumstances. We have all experienced that, and we have to say, well, we make our own mistakes and we live with the consequences, and we've broken hearts—even our own—and hopefully at the end we can look each other in the eye with love.

RT: It's not too late to ask for a refund for that tour!

EC: There's no gig I've ever seen you play where I would ask for a refund, whatever the circumstances. The same cannot be said about me, I have to say! But definitely not you. You have found music in all of this.

RT: I've seen you many times and I've never been disappointed. Just so you know.

EC: A part of the book that I did also want to talk about is your inclusion of a series of dreams. Was that a structural device that you felt was a way of encapsulating the way your mind worked? Were these dreams that you wrote down at the time?

RT: They're dreams that I remember. They were that vivid that I can remember them absolutely lucidly. Originally, I was going to put them in the main body of the text, but my editors kind of talked me out of it, and they were probably right. But I wanted to show that it wasn't so linear. Here I am, writing chronologically, and I'm going through this, but it was crazy at the same time, and there were things where you're thinking, "What's real? Is this real? Or what's going on in my mind, is that real?" There were times when it was really on the edge. And I think the dreams just show an insight, perhaps, even into the creative process; you know, the fact that if you're a writer, if you're a creative person, there's this other stuff going on in your brain, and sometimes it overlaps into dreams. Sometimes you wake up from a dream that seems more real than reality, and you really don't know what's going on. I sound like some nutcase, some lunatic!

EC: That is a very beautiful way to put it. I'm extremely fortunate that I rarely remember my dreams, and I'm always exhausted in the mornings when I do recall them, because they are as vivid and as roller coaster as some of the dreams you recount here. But I love the way they brought us inside your mind, because you're dealing with an awful lot of things which are very emotional, and you speak with great love and respect for music, and respect for people and love for people and lament for people. I think it was a very good decision. I wouldn't have minded them dropped within the chapters, but it wouldn't be for everyone, and I can understand editors are literal-minded in that way.

Do you feel in any way that by writing this book, "People know stuff that I kept to myself before this moment"? Do you feel any self-consciousness? Was there any trepidation?

RT: Trepidation, absolutely. It's laying yourself bare, but then, as singers and songwriters, we're used to laying ourselves bare on the stage every night, really. We're bringing stuff out from our insides and holding it up to the audience, saying, "Look at this, look at this shit that I deal with," and seeing if the audience recognises it. If the audience says, "Well, this is common human experience," then you've kind of achieved something, but you are laying yourself bare all the time. And I know you play solo sometimes, and how naked is that, to be up on stage solo in front of the audience, and there's only you? You can't blame the drummer, because there isn't one! You're absolutely naked.

EC: I love solo performance. I spent three years doing a show where I talked a lot, and it was entwined with the publication of my book. I didn't read from it during the tour, but I did tell some of the same anecdotes and maybe pointed out the songs that particular episodes had led to. So that was a very joyful thing to do; sometimes very upsetting, when it was to do with members of my family that had passed, but different to rock and roll, where sometimes it's basically like running around with your underwear on your head—preferably with all your clothes on! It's something ludicrous, and you have to kind of just let yourself go. Think of all the rock and roll people we love the most of all. They have an abandon. People say rock and roll and they mention a bunch of names, and you go, "None of those people are rock and roll. Little Richard, that's rock and roll. Get to where he's at, and then you can talk to me about it. All these people you're mentioning, they don't have the first idea, they're just smoke and mirrors compared with that."

EC: The last time we were onstage—the last show of mine that my father attended—was your Meltdown [Festival] at the Royal Festival Hall, when we played together.

RT: That was a wonderful show.

EC: So that will always live in my heart forever, as will many songs, and it's been a beautiful thing to listen to the songs, particularly from the period that you're writing about, but of course it's made me listen to more. I encourage everybody to read this wonderful book of Richard's, because you will laugh so many times, you will sense the love, the respect. And it's been a real pleasure to speak with you, Richard.

Index

Richard Thompson is a world-celebrated and influential guitarist, singer, and songwriter. His widely beloved early work within the band Fairport Convention revived British folk traditions, and his duet albums and performances with Linda Thompson are legendary. His songs have been covered by Elvis Costello, David Byrne, Bonnie Raitt, Emmylou Harris, and REM, among others. He continues to write and perform and tour widely. He lives in New Jersey.